VARLAM SHALAMOV'S
KOLYMA TALES

STUDIES IN
SLAVIC LITERATURE
AND POETICS

VOLUME XLI

Edited by

J.J. van Baak
R. Grübel
A.G.F. van Holk
W.G. Weststeijn

VARLAM SHALAMOV'S
KOLYMA TALES
A FORMALIST ANALYSIS

Nathaniel Golden

Amsterdam - New York, NY 2004

The paper on which this book is printed meets the requirements of "ISO 9706:1994, Information and documentation - Paper for documents - Requirements for permanence".

ISBN: 90-420-1198-X
©Editions Rodopi B.V., Amsterdam – New York, NY 2004
Printed in The Netherlands

CONTENTS

Preface

I have used John Glad's translation of *Kolyma Tales* throughout this study and all quotations are from this edition. The meanings of any Russian words will appear in the footnotes as required and were for the most part obtained from Robert Reid of Keele University. Throughout this study I have constantly used the male pronoun in reference to the protagonist, focaliser, narrative voice and unnamed convicts. This is simply because the criminal world of the Gulag was primarily made up of male prisoners. There were, of course, women in the camps, but Shalamov makes little reference to them in his *Kolyma Tales*, and none appear in the tales chosen for this book. For the transliteration of proper names I have used the Library of Congress system, but to avoid confusion, Shalamov's fictional character names are from J. Glad's translation.

Acknowledgements

I would like to thank Robert Reid for his total and unquestioning support throughout the whole process of writing this book. His patience and encouragement have been invaluable. I would also like to thank the other members of the Russian Department for their dedication and help. I would also like to thank the many scholars around the world who have enabled me to locate valuable documents and materials. I would also like to thank Laura Kline in raising both Shalamov's profile with her official Shalamov website and for highlighting my own research. I would like to thank my parents, Dorothy and Frank and other family members, for supporting me when I needed it most. Finally, I would like to thank Kay for all her help and strength for me to complete this work and for her total commitment and support in my academic career.

Introduction

'A man can be destroyed but not defeated'[1]

'He who has a why to live will always bear a how,'[2]

'The short tale is the perfect narrative form because it can be read at one sitting and thus attain a "unity of effect or impression" that cannot be conveyed by longer forms.'[3]

Upon his death, Soviet officials described Varlam Shalamov[4] as the 'well known Soviet Poet', but his works and literary reputation during his lifetime only reached a small circle of admirers.[5] *Kolyma Tales* were first published in 1970, in the émigré publication *New Review* over a period of six years, but were mainly used as a political tool against the Soviet regime.[6] His verse, however, is famous inside Russia, but has not been made available outside that country in any meaningful translated quantity. His poetic background is evident in the tales; indeed, the layering of symbolism and metaphors combines to produce exquisite works of art. Each tale can be read as a Gulag testament, and can also be read and understood as a portrait of one of the most harrowing eras in Russian history. Solzhenitsyn is of course a close contemporary of Shalamov as both author and survivor, but that is where the similarities end.[7] Shalamov does not preach or moralise about his experience within the camp system; rather he presents events impartially.[8] He employs a distancing technique in order for the reader to make his or her own judgement. In a way, he is relying on a reciprocated dialogic process and in some cases effectively directs a question to the reader: 'Can you believe this happened?' Toker argues that whereas Shalamov's tales are neither fiction nor reality, Solzhenitsyn's works are wholly fiction and are a replicating model of human attitudes and fates: 'Essentially, the pact the reader is invited to enter is *metafictional*: it promotes attention to the links between the texts and the reality that they point at, as well as to the nature, extent, and purpose of the fictionalisation.'[9] Shalamov challenges all forms of reality, and attacks the idea that the representation of life is one-dimensional. Man exists in a three dimensional world, where he is exposed to tangible and intangible forms. Dipple states 'Realism insists that life is multiform and must be rendered not singly but in its puzzling multiplicity.'[10] Shalamov's works embody this multi-layered universe and his approach to situations, characters and events in *Kolyma Tales* is primarily to reverse any pre-conceived notions of normality or reality. Thus, it is difficult to differentiate what is real from what is fiction, but this is Shalamov's point. He requires the reader to experience the physical, emotional and psychological disorientation of the Gulag system.

The tales do not read as a factual account of life in a Gulag, nor are they pure fiction; rather they fall somewhere in between. Toker describes the tales as 'documentary prose'; that is, where real names, events and locations are incorporated into a tale to give the impression of authenticity.[11] They are also testimony: 'understood not in the narrow legal sense but, more broadly, as the word of another providing a source of knowledge.'[12] Shalamov's tales are angled toward events he either witnessed or heard about, and the presentation of each tale specifically acknowledges the author's position in relation to events. Thus, an occurrence that Shalamov heard about second hand is not written as if 'he' were there; rather he reports the facts from a third-person perspective. Also, his first-person perspective demonstrates a greater awareness of details and factual information. Thus, the over-arching structure is dependent upon Shalamov as author and Shalamov as witness. Meaning within the tales 'is a function of the relationship between two worlds: the fictional world created by the author and the "real" world.'[13] His tales are not only representative of his experience, but are an essential part of Shalamov himself. He is the central point of reference in most of the tales, as observer and witness, but because of the basic truism of his own survival, many of them focus on the death of others. Shalamov assumes an authoritative position, and to some extent acknowledges this to the reader. This is a result of his need to explain what happened in the Gulags, because there are many millions who cannot. As Toker says 'Like most Modernist works, his texts challenge the reader not to seek a meaning but to help create it.'[14]

Shalamov makes few references to intimate acquaintances in his works, basing friendships on *quid pro quo*. His life in the camps was established on the principle of convict autonomy; that is, the convict could only rely on himself. This distancing of one man from another could be symptomatic of Stalin's own personal paranoia. His inability to trust even his closest advisors radiated from Moscow to encompass the whole of the Soviet Union. Where a man finds only mistrust in his fellow men, then normal human relations do not apply. The general tone in *Kolyma Tales* is of indifference born of an anti-social environment. Life and death have no realistic meaning when all around death and near-death are prevalent. Less important human abilities such as religious convictions, idealism, hope and memory cease to function at all, and consequently baser needs such as food, sleep and warmth are foregrounded. Hosking argues that under extreme conditions, human survival can only be achieved when 'human psychology is blunted by cold, hunger and overwork to admit of only the most basic responses.'[15]

This study in its endeavour to analyse *Kolyma Tales* will use an adaptation of Russian Formalism. The early Formalists tended to base their analysis of fiction on the *form* and not the content of a work.[16] The Formalists learned from Potebnia and Veselovskii, who researched language and folklore respectively. Their work consisted of studying the use of words and how words become metaphor.[17] Propp's analysis of folktales was instrumental in the development of Formalism. He was not an 'official' Formalist, but can be considered in some ways to be 'more formalist' than Shklovskii, Tynianov and Eikhenbaum.[18] His work identified the basic building blocks of folktales, and interestingly enough, his definition of a minimal set of functions answers the question 'how can a tale be re-told from generation to generation and still retain its essence?'[19] Folktales are carried by the human mind and are not a social construct; they exemplify certain human characteristics, such as greed, love, deceit and death. All these inherently exist wherever humans are found, but they are not merely functions of society or politics. Propp found that plot structures exist everywhere independently of textualisation. In a Proppian sense Shalamov's tales exist, not because he created them, but because humans act out repetitive actions every day, even in such a place as the Gulag. Shalamov has merely written down what he has witnessed and to this extent the plots have written themselves. According to Andrew, Tomashevskii and Shklovskii were two of several proponents of Formalism who were accused of 'standing outside history' in their approaches to the analysis of literature.[20] Their method also precluded a text from any social, historical or political influence,[21] and viewed an individual work as being wholly distinct from any former or contemporary text. However, *Kolyma Tales* exist precisely because of the environment they depict; if the Gulags did not occur, then neither would *Kolyma Tales*. Paradoxically, in fact, a Formalist approach to *Kolyma Tales*, such as the present work, only serves to emphasise (through, for instance, analysis of characterisation and setting) the close connection between the stories and the environment which provides them. Thus, a literary tradition cannot exist in a vacuum, and it is not surprising that the Formalists were forced to revise their methods.[22] Formalism went through several re-workings until its eventual 'demise' was hastened by the rise of Socialist Realism.[23] However, the basic form of analysis continued and Formalism made a slow return form the 1950s onwards. In 1970, a group of British Slavists got together and began to rediscover the techniques of the early Formalists.[24] O'Toole's seminal structural analysis of Chekhov's *The Student* raised awareness of how Formalism can be reapplied to particular texts. The short story has been identified as a medium for which a Formalist approach is particularly suitable and it was therefore thought fitting to use this technique for analysing *Kolyma Tales*. Thus, Neo-Formalism as it is known today, provides the basic methodology of this study, in particular Professor L. Michael. O'Toole's work *Structure, Style and Interpretation in the Russian Short Story*.[25]

The Formalists created a system to identify and explain the structural level in any work of fiction. That is, a particular structural feature is foregrounded above the rest. The 'flexible' dominant 'could be conceived of as operating on more or less any level of the text – imagery, character, language, plot and so on.'[26] O'Toole names six separate levels, and in each literary work, only one becomes dominant, with the other levels fulfilling a secondary function. The levels are: narrative structure, point of view, fabula, sujet, character and setting.[27] Determining the dominant level of analysis involves applying each level in turn to see which fits best. When analysing a poem, a short story or novel, one must always beware of trying to force a square hole onto a round peg. It is theoretically possible for the 'wrong' dominant level to be identified, but the short story medium generally concentrates on one thematic idea and thus reduces any risk of this occurring.

O'Toole's technique is certainly useful for analysis, but he prefers to use a general approach rather than to 'nail his colours to any single theoretical mast.'[28] His analysis is rather eclectic in that it incorporates a number of critical theories, including structuralism. This flexible approach also makes it congenial to adaptation by allowing those wishing to use his 'method' to utilise other approaches rather than stick to hard and fast Formalism. Indeed, the approach is dependent upon the text itself. My analytical approach to *Kolyma Tales* has led me to seek sources other than those mentioned in O'Toole's text. In particular, I have drawn upon Leona Toker and Laura Kline's[29] English language works which offer arguably the most detailed analyses of *Kolyma Tales*. For example, Toker highlights Shalamov's interesting use of the focaliser and Kline demonstrates the extent to which Shalamov's worldview is located in his works. I have also drawn upon van Baak's analysis of space, Shukman's theory of time and Scholes and Kellogg's *Nature of Narrative* as useful tools for analysis. Finally, I have established links with several international theorists who have provided published and unpublished articles on Shalamov. This in turn has led me to draw upon unpublished theses and websites for unusual and pertinent information which has enabled me to present a better understanding of Shalamov's Gulag experience.

This study will analyse eleven *Kolyma Tales* by assigning each one to a particular structural level. Each tale was chosen as exemplifying a dominant level for analysis, but this is not to say, of course, that there are not many other tales that could equally convey a strong level.[30] This book is divided into five chapters, each chapter concentrates on a particular structural level and a particular text from *Kolyma Tales*. Each tale is then further analysed via the secondary levels; for example, the narrative structure of *The Train* will be analysed via point of view, fabula and sujet, characterisation and setting. This method enables the reader to pinpoint precisely how a tale is organised and how one level affects another. The tales chosen are listed below against the dominant feature which they illustrate:

Narrative Structure	- *The Lawyers' Plot* and *The Train*
Point of View	- *An Individual Assignment, Berries* and *Quiet*
Fabula and Sujet	- *Sententious* and *A Piece of Meat*
Characterisation	- *In the Night* and *Major Pugachov's Last Battle*
Setting	- *Lend-Lease* and *Fire and Water*

The tales chosen for narrative structure involve forms of travel, and as such, emphasise the narrative stages of this level. Both *The Lawyers' Plot* and *The Train* are journeys that possess all stages of a structure, because, although they retain a short story feel, they are significantly longer than many other *Kolyma Tales*. The longer tale therefore has the ability to retain and impart a fuller sense of story and these two tales are illustrative of how a narrative structure gives a story a sense of completion.

One of the main features of Shalamov's use of point of view resides in the difference between the *narrator* and *focaliser*.[31] The knowledgeable, indeed, omniscient narrator is rarely used for a simple reason. Shalamov as author places himself as a near or distant protagonist within the tales.[32] Indeed, narration in the three tales chosen to illustrate point of view demonstrates flexibility of narratorial perspective, but with a common thread. It is not only Shalamov, the future and knowledgeable narrator in the tale, but also Shalamov as a near-death focaliser with a limited perspective on proceedings. Shalamov passionately believed that a person can only write about such harrowing events if he or she has personally experienced them.[33] Thus, it is his belief that no sense of realism can exist, if information from second or third hand witnesses is used.

The fabula and sujet are considered in this study as a single topic under one chapter, whereas in O'Toole's text, they are treated as separate topics. The reason for combining them is that in the case of Shalamov's stories temporal and causal relationships have proved (on analysis) to be consistently inseparable. When Shalamov withholds information from the reader, he automatically interferes with the temporal flow. When the reporting of an event is delayed, this affects the reader's interpretation of actions. Thus, when the narrator initially reports Golubev's operation in *A Piece of Meat*, both the order and cause of events are affected. The trajectory of the tale is therefore based on the discovery of why and how Golubev gave up his appendix. Equally, Shalamov localises cause and effect within a tale by presenting a scene and then explaining the event or actions. Thus, the fabula or action is closely linked with the sujet or causes of action. In a sense, Shalamov does not reveal the full fabula because he limits the release of any information. It is possible to view each tale as incorporated within a wider fabula in space and time, but the given information is usually contained within the protagonist's limited sphere. Shalamov also uses the medium of memory to modify the presentation of the fabula. The focaliser in *Sententious* completely determines the presentation of facts, because this depends on his slowly returning memory. When he has recovered his health sufficiently, then more of the fabula becomes available. Thus, time, memory and the presentation of information become entwined within the structure of a tale.

Characterisation, like setting, is strictly limited and without unnecessary embellishments. The two tales chosen to illustrate it offer widely differing approaches to character, but both emphasise Shalamov's insistence of limited characterisation. The two grave robbers in *In the Night* only know each other vaguely, but sufficiently enough to enable them to carry out a morally reprehensible deed. Shalamov reports how a man's identity alters in order for him to survive the Gulag. In effect he has altered man's function, both as a real and fictional character. 'Function' is also present in the 'Proppian' sense: the lead character Pugachov, in *Major Pugachov's Last Battle* does indeed fulfil Propp's definition of a folkloric hero. Folk tale heroes perform a 'heroic' quest to attain a specific goal, but, in general Shalamov portrays his heroes somewhat differently. In essence, he is arguing that there are no heroic or villainous people in the Gulag, because there does not exist the fundamental human trait of freedom of choice: free will.

The final chapter, 'Setting', concentrates on *Lend-Lease* and *Fire and Water*. Here, the environment fulfils two functions: firstly, it is a backdrop for the characters and secondly it acts as part of the plot. With Shalamov's limited use of setting, any descriptions must fulfil an important function, and in *Lend-Lease* the large grave acts as a function of memory. Nature repulses the work of humans and therefore Man's attempt at burying his secrets is doomed to failure. Natural features *in Fire and Water* are dynamic and are used to emphasise Man's temporary and ultimately feeble ability to tame the elements. It is Shalamov's aim to compare the strength of natural forces with the weaker force of humanity and he concludes that Man and human creations are merely ephemeral. The protagonists in both

Lend-Lease and *Fire and Water* are therefore merely temporary witnesses to Man's injustices to Man.

Finally, it is worth mentioning that Shalamov began writing during the nineteen twenties, but spent a great part of his adult life in the camps. Thus, his literary influences derive in great part from pre-thirties Russia. Indeed, he was more influenced by the literature of his youth than by contemporary authors. There are instances of intertextuality in the *Kolyma Tales*, where Shalamov clearly draws upon Russian literary texts. For example, *On Tick* brings in several elements of Pushkin's *Queen of Spades* and is understood better when read against this work.[34] Yet, Shalamov denounced nineteenth-century humanist literature because of its incorrect assessment of the human condition.[35] There was no moral gain, nor redemption through suffering, and these tales arguably demonstrate that he was right.

NOTES

[1]   E. Hemingway, *The Old Man and the Sea*, (London: Cape, 1952) p. 103
[2]   In V. E. Frankl, *Man's Search for Meaning*, (Washington: Washington Square Press, 1963), p. 35
[3]   Quoted from W. Martin, *Recent Theories of Narrative*, (Ithaca, New York: Cornell University Press, 1986), p. 82
[4]   Shalamov's first name was initially spelt Varlaam, after the patron saint of Vologda Cathedral. However, as an act of defiance against his father and the Orthodox religion he dropped the third 'a'. See L. Toker, *Return from the Archipelago: Narrative of Gulag Survivors*, (Bloomington: Indiana University Press, 2000), p. 143
[5]   Indeed, in order to be published, Shalamov signed a statement to the effect that 'the thematics of his work were no longer topical.' In J. Glad, 'Art out of Hell: Shalamov of Kolyma', *A Journal of East and West Studies*, CVII, 1979, pp. 45-50
[6]   In 1967, the works were first translated into German, then French, then into Afrikaans, before being translated back into Russian from the French translation. See M. Brewer, 'Varlam Shalamov's *Kolymskie rasskazy*: The Problem of Ordering', University of Arizona, Masters Thesis, 1995
[7]   Their respective prison sentences and the conditions to which they were exposed were also completely different. Shalamov spent seventeen years in total, in and around the Gulags: L. Toker, 'A Tale Untold: Varlam Shalamov's "A Day Off"', *Studies in Short Fiction*, XXVIII, 1, 1991 (Winter), pp. 1-8
[8]   Solzhenitsyn has been likened to Tolstoy, whereas Shalamov is thought to resemble Chekhov. Glad makes this assessment in his Foreword to the complete *Kolyma Tales*: 'Chekhov, a writer who respected the rights of the reader in the artistic process, consciously avoided drawing conclusions for his audience. Tolstoy, on the other hand (like Solzhenitsyn later), constantly lectures the reader.' J. Glad (Translator), *Varlam Shalamov: Kolyma Tales*, (Harmondsworth: Penguin, 1994), p. xvi
[9]   Toker, *Return from the Archipelago*, p. 188
[10] E. Dipple, *Plot*, (London: Methuen & Co., 1970), p. 5
[11] L. Toker, 'Towards a Poetics of Documentary Prose: From the Perspective of Gulag Testimonies', *Poetics Today*, XVIII, 2, 1997, pp. 187-222
[12] Toker, *Return from the Archipelago*, p. 123
[13] R. Scholes & R. Kellogg, *The Nature of Narrative*, (Oxford: Oxford University Press, 1971), p. 82
[14] Toker, *Return from the Archipelago*, p. 158
[15] G. Hosking, 'The Chekhov of the Camps', *TLS*, 17 October 1980, p. 1163
[16] The Formalists did not of course attach this name to themselves. Anti-individualist theorists, such as the Marxists, labelled them as such. Also, it is important to differentiate the Formalists from the Symbolists who also concentrated on the 'form' of the work. The Symbolists' concept of form is the 'perceivable part of a work of art' e.g. the sound of the words. The Formalists believed a work should be treated as a whole. See T. Todorov 'Some Approaches to Formalism', in S. Bann & J.

E. Bowlt, (eds) *Russian Formalism: A Collection of Articles and Texts in Translation,* (Edinburgh: Scottish Academic Press, 1973), p. 11

[17] Potebnia found that the basis of poetry was metaphor. That is, a word or phrase transcends its own meaning to represent something else. This is an important point to consider in relation to Shalamov's poetic background. Shalamov uses a poet's prose in the construction of the tales and consequently he makes significant use of the metaphor in the process. L. T. Lemon, & M. J. Reis, (eds) *Russian Formalist Criticism: Four Essays,* (Lincoln: University of Nebraska, 1965), p. x

[18] A. Shukman, 'The Legacy of Propp', *Essays in Poetics,* I, 2, September 1976, pp. 82-94

[19] The answer is that Propp identified all the functions that are the basis of a folktale and these never change. It is only the extra 'padding' of names and locations that change, whereas the structure never deviates. Ibid, p. 83

[20] J. Andrew, Introduction to 'The Structural Analysis of Russian Narrative Fiction', *Essays in Poetics,* 1, 1984, pp. i-xxix

[21] Lemon & Reis, p. x

[22] Russia in the twenties was a country undergoing all forms of change, and literature could not avoid this revolution. Writing is a dominant medium for propaganda, and the Marxist unofficial policy was to dehumanise the 'author' and make all writings socially responsible for promoting the 'people' and consequently the state. Thus, a paradox was created; if a text has to acknowledge history and society, then the so-called 'bourgeois' authors of the nineteenth century had to be acknowledged. This of course ran contrary to Marxist criticism, which desired a move away from any bourgeois literature.

[23] Works like V. P. Kataev's *Time Forward!* were hailed as the embodiment of this form, and was considered one of the best five-year plan novels. This medium stifled any writer's 'freedom to select themes and treat them as they thought fit.' L. Kochan & J. Keep, *The Making of Modern Russia,* (London: Penguin, 1997), p. 386

[24] J. Andrew, (ed.) *Poetics of the Text: Essays to Celebrate Twenty Years of the Neo-Formalist Circle,* (Amsterdam: Rodopi, 1992), p. iii-iv

[25] L. M. O'Toole, *Structure, Style and Interpretation in the Russian Short Story,* (New Haven & London: Yale University Press, 1982)

[26] A. Bolshakova, 'The Theory of the Author: Bakhtin and Vinogradov', in *Essays in Poetics,* XXIV, Autumn 1999, pp. 1-12. This is with reference to Andrew's introduction to Formalism.

[27] Symbolism could also be considered as a separate level, but its inclusion is beyond the remit and scope of this study.

[28] A. Jefferson, 'L. Michael O'Toole, *Structure, Style and Interpretation in the Russian Short Story:* A Review Article', *Essays in Poetics,* VIII, 2, 1983, pp. 75-87

[29] L. Kline, Ph.D., Dissertation: 'Novaja Proza: Varlam Shalamov's *Kolymskie Rasskazy*', University of Michigan, 1998

[30] Shalamov wrote 147 tales in total.

[31] Genette defines a focaliser as the character (or implied character) through whose eyes the narrated events are presented. In G. Genette, *Narrative Discourse,* (Oxford: Blackwells, 1980), pp 186-9. The focaliser in *Kolyma Tales* occupies an important role for both Kline and Toker, and this point will be pursued later in this present work.

[32] Toker, p. *Return from the Archipelago,* p. 165

[33] V. Shalamov, 'O Proze', p. 549. Cited in Kline, p. 225

[34] This is intertextuality in the sense defined by Martin: 'Intertextuality is where literary techniques or phrases/ideas are transported from one text to another; therefore aligning texts to a literary tradition.' Martin, p. 123 Other tales such as *In the Night* and *Shock Therapy* refer to Gogol's *The Nose* and *Taras Bulba* respectively. Also, Shklovskii always maintained that the reader always perceives a text in relation to others. In T. Todorov, *Introduction to Poetics*, (Brighton: Harvester Press, 1981), p. 23

[35] Kline, p. 6

Chapter 1

Narrative Structure

'The song is beautiful through its harmony, and the tale through its narrative composition.'[1]

O'Toole describes narrative structure as '...the shape of a story's trajectory. Every story is projected from a state of rest by a force of some kind in an arc of rising tension until it reaches the apogee where it begins to fall towards a point of impact.'[2] This brief description is essentially what this chapter will attempt to recognise and further elaborate. O'Toole notes that the theme of a story is inseparable from the narrative structure and is built of thematic motifs. These motifs have positional implications for the tale and are directly related to how a story is moulded together.[3] The motifs are the building blocks of a narrative work and their use creates an understandable and coherent tale for the reader. My analysis of the narrative structure in *Kolyma Tales* derives from Tomashevskii's five-stage model: exposition, complication, peripeteia, dénouement and resolution.[4] Each stage identifies the progress of a story, but there are also two other stages recognised by Petrovskii: prologue (specific and general) and epilogue (specific and general).[5] A story using a simplistic beginning, middle and end, usually has most of these stages as it progresses to a satisfactory conclusion.[6] The literary quality of a tale derives in part from how well the narrative structure is manipulated. A good structure ensures a satisfactory reading whereby a tale progresses seamlessly from one stage to the next. The prologue sets out general and specific information relating to the protagonist(s) and the surrounding setting and therefore sets a scene. A complication occurs to disrupt this scene, thus creating a sudden difference and challenge to the protagonist. It is this disjunction, which creates the beginnings of a story. The complication is not usually just a single event, but a linear series, culminating in the peripeteia. A complication is due to the presence of an obstacle and causes a necessary development or change in a tale. This obstacle has to be overcome in order for a semblance of the status quo to return. Andrew neatly describes how this narrative structure unfolds:

Tomashevsky saw the narrative structure as an extension of the dialectical unfolding of the fabula which moves from state A to state B by means of conflict or intrigue. The exposition, or opening harmonious state is 'disturbed' by a dynamic motif that leads to the *zavyazka* or complication. This in turn leads on to the central turning point, or peripeteia which produces a state of suspense or tension, which is resolved by means of the *razvyazka* or dénouement.[7]

The epilogue therefore is considered as a return to a normal state; that is it mirrors the state from which the tale began. However, Shalamov's use of epilogue, as with other levels of the structure, is particular to *Kolyma Tales* and for him there is no return to a 'normal' state of affairs, as such a condition cannot be said to exist in the Gulags. This will become apparent in my close readings of the *Tales*.

In essence these tales are fixed mainly on a static incident and the narrative tone is rather that of an observer than of *skaz*. Therefore, a complete narrative structure is redundant and tales such as *Lend-Lease* focus more on characterisation, than narrative structure. However, *The Lawyers' Plot* and *The Train* do indeed stand out because of their strong narrative structures.[8] What is explicit in both *The Lawyers' Plot* and *The Train* is the completion of a journey and it is for this reason that specific elements of narrative structure are foregrounded. A journey presupposes a departure from a certain place and an arrival at a destination, whether metaphorical or physical. Propp found a journey into the unknown to be a constant presence in oral tales.[9] Hence all journeys were symbolic of the hero's dealings with the unknown, in an unknown land and with unknown peoples. Shalamov's tales deal with such an unknown, where the culture of Stalinist secrecy invades every aspect of people's lives. Another prominent feature is the medium of travel and the use of vehicles throughout the tales. Local travel in such a vast area as Kolyma is mainly on foot, for several reasons, including lack of transport and the sheer number of convicts on the move. A journey by truck is thus a special occasion and in *The Lawyers' Plot* this provides the basis of the tale.

The themes of *The Lawyers' Plot* are fear and the inevitability of execution; *The Train,* by contrast is about resurrection in escaping the camp (metaphorically as well as physically). While both stories are filled with complications, *The Lawyers' Plot* uses them to build the tension and these are not resolved until a final dénouement. In *The Train*, each crisis is resolved as it is reached. *The Lawyers' Plot* is about an unwilling hero's journey to an unknown destination, while *The Train* has the hero using his own initiative to reach a known destination. The results are two contrasting pieces of work, which, while generally obeying a common narrative structure, embrace it differently. *The Lawyers' Plot* can be broken down into its narrative structural sequence as shown:

General Prologue	- description of life in the camp
Specific Prologue	- description of his standing in the camp
Exposition	- getting ready to work night shift
Complication (initial)	- a call to see the duty officer
2nd complication	- Sent onwards by Romanov to Khatynakh
3rd complication	- Sent by Smertin to unknown destination (Serpentine)
4th complication	- Onwards to Magadan by unknown figure
5th complication	- Office of Atlas
6th complication	- Rebrov office
Peripeteia	- 'Why are we here? I was in wing…'
Dénouement	- 'We're being released,'
Resolution	- Transit prison
Epilogue	- No details, the reader is left, as is the hero in a transient state

There could conceivably be other narrative structures, all based on the same sequence of events. Omniscient narration would give us another perspective on the affair, but the events of those days were lived by Shalamov and to fully appreciate the fear and consequences of such a journey, a first person narrative would seem in order. Captain Rebrov's viewpoint could also be dominant, but again we lose the personal experience that Shalamov went through, coupled with an improbable paradox: if Rebrov was executed who wrote the tale? Another factor to note is the interweaving of the narrative between the hero and other characters. The narrative exchanges pass from one character to another, as if handing on a baton in the narrative race. The activities of the secondary characters are hidden behind the scenes and they come forward only at strategic points in the tale. They are the ones who carry the tale, by appearing at designated complications, and handing the hero on to another official. Rebrov's dénouement is arrest, while the hero's fate is still uncertain. Shalamov's use of the title 'Lawyers' Plot' seems to parody Stalin's conviction of a 'Doctors' plot', as a result of which many doctors (all Jewish) were arrested for plotting to kill army officers and two long-dead officials.[10] This seems to indicate a continuation of the story, with another wave of arrests, which once again may involve anyone.

In *The Train*, the narrative can be divided into two interlinking structures. There is a psychological as well as a physical journey undertaken by the hero. The negative mental state created by the camps is just as important an obstacle as the malnourished body to escape from Kolyma. Shalamov makes this connection many times in his tales, but as in *The Train*, it is rarely a dominant motif.[11] However, when a man's mind has been thoroughly disabled through suffering, it is resignation and an unquestioning acceptance of events which become the dominant mental state. No more so than for the hero in *The Lawyers' Plot*. The theme of *The Train* is the race to escape, one the hero must win. Once the journey has been 'won', there is a period of reflection and a feeling of relief at having made the escape. Shalamov achieves this by making *The Train* into almost two separate tales: that is, prior to the train leaving Irkutsk and after its departure. The first part is fast, filled with nervous tension, while in the latter, the atmosphere is relaxed and the hero's mind is able to metaphorically wander away from Kolyma.

The rest of the Chapter is devoted to consecutive analysis of *The Lawyers' Plot* and *The Train*. The analysis of both tales will be further broken down to highlight how the narrative structure imposes itself on the secondary levels.

1.1 *The Lawyers' Plot*

1.1.1 Point of View

The Lawyers' Plot can be thought of as a survivalist journal, inasmuch as Shalamov himself did indeed manage to survive. Shalamov comments: 'There are no memoirs, there are only memoirists; those who live longer, triumph of the emotion they project.'[12] This tale is a testament to those who survived and those who perished because of the very injustices of a society that revolved around persecution and fear. Shalamov uses a first person point of view, whereby the reader only learns of the protagonist's journey through his thoughts and words, i.e. experiences events as Shalamov did. Shalamov intends this type of narration to create the intrigue and mystery surrounding the journey and we, like the hero, are privy only to a certain amount of information. The 'author is supreme' here, because he has complete knowledge of the hero's situation from start to finish.[13] There are three ways in which the tale delays our understanding of events. Firstly, Shalamov withholds information from the reader at crucial points, thus ensuring that a sense of mystery and fear of the unknown become paramount. Secondly, the reader is also only able to gain a little information surrounding the hero's reason for being in the camp, his present troubles and his prospects for the future. Finally, the hero deliberately states that: 'I made no attempt to clarify anything...' in response to the officers questioning.[14] Shalamov's use of these techniques is crucial to the ordering of the narrative structure and creates the necessary levels. We are therefore in Shalamov's shoes during these events, and we see and feel only what he saw and felt. The narrative structure in essence retains the events as they happened to Shalamov, and it is reflected in the use of point of view.

The point of view in the prologue, both specific and general, is from a first person perspective and allows us details of the narrator's and his fellow inmates' positions. The exposition also retains this point of view and we are led directly into the first complication, with the introduction of Shmelyov the foreman. The focus transfers to Shmelyov and immediately back to the hero, who questions the foreman: '"Have I been transferred to the morning shift?" I asked *suspiciously.*'[15] We can infer that this event is not to be treated as unusual but rather with apprehension. Shalamov allows a moment of uncertainty, before a positive attitude is adopted for the immediate future. Ricoeur observes: 'Narration implies memory and prediction implies expectation.'[16] The hero has still not '...reached the shoving stage,'[17] and therefore he still retains a sense of curiosity based on self-preservation and memory. The narrative restrains the point of view from making bold predictions about the future, thus ensuring that tension is allowed to build up unimpeded. The hero has kept a semblance of curiosity, but only just enough to filter his own worries to the reader. A little information works far better here than would an excessive dialogue between Shmelyov and the hero.

As the complications build up, so do the small doses of information and there is a decreasing need for the hero to worry. But, if this was true, then the reader becomes unconcerned and detached from the hero, thus drawing us away from the building tension. Shalamov, although using this technique does not in fact lessen our fear for him: it increases instead. So how does he do this? Initially, we become completely entwined with the hero in his quest, and we want to find out what happens to him. The hero wants to find out, but only to a limited extent and he is more concerned with the rules of working practices and his chance to miss a shift than with his future. On finding out that his work gang are also off, he avows, 'I hadn't been so lucky after all.'[18] Shalamov creates intrigue, both for the hero and the reader, but immediately draws him away from speculation, leaving us in need of facts: 'This - new thing – had nothing to do with the mine...That meant I was being taken to a new place.'[19] The next complication has Shalamov using the same technique and informs us of the 'Serpentine' the 'infamous pre-trial prison where so many people had perished the previous year.'[20] But after moving from here the narrator merely states 'Where was I being taken?' There was no sense in asking...'[21] His ambivalence recurs when the hero meets the pock-marked man, who testifies that he is to be executed. This immediately draws the reader to the idea of a similar fate for the hero. Thus begins the resurrection of the hero who quietly remarks on the fatalist manner of this man, indicating that he begins to see himself as alive, or as near as possible: 'I didn't like this piece of news at all. Embarrassed, I fell silent,'[22] The ability to recognise death or life in others is crucial to the hero's awakening, but paradoxically he does not take any more interest in his own fate. The series of complications has drawn the protagonist away from any thoughts on the future, and consequently he merely enjoys the scenery.

The point of view as we have already noted, is given to us via the hero, and thus the reader is only made aware of officer's questions and certain mannerisms. We only receive the interrogator's questions in simple form. Captain Rebrov however, receives more narrative attention than other officers and the dénouement allows us to understand why. Shalamov allows us to hazard guesses as to Rebrov's personality and why he chose the hero for questioning. Shalamov does not give us information as to why he was arrested, but through re-reading we learn that events have already occurred before the tale starts. The hero's technique of delaying information to the reader enforces our suspense and allows only specific and related material to leak through. It is a steady drip-drip of information, reminiscent of water-torture that passes from the metaphorical to the actual. Other characters are either given a limited narrative domain or else given no narrative at all. Where the guards are particularly friendly or unfriendly, we are given narrative exchange: however, when this is not available or unnecessary then we are not: 'After some brief negotiations at the entrance I was admitted into the yard of Vaskov's House.'[23] The resolution occurs swiftly and unexpectedly. The background information as well as personal insights are then given to the reader. We know of Rebrov's fate and the hero's relationship with other prisoners. He explains 'All convicts in the northern mines who had formerly been lawyers were brought in. The rest was simply a matter of the usual investigative techniques.'[24] The hero's lack of memory and interest in affairs is diminished and he is able to think and pass on this information to us. Therefore, we begin to see how Shalamov has deliberately organised the trickle of information, not as a deliberate narrative necessity (although this is part of it), but as a vital aspect of the hero's awakening from death to life. The delicate and timely release of information therefore constructs the narrative tale, with the hero's and others' point of view significant to its creation.

1.1.2 Fabula and Sujet

The narrative structure is based on those facts which the reader is given during the course of this tale. However, with events narrated from the first person, care has to be taken in differentiating the fabula and the sujet. The motives behind the initial summons create a fabula that can only be worked out from the end. In other words, the sujet forces us to live in a state of permanent suspense until events are revealed and the whole fabula is therefore exposed. The narrative in this tale is about expectation and memory. The reader is asked to anticipate the likely ending in the beginning and find the beginning in the end.[25] However, Shalamov encourages the reader to question reality in the course of this tale since in his view 'Soviet Reality' is an oxymoronic concept. Everywhere, lies, deceit and fear have become the normal currency and therefore in Shalamov's tales, fact and fiction are interwoven to represent this terrible confusion. The narrative structure whilst displaying a semblance of order, in fact deliberately blurs the fabula and sujet. There exist several story lines, but what is real and what is fiction are twisted to such an extent that the hero is in the dark as much as the reader. The creation of untruths and suspicion characteristic of Soviet Russia are prevalent in the tale and therefore the ordering of the narrative structure is based on unreal occurrences and a fear of the future.

The opening prologue and exposition are the main events, which go some way to indicate a sense of normality. Life for the hero is even described as 'better' 'unexpected joy' and 'I was still a person'.[26] Shalamov therefore requires that a bubble of equilibrium be present in order for it to burst. Although the events are presented in the present tense, the facts and especially the motives behind the interruption in the hero's life, are anonymous and here we detect a split between the fabula and sujet. The fabula therefore exists before the story starts, and the sujet presents the immediate consequences of external actions. When the author introduces an action without apprising the reader of its motives, he has introduced a form of 'suspense'. It is this suspense, which precipitates the search for the motive.[27] By splitting the fabula from the sujet in this way, Shalamov has deliberately presented a false sense of reality for the hero. In other words we begin to view how Soviet Reality was perceived by its citizens, causing confusion and uncertainty amongst them. Rebrov initiated the summons, drawing the hero out of his sphere and into Rebrov's, but we, like the hero, are not aware of this fact. We are only made aware that the hero has left his sphere for an as yet unstated reason. The sujet is strictly from the hero's point of view, and the true fabula remains at a distance from him.

Shklovskii found that in all stories there existed bound and free motifs in all stories. Free motifs are secondary, yet important aspects of a tale that give it a poetic or artistic setting. Bound motifs are essential to the plot: they are needed to advance the tale or explain a particular situation. The introduction of characters at strategic points seems to indicate that they are bound motifs. Their introduction is structural, and they contribute towards the causal chronological course of events in order to further the tale.[28] They can therefore be considered both bound and dynamic motifs, that is, motifs that change a situation. These motifs thus contribute to the presentation of the sujet, keeping it separate from the fabula.[29] They in turn create the linear complications of the narrative structure. However, in *The Lawyers' Plot*, this linear process does not conform to an ordinary day-night sequence. Sleep is disrupted, and a day has ceased to exist in anything other than name: 'It was the usual Kolyma morning – without light, without sun, and in no way distinguishable from night.'[30] The hero is sent on, sleeps, wakes and is sent on again. He is deprived of sleep, a fixed abode and is in a perpetual state of uncertainty.[31] The narrative structure therefore creates a sense of disorientation within the sujet, where travel becomes extended and rest periods are sporadic. By using this process, Shalamov has further emphasised a convict's disorientation by destroying the traditional sequence of day and night.

Hints of death and execution are frequent and increase as the tale continues, thus making the reader believe in the likely outcome of the tale. In building up a related series of complications in the form of interrogations the sujet resembles the fabula. We are made to believe that the interrogations are vital and necessary steps to achieving the expected conclusion. This can be seen in the five interrogations:

1st interrogation ascertains that the hero was a 'lawyer'
2nd he is asked if he is a lawyer and one who wrote complaints about the bread ration
3rd a lawyer again

4th a lawyer with knowledge of high-ranking officials

5th he is questioned by Parfentiev again about these officials (of which he is one)

These events are working up to an expected ending, that is, the execution of the hero, but the outcome has altered owing to external events, i.e. the arrest of Rebrov. The narrative structure therefore includes both external influences that drive the story (i.e. Rebrov arresting the hero and Rebrov getting arrested himself), but these are only revealed at the peripeteia. The 'plot' of the lawyers was not a creation based on reality, but a fictional plot fashioned by Rebrov, based on unsubstantiated reports. Thus the title *The Lawyers' Plot* represents a false reality. The peripeteia itself is therefore something of a surprise, but not to the hero, who calmly explains what and whom he knows to the reader. Shalamov subtly conveys to the reader, that the hero is ignorant of events, but in fact he is described as beginning '...to put two and two together.'[32] The hero therefore becomes an unwilling detective in this tale. With the mystery solved, there still remains the problem of 'what happens next?': now the fabula is reunited with the sujet, and the reader can piece the story together. The resolution does not resort to type with a happy ending, and a return to the status quo, but a change has developed. The hero instigates the dénouement and he suddenly becomes a dynamic force in the tale. The hero has been woken up by this fabula and he develops a tongue. The hero has not remained static throughout the journey's passage, but has changed or, as Propp puts it, the hero is 'transfigured'.[33] The state of equilibrium has not been restored, but unknown and uncertain events lie in wait for the hero. Since there does not exist an explicit epilogue, the tale has to finish here. However, with the hero in a state of transformation a transit prison is the only place to move on to. Given the state of Soviet Reality, there is no place for 'normality' or freedom, so a transit prison seems proper for a hero in transformation. The narrative structure draws the fabula and sujet together at the end of the tale, but Shalamov illustrates how a simple sequence of events can be lost under a system of secrecy and illusion.

1.1.3 Characterisation

To a large extent the narrative structure dictates the limits of characterisation in *The Lawyers' Plot*. The focus remains firmly on the hero and his perspective on events, and the other characters remain incidental to the tale.[34] This distancing effect enables the hero to be presented alone against the odds, and a more dominant presence by other characters would take away the specific personal horror of the hero's plight. The narrative structure only uses characters when necessary and fellow prisoners generally remain anonymous and fixed to a scene or event. The secondary characters exist in a 'closed' setting, whereas the hero is free to move around.[35] The passing narration therefore fixes each character to a set place and time, that is, when the narrative eye focuses on the character in front of it. So each stage of the narrative structure is pushed along by the introduction of a relevant character or characters. *The Lawyers' Plot* could not be said to be completely about the hero's journey, but about the lawyers and others caught up in it. It is likely that all the other lawyers were brought to the House of Vaskov in the same manner. It could also have been primarily about Rebrov or even Vinogradov. Their narrative journeys are not reported, but they are active participants in the tale and their actions directly relate to the hero's. In fact it is because of their actions that the hero finds himself on an unknown journey.

The tale opens with a description of the hero and his compatriots: 'Into Shmelyov's work gang were raked the human rejects, they were the by-products of the gold-mine.'[36] This description is not further elaborated, but concentrates on the gang leader instead, who possesses important distinctive features. This leader's face is cloaked, thus acquiring a form of anonymity. Shklovskii describes this process as masking, whereby only certain aspects of the character are described in order to foreground these at the expense of others.[37] Indirect characterisation refers to characters whose attributes are hinted at by indirect comments or observations. The narrator in *The Lawyers' Plot* uses this technique for the other workers as they wait to be begin their shift: '...before the half-opened doors with their cold drafts, each man's character was revealed.'[38] Most characters resist making the final move outside and use some braking technique to retain a sense of warmth and feeling. One however, leaves straight away to 'resist the shivering'.[39] Therefore one gets the sense that they were coming to the end of their useful lives in the camp. This raises the expectation that at any time someone will be called up for 'deceiving the state' by not fulfilling the quota.[40] Thus the exposition has created an impression of a brutal experience to come, which must be resisted at all costs. The approach of Shmelyov would therefore bring a welcome sense of release, whether or not it brings a known threat. To escape from the work regime is a priority for any prisoner, but this gang has the most to fear.

The first complication brings a '...joyous exhaustion,' thus indicating that the hero is exhausted before he has even got to work.[41] The question has to be asked here: just how long could this character go on for? The interruption of his shift has most likely saved his life and it is here we first learn the hero's name, Andreev. This personalisation signifies an awakening from near death and a small return from the abyss for which the hero was destined. The complication therefore brings back a sense of humanity to the hero. The introduction of Romanov creates intrigue with, 'so we meet, Romanov kept repeating ecstatically...so we meet,'[42] indicating that the meeting was inevitable and desired by Romanov. There exists the notion that others know the hero, but he does not know them. Romanov knew of Andreev, but the hero asks 'Romanov, who's Romanov?'[43] The atmosphere of suspicion and spying exists in the camp as it does outside, where it would seem authority figures make it their business to know yours. His house is also a jail within a larger jail. The vast selection of bolts and chains keeps Rebrov locked inside; the jailer has the status of the jailed. The hero's dishevelled and dirty appearance is in strong contrast to Romanov's music and cologne. The contrast between Romanov and the hero is emphasised by the officer's ability to change a complete uniform, while the hero can only change his boots. Yet, in the camp, a secondary set of clothes, or even a scarf would be a liability and prone to theft. The situation is surreal, but the complication is made more concrete with Romanov's question: 'You know where we're going? To Khatynakh itself, to headquarters! Ever been there? It's OK, I'm only joking, just joking...'[44] This black humour is out of place, but the hero only cares that he is not working a shift.[45] The characters are beginning to be portrayed more as caricatures than real people and the name Smertin (Death) is both a pseudonym and a mask. The second complication reveals a command chain, whereby Romanov plays up to Smertin and 'helps' him find the necessary papers. Smertin is also 'jailed' by Stalin with the ever-watchful Secretary's picture occupying one wall. The hero observes that this '...is a man who had spent his entire life in precisely this sort of room.'[46] The narrative once again moves on to another destination, where fellow prisoners are met but are once again anonymous. The isolation of the hero is reinforced, keeping each crisis fresh and the hero distant from any sense of being in control of events. The two new guards are wary of the hero, and after much whispering to Romanov receive a 'note'. Andreev has taken on a special status and this is further reinforced by the offer of the felt boots. With two days of rest, food and warmth, one gets the impression of 'fattening up the goose' for slaughter. The cafeteria is the main meeting point for all types of people in the North and these establishments are also a collection point for other prisoners.[47] However, non-convict clientele consist of bounty hunters, geologists and black market dealers. As Shalamov puts it: 'These were the heroes and the scoundrels of the north',[48] and by including this road stop, Shalamov has drawn on a wider community. The good treatment meted out quickly gets worse and the doomed travelling companions create an image of fatality for Andreev. The exhausted prisoner says 'How warm!'[49] but the hero comments, '...his eyes were clouded and expressionless.'[50] Shalamov comments: 'The lightness of the future corpse has not been described in literature...the return to life is hopeless and does not differ from death.'[51] Nabokov described the state of waiting for the future in just such a negative light: 'In fact the future contains only anguish-creating transitions or the sluggishness of habitual action.'[52] To recognise death in others is the start of recognising life in oneself, but for the prisoner certain death awaits.

Finally, the hero is introduced to Atlas, the Director of Magadan, yet he is of junior rank to Captain Rebrov (or maybe Zeus!). The masking name Atlas creates images of a Titan ordered to carry the Heavens on his shoulder,[53] but it is Rebrov who has the authority. Authority figures are thrown upside down during this period (1938-39) and the accusers become the accused. The peripeteia occurs only when the main characters are together. Parfentiev and Andreev and various other lawyers are present when the reason behind their release becomes apparent. In the space of three days Andreev is reprieved. This Christ-like resurrection is the time between Rebrov's accusations and his own arrest. The hero has metaphorically died during this period, in the course of which he has lost all hope and strong emotions. His coming alive at the dénouement is however, not succeeded by euphoria, but rather anger. According to Shalamov the first emotions to return after 'awakening' are indifference, fear and bitterness, but here there is suppressed fury at the hero's treatment. After receiving a verbal attack from an anonymous prisoner, the hero shouts 'What are you, a friend of the people?'[54] There is no escape from persecution regardless of whether you have committed a crime or not.

1.1.4 Setting

The setting in *The Lawyers' Plot* is not static, but necessarily dynamic.[55] There are brief stops, and even briefer descriptions of the environment, which once again, make it resemble Bakhtin's paradigmatic Greek *adventure tale*.[56] Shalamov ensures that all settings are relevant to the tale, but keeps them limited and symbolic. The structure enforces a change to the setting each time another complication is reached. There is little 'story-time' here and any 'real-time' is swiftly skirted over. The tale continues by concentrating on the transient nature of setting and each time a new setting is reached, little is said until departure and a new setting come into focus.

The prologue is set entirely on the eve of another night of work, with the workers waiting in cold dark barracks. We are informed of the severe temperature, but immediately told that life is better here than in an ordinary day gang. Shalamov seems to create a paradoxical image of a better life, where none would seem to exist. However, to Shalamov it is a small matter of degrees that create the difference. The 'ordinary' setting he has created is the 'settled' state the hero is familiar with. This makes an anonymous journey to the unknown even more frightening; the narrator is asking us what could be worse? This extends to the 'safe' exposition until the introduction of Shmelyov disrupts this situation. The narrator further emphasises the dark, expectant setting with a singular remembrance. '...it is torturous even now to recall those last minutes before going into the icy night.'[57] The first complication brings a welcome relief for the hero and the barracks become magically warm, bringing to life the parasitic lice.[58]

Shalamov employs a handy technique to halt time in the text by 'putting the hero to sleep' and awakening him in time for the narrative to move on. After each halt there is a sudden movement forward of the narrative and another level has been reached. The setting becomes important to the structure in this way, as it defines where and how the tale has arrived. Setting emerges as a binary, with a stark division between warmth/life inside and cold/lifelessness outside. Romanov's front door can therefore be looked at as a barrier between survival and death. For van Baak, houses represent man's creation to withstand the elements. In a sense the house symbolises a barricade against external chaos, and the ultimate barrier for withstanding the elements. In Siberia, it represents man's triumph in surviving the harshest conditions.[59]

The use of transport further heightens the tension, with larger vehicles brought in, carrying with them an increasing number of passengers. The initial journey from the barracks to Romanov's house is not described, but the closer the hero gets to Magadan, the more detail and scenery is revealed. Shalamov also uses the light and dark binary to emphasise the complications. The arrival is surrounded in darkness, thus increasing the luminosity of a solitary lit room. This effect also causes Smertin's house in the morning to '…appear smaller than it had at night.'[60] Darkness furthermore, magnifies the portentousness of the officials' houses. Only the inside of an office has the life-giving qualities of light, but it is in these offices that life-and-death decisions are made. The artificial light and warmth of each official building reflects the irony of a state that conserves or takes life in these microcosms. In Siberia nature does kill, but it is with impartiality and benevolence. Every prisoner has no chance of survival against authority or the elements and therefore is threatened with death from all quarters. In a way, these two concepts have become one large unchangeable monolith where dark deeds and death are the only truth. Ironically, the hero also has a chance to recoup. In contrast with the offices, when the hero is with the other prisoners, there is no light, and he is thrust back among the horde. Darkness represents the anonymity of death, where the hero is metaphorically on his own. Shalamov illustrates how we will always die alone even surrounded by many others. These 'coming into the light' scenes although not replete with narrative fact, enable the reader to gain an insight into how the pre-trial system works in Kolyma.

The narrative of the first truck journey focuses on the hero's ability to keep warm. As the subsequent journeys continue, the environment, other people and the guards begin to occupy significantly more narrative. The journey towards the 'Serpentine' is long and winding, taking most of the day to cover just 17 miles. This journey indicates the futility of the penal system, with snaking roads and detours. There is no straight path in Kolyma, but a series of winding journeys with only disorientation as its goal.[61] The 'Serpentine' is described in relation to the prison area, but later as the truck descends nearer to Magadan, ironically the bringer of death, life begins to flourish: '...we were so warm that we didn't want to go anywhere; we wanted to wait, to walk a little on this marvellous earth.'[62] Nature is warming the prisoners, bringing them back to a temporary life. The tension before the final descent into Magadan is heightened and it seems the whole world is holding its breath with the '...ringing silence of the taiga.'[63]

The major peripeteia takes place in a small cell from which access is gained via a dimly lit corridor. There is a window in the cell, although tiny, and it is locked with a 'massive iron latch' thus highlighting the forced occupation. The 'House of Vaskov' brings with it not life but death. The enclosed space is used to bring together the protagonists. Shalamov uses this technique to create an environment from which the hero cannot escape. The resolution swiftly arrives and the men are 'released' from the cell to meet the other lawyers. The closure of the story neatly mirrors the beginning of the exposition. The hero is standing amongst a group of men just at the 'exit' to the external harsh world, whereas at Magadan, the hero, although with a similar group of anonymous men, is standing at the 'entrance' to a better world. Van Baak's concept of framing is relevant: the doorways are partly open, thus enticing the men out. To leave the 'safety' of the cell or barracks is to embark on a journey into the unknown, for the cell and barracks have reduced men to existing in a 'womb state'. Consequently, they fear what they would have to experience outside.[64] To leave the womb is to experience a 'primal scream', where innocence is destroyed. Yet Shalamov does not force a birth at the barracks at Kolyma, instead the birth is delayed throughout the tale and it is the dimly lit corridor at Magadan, which promises the birth proper. Therefore the promise of death gives way ultimately to life, albeit a Kolyma life.

1.2 *The Train*

'Images are given to poets; the ability to remember them is far more important than the ability to create them.' [65]

The narrative structure of *The Train* is not reliant upon the interjection of external characters to further the tale. Instead it relies on a battle in the hero's head, where the mind is imploring the external body to make the escape. The hero now has to embark on two journeys: a psychological rediscovery of freedom coupled with a physical departure from exile. In bringing this about, Shalamov creates a sense of estrangement from what the reader would perceive as a 'normal' train journey. Without the psychological thoughts and fears the hero expresses, the tale would simply read: arrived at station – boarded train – arrived in Moscow. For a 'goner' this basic idea of a journey would not exist. Instead we are privy to the fears, uncertainties and suspicions of a convict finally leaving his physical and 'mental' incarceration. There seem to be two levels of narrative structure in the design of this tale, as this momentous event cannot be reliant upon a simple one-dimensional structure. Therefore, the structure of *The Train* is as follows:

Psychological	Physical
General Prologue –	Description of Station
Specific Prologue –	Hero arriving at station
Exposition – 'I woke'	
Complications – Criminals	Boarding train
Fear of buying a ticket	Finding a seat
	No locomotive

Peripeteia – A '…battle, a terrible battle' for room.
Dénouement - 'Forced myself to realise I was
headed for Moscow.'   Whistle not
                                                       heard
Resolution – Relaxes into journey   Train moves
General Epilogue - Future thoughts
Specific Epilogue – Wife waiting   Train arrives
                                                       at Moscow

The two structures cannot truly be separated, as they require each other to move the story forward. It is a case of the physical acting upon the psychological and vice versa in order to allow the hero to begin and finish the trip to Moscow. We are privy to the reality of the criminals' threats, and this creates tension for the hero on a physical level. We are also made to experience the anxiety of the hero's thoughts on buying a ticket or finding a seat on the train. The tale operates across both structures because of this duality of experience and the effect is one of both internal and external forces, which act alongside each other to hinder the hero's progress. The hero is not reliant on others to push him and the plot forward, as in *The Lawyers' Plot*, but he is able to exercise free will and determine his own future.

It is usual in a traditional narrative structure to find the peripeteia well towards the 'end' of a tale.[66] This ensures that there is a build up of complications, thus placing the dénouement at such a position that any further material is 'merely' resolution and epilogue. The length of the tale prior to the peripeteia is therefore longer than the concluding part. However, in *The Train* the peripeteia appears to fall in the middle of the tale. A peripeteia is marked by a change in tone or other similar literary device[67] and prior to the peripeteia in *The Train* the tone is fraught with danger and tension, and immediately after changes to almost one of serenity. Shalamov ensures that the carriage has now become a peaceful haven for the hero. The re-emergence of the criminal, who 'saved' him at the station, is not allowed to interfere with this serene environment and any danger he might have posed is negated. The carriage becomes a microcosm of Russia, full of former camp inmates but it has become a safe environment. The dénouement then slows the tale down to take in the journey (three days), and emotions and physical travel become one.

1.2.1 Point of View

The Train opens in a similar way to *The Lawyers' Plot*, where the narrative is in the standard linear sequence, i.e. from prologue to epilogue. The prologue again sets the scene where the narrative is from a prisoner's first person perspective. The reader is therefore also required to understand the tale from this personal, subjective experience, in the same way as *The Lawyers' Plot*. The opening line informs the reader of the hero's arrival at the train station. So, unlike *The Lawyers' Plot*, the hero has arrived at an intermediary stop and therefore he is in a period of transition. Secondary characters determine the hero's journey in *The Lawyers' Plot* unlike the hero in *The Train,* who has set the path for himself. Therefore, the obvious difference between the two tales is how their paths shape the direction of the hero.

In *The Train*, the hero comments: '...I lay down in the clear, sharp light of an electric bulb.'[68] We are again faced with an image of prison and authority, with a patrolling policeman and a military patrol. The end of the paragraph has the specific prologue using a similar motif as in *The Lawyers' Plot*: 'I had lost any sense of fear much earlier.'[69] Therefore, the two heroes are presented with a similar outlook, where both men are only able to concentrate on the present. The future is deemed to be unreliable and ultimately dangerous and this is contrasted with their present, relatively safe situation. The second paragraph in *The Train* mirrors *The Lawyers' Plot*, where the specific situation of the hero is one of fear and uncertainty, but also of sheer exhaustion. The hero in *The Lawyers' Plot* comments: 'Let come what may!'[70] The hero allows us to feel this exhaustion for ourselves, with timely and relevant thoughts of fear, brought on by lack of sleep. We get jumbled and disjointed inner thoughts, as one does before falling asleep in an uncomfortable or dangerous place: 'I was frightened by the terrible strength of man, his desire and ability to forget.'[71] This is resolved by 'and I regained my calm.'[72] Shalamov places us with a man who has 'escaped' and is just beginning to come to terms with remembering his ordeals, rather than just 'experiencing' relentlessly. Thus, Shalamov has created a general prologue followed by a specific and through the use of the 'sleep' and 'waking' technique, used here for the first time in this story, the reader is led directly into the exposition. Also, it is important that Shalamov has again referred to 'himself' as essential to the existence of the tale. He states: 'I would not permit my memory to forget everything that I had seen.'[73] It is the same voice that draws attention to the importance of memory in *Lend-Lease* when the hero views the mound of frozen bodies. In effect, what Shalamov has done is to build his own future self into the story using what we could term a 'forwarding device'.[74] Narrative structure in *The Train* is in one aspect a direct memorial experience of events and as such the tale will be narrated as fully and accurately as possible.[75]

The exposition begins with 'I woke...' and continues with the first person singular pronoun, 'I' until it changes to the inclusive plurals 'us', 'we' and 'our', concerning his comrades. Their presence is transient to both the hero and the tale and, almost immediately, the narrative returns to 'I'. The narrative reinforces the fact that the prisoner has only just left the camps, and has not arrived at his destination. He is in a limbo world where both criminals and civilians are present, and therefore he cannot be expected to be at ease in his present location. The narrator also creates an unlikely hierarchy of survival. In anticipating the pleasure of standing next to a book counter, he likens it first to 'a dish of hot meaty soup' then to 'a glass of the water of life.'[76] Thus water first, food next, and intellectual stimulation last. It is Shalamov's process of re-socialisation put in order of necessity, which marks the exposition as a beginning of the self with the consequent revival of the spiritual 'I'. Civilisation and safety are only found when the hero feels most at ease, and therefore there would be no intention of buying of books '...until [he] got to Moscow.'[77]

The first complication brings in significant others and dialogue is employed. The reader is given both sides of the dialogic exchange; thus the narrator distances himself from the tale and the point of view changes to indirect narration. He is relating events from a familiar yet hazardous situation, in contrast to the hero in *The Lawyers' Plot*, where the situation is unfamiliar, and not immediately dangerous. However, by conceiving the complications through indirect narration, both tales create an atmosphere of fear on the part of the hero. This technique ensures that elements of tension are created and once again the reader is forced to read on, in order to find out the consequences. The tone used by the hero is one of resignation but with an added 'luck was my only hope.'[78] He also uses the inclusive 'us', when referring to his fellow convicts back in the camp. The incident with the criminals dispels the notion that the hero is safe in having left the camps.[79] The reverse is evidently true and recognition of this puts the hero into a nervous state. He says that he had '...an excellent memory for faces,' yet does not recognise those of the criminals threatening him and the narrative exchange reflects this. He uses defensive language whereas the thief maintains an aggressive tone. Shalamov has placed the thieves in the ascendancy: they initiate contact and dialogue and the hero consequently answers from an inferior position. Memory operates on two levels in this tale: it is an immediate survivalist tool as well a medium to concentrate on distant experiences.[80] Memory is also used to judge others, as when the convict boss comments '…he was a decent sort.' Thus point of view can be linked to judgement via the process of memory recall and later in the tale the hero's judgement of others becomes more explicit as he has time to think and make the connections between Kolyma and its effect on fellow passengers.

It is another thief who takes control of both the dialogue and the other criminals, to resolve the physical threat. The complication is now established and the hero has fewer threatening problems to deal with. The psychological and physical environment now begin to surface and the mind has to force the body to take charge of a situation and act without hesitation. In a way this is representative of the hero's gradual re-assimilation into society. He was always told what to do, but now he has to find the necessary tools to achieve his aims for himself. The narration closely informs the reader of the hero's intentions, but the text also makes explicit the fact that it is not easy for the hero to initiate proceedings. The hero makes another analogy when he gets his ticket. He hands his money through the window 'where [it] would disappear as inevitably as my life had disappeared until that moment.'[81] The ticket itself is described almost as a prisoner 'rough, hard and thin', but a 'wafer of happiness'. This could also refer to Orthodox Communion, where the wafer of bread is regarded as the hero's guarantee of salvation.[82] His psychological turmoil at purchasing a ticket is intermingled with the physical necessity of queuing and waiting in expectation. Only his voice stands out from the crowd, with the cashier and her orders reduced to shouting 'something to the effect…'[83] This use of an estranged and disembodied voice allows the hero's voice to become central and essential to his own plight. We are reliant on the hero to supply us with this information, but only he has heard it.

The third complication involves getting the right train, where carriages are used both as living spaces and for travel. The hero's train does not have a locomotive like the static carriages and 'looked like a dormitory.'[84] There is ambiguity between what constitutes a train or a home. The vast distances travelled Russian trains required them to be 'homes', at least temporarily. Therefore to catch the right 'home' is especially important to the hero and the narrator makes the reader relive and share the hero's fear of catching the wrong train. This fear of obstacles continues when he finds a drunken lieutenant in his 'reserved' bunk. However, the hero's momentum in dealing with complications ensures that this hitch is dealt with quickly. The sound of the whistle marks the physical peripeteia, as it signals the longed-for motion of the train. However, significantly it is inaudible to the hero and therefore Shalamov ensures that there is not a definitive moment that marks the transition from uncertainty to certainty: 'In the confusion, amid the shouts of this prison car, I missed the main thing that I needed to hear...I hadn't heard the train whistle.'[85] This external action is crucial in marking the beginning of the physical journey and psychologically the hero is now ready to look forward: 'I forced myself to realise that I was headed for Moscow.'[86]

The hero now relates the events of the train journey as a passive observer. He attempts to distance himself from others and comments on a travelling companion who, '... sized me up in detail, no doubt very correctly despite the fact that I had said nothing of myself...'[87] The traveller only has a voice through the narrator, and indeed when the 'saviour' from Irkutsk joins the carriage, he merely reiterates what the man had said to him: 'I just want to go home and see my family.'[88] The narration, rather than concentrating on the hero, expands to include observations on others. He even engages in conversation with the lieutenant. Shalamov builds up confidence in his hero as the train travels away from Kolyma. The physical and psychological departures from Kolyma are now reported as a single experience and the narration reflects only his state of mind. The physical is being taken care of, while the psychological side is left to develop. The hero ceases to introspect and we are left solely with his thoughts that objectify Kolyma, its inmates and his experiences. It is only in the epilogue that thoughts of the future surface. The happiness he feels is in contrast to the 17 years away. The point of view changes here to the present day when he exclaims 'This is all I remember as my first happiness, the unending happiness of "freedom"'[89]

1.2.2 Fabula and Sujet

The narrative structure in bifurcating into two distinct areas (psychological and physiological) makes an interesting impact on the fabula and sujet. The fabula relates to the physical journey, but the sujet is presented through psychological understanding of events. The changing psychological states are clearly Shalamov's interpretation of his own journey, but with the physical journey as a backdrop. We once again have a story in which the sujet closely corresponds to the fabula, but there exists a difference between *The Train* and *The Lawyers' Plot*. This difference is in the 'why' of the journey. In *The Train* the reason for the journey is fully known. By contrast, understanding *The Lawyers' Plot* stems from finding out the reason for the journey in the very last passage. Here it is mentioned in the fourth paragraph of the exposition. Shalamov has explicitly made this tale very easy to interpret and the need to create a hidden agenda for the hero is not required. The theme of *The Train* can be classed as 'static' because the reader does not redefine it as new information is acquired. Culler maintains that a process of 'double reading' is enacted by the reader to read events forward and meanings backwards. Shalamov 'helps' this process by filling in past and future events during the course of the tale.[90] *The Lawyers' Plot* would seem to have a 'dynamic' theme during the process of reading, with the reader carefully revising expectations in the light of the new information. It is only after reading that the themes become singular and transparent. *The Train*'s theme is different because it traces the 'how' of the journey rather than the 'why' (as in *The Lawyers' Plot*).

The sujet in *The Train* repeatedly leaps back in time during the first part of the tale by using distinct memories of near and historical past. Shalamov uses a retardation technique throughout the prologues and exposition.[91] Each current episode is firmly placed next to a similar past situation or it leads to an expansion into the future. For example, when a light is shone in the hero's face, he thinks '...but lights had shone in my eyes thousands of times before...'[92] and when he reminisces about his homeland he identifies Irkutsk as 'my Moscow.'[93] The flashbacks do not relate to Kolyma, but further back to the time before his incarceration. He tries to remember his clothing size, but cannot. This situation is further explained by a flash-forward of '...my size was fifty-one. I learned that in Moscow.'[94] Time therefore becomes a confused reality, where the fabula is blurred by the sujet. As his travel progresses away from Kolyma, so thoughts on the future are filled with more details. The exposition is directly concerned with his travel to and within the train station, but, in a way, the actual process of travel recedes from the narrative as the tale progresses. That is, the hero foregrounds his immediate surroundings at the expense of the experience of travelling. Since the tale is 'bound to an end point' or foreknown ending, Shalamov utilises many delaying and retardation techniques to supply further information, not directly related to the process of travel.[95] The sujet imposes itself during the exposition, with a short and precise summary of his flight from Yakutsk to Irkutsk, as if this detail is less important. In an aesthetic sense, this may be true, because of Shalamov's insistence on the train being the dominant feature, and necessary to form the other half of a symmetrical journey.[96] The hero repeats 'A prison car, a prison car.'[97] This mirrors the exposition, where the hero had just 'awakened from a dream that had lasted for years.'[98] Arrival at the station is an exact replica of his arrival there 20 years before; only it is in the opposite direction. To the hero, this series of events is a confusing and precarious time in his need to remember. It is perhaps an easier option to forget the time between the two arrival points at the station and concentrate only on the future. The fabula does not focus on the 20 years of camp life, and the sujet does not give the reader any information either. It is only the time at the station that is important. Rimmon-Kenan's view is that: 'if there is no temporal succession there is no story,'[99] but Shalamov's focus on the sujet rather than on the fabula, means that time is still ticking away during both the reading of the tale and in the tale itself, but at different rates. That is, when the tale concentrates on the psychological sujet, and not on the hero's physical actions, the hero's time on the station and the reader's time do not correspond second by second. Time for the reader is in seconds, whereas time during the hero's thoughts is hours. Time is therefore used as an arbitrary background from which events flow. The sujet does not dominate the trajectory of the tale; rather it is forced to play a secondary role by the 'physical' fabula at several points in the text. The encounter with the criminals, buying a ticket and boarding the train are all physical actions that are essential components to the theme of the tale. The sujet then has to reunite with the fabula in order for the tale to continue at these crucial points.

Shalamov also introduces the disorientation process of sleep in a similar way to *The Lawyers' Plot*. Day and night have ceased to exist again as a tangible measure of linearity. After the incident with the criminal the hero thinks 'The train was leaving for Moscow in the evening.' Yet the next sentence begins 'In the morning the light from the electric bulbs seemed heavy.'[100] This apparent contradiction seems to indicate that the incident with the criminal had taken place in the early hours of the morning, in darkness, and therefore it can be called night-time, but to the hero this is not night. Sleep and awakening are used as endings and beginnings in the structure of the tale, with the prologues, exposition and the dénouement all incorporating this opposition. It is a means of temporal acceleration, the purpose of which is to bypass non-important information. Once the dénouement has passed time completely ceases to exist in any meaningful capacity. The two references made to it are almost an aside: 'On our third day of our life in this rattling car...'[101] and 'But there was no more sleep for the passenger who had slept for two days....'[102] Ricoeur considers 'narrative...meaningful to the extent that it portrays the features of temporal experience'[103] but Shalamov does not make narrative and time explicit here. Rather the reader is asked to infer any temporal changes and 'assume' that travel is taking place. Shalamov has kept time outside this microcosm of Russia and the incidents and observations by the hero could quite conceivably have been reported in a different order. The specific epilogue condenses the main events of the journey into a brief listing of key events. A certain perspective and distancing from past events can now be perceived: 'I was returning from hell.'[104] The tale does not attempt to evade closure, because closure does not exist in any meaningful sense of the term in Shalamov's tales.[105] Although the reported events finish in the tale, Shalamov acknowledges that trials will continue after the tale finishes. He may survive in Moscow, but there again events may overtake him and force him to return. There is more certainty of the future than in *The Lawyers' Plot*, but never a complete surety. The hero's need to remember is reflected in Shalamov's use of future projection and therefore, the boundary line for closure has been breached. He ensures that the story does not remain within the confines of plot, but is projected beyond the events narrated and into the future.

1.2.3 Characterisation

As in *The Lawyers' Plot,* the prologue gives a general description of both the hero and the characters around him. The narrator distances the policeman from the 'dirty, stinking, ragged bodies' by having him patrol around and over the other convicts.[106] The scene effectively demonstrates the breakdown of law and order in the outer reaches of Russia and beyond. Shalamov portrays citizens as belonging to one of two camps: the law enforcers or criminals. Traditionally, the hierarchy of coercers in the camp has the guards heading the list with the common prisoner gangs next. On the station, however, there is a subtle change in the nature of coercion, where it is unknown who holds the most influence and the police do not possess absolute authority. The hero is aware of the danger of this place, but is comforted by the presence of an armed military patrol with what could be described as 'blood' red armbands.[107] The hero comments 'There was no way the policeman could have controlled the criminals in the crowd, and this fact had probably been established long before my arrival at the train station.'[108] The situation then is that the hero is not put at ease by the presence of the police, but is inevitably treated as one of the criminals who perhaps frequently create a scene. Descriptions of the hero's clothes including the 'pea' jacket and the camp way of wearing clothes for maximum warmth are necessary to ensure that the hero is not miraculously transformed into a 'human', but still remains a convict. His character appeals to our emotions and in a sense he is neither superior to the other prisoners nor to the environment: in essence we are asked to respond to his sense of humanity.[109] Shalamov uses a retardation technique to withhold any sudden psychological changes. By employing this, he ensures that a transformation is only achieved through travel away from Kolyma. The hero, by stoutly refusing to forget his Gulag experience, slows down any basic reintegration that will inevitably occur, once the physical persecution has ceased.[110]

The exposition continues with the hero first ridding himself of Kolyma by washing himself in the snow: 'Black splashes flew in all directions'.[111] But the transformation falters as he finds himself ill at ease with his new freedom and 'civilian' people pose a challenge to him: 'All the salesgirls were dressed in identical blue dresses.'[112] Through the hero's eyes we are able to view what he sees; life outside the camp is not so different from inside. Civilian life like camp life, is militarised and the ubiquitous queuing is suggestive of regimentation. The train station where the hero first sleeps and where he goes to collect his ticket are a sea of bodies, nameless and constantly moving. Pedestrians in Irkutsk are also hurrying in a nameless direction. We thus get an image of directionless people, yet only from the hero's point of view. His time in the camp would have been dominated by constant purposeless movement and so the analogy is carried on here. However, the hero and his comrades move in unison towards their goal and they adopt a position of strength in numbers. Their military movement ensures a collective force against their 'new' surroundings, but when this is dissolved the single prisoner can become a target.

The introduction of the first complication brings with it a collection of faceless, yet distinctly portrayed criminals. The hero is still subservient to others and the narrative exchange reflects this. He reacts to the thieves as a powerless figure, with only a brief reference to his newly bought penknife. This 'talisman' represents a valiant, but ultimately useless force against overwhelming odds. The narrator has generalised the criminals to such an extent that he has created an easily recognisable criminal type. Although each criminal has distinctive attributes we are not allowed past a standardised idea of what a criminal is and how he would behave.[113] However, Shalamov has exaggerated particular attributes in order to create non-humans, and what would seem to be gothic creatures of darkness: snouts, long fingernails, sharpened stakes and pale earthy skin. The vampire image is further reinforced when one remarks of the hero's profession in Kolyma: 'A paramedic? A doc? You drank the blood of people like us.'[114] Shalamov has accentuated the animal in the thieves and their predatory hostility is directed towards the political prisoners. Like the 'friend of the people' in *The Lawyers' Plot*, this discrepancy between the two types of prisoners evokes a mutual hatred. Criminal convicts habitually oppressed and harassed the politicals and their baleful influence extends outside the camps. The long fingernail of accusation seems to represent the internal justice meted out to any political prisoner who strays away from safety.[115] As the hero comments, '…neither the policeman nor the patrol could render any help here.'[116]

The 'fight' against his old foes makes way for the new physical challenge of freedom, which presents itself when the hero has to catch the train. The 'battle, a terrible battle' to get access to the car, results in a victory for the hero, who defeats the lieutenant to claim his berth.[117] It is only after the lieutenant's defeat that the story progresses. This lieutenant proves to be a good friend for the hero and as the journey proceeds, so does their companionship. However, it is invariably the lieutenant who embarks on conversation with other passengers, whilst the hero retains his distance. The hero is therefore able to begin a gradual relationship with others, where mistrust and self-interest, (the tools of survival) have been discarded.

After the dénouement, the tale presents a panoramic view of character. The train starts and stops at unknown locations but takes in and discharges various new people. However, the lieutenant and the hero place themselves in a superior position. By surveying the rest of the carriage and making critical judgements, they have effectively put themselves above their fellow travellers. The hero is a convict, yet regards others from a position of authority. He unfolds the complex story of a small boy and his father who are on the train and the absent mother who has remained at Kolyma. Shalamov informs the reader of the various ways in which the Soviet system alters and deforms lives to such an extent that there remains no sense of normality. The narrator hazards many reasons why the mother did not return, but importantly states 'I neither learned nor wanted to learn anything.'[118] Since no dialogue is exchanged between the hero and the father, we have to infer that this conversation has taken place. What is also significant is how Shalamov juxtaposes the boy's play with 'card-sharks' and 'wheeler-dealers' with his suggestion that the boy and his father were 'of course, happy'.[119] Their inner happiness transcends any spatial boundaries and therefore the physical location cannot detract from their freedom and ability to be in each other's company. Shalamov suggests that the boy and his father do not need a particular external environment in order to be happy, as long as they are together. An important point about this mini-tale is that, of all the thousands of anecdotes which Shalamov had at his disposal, he chooses to tell a story about a family, the one entity that did not exist in the camps. This allusion to the hero's own family points to a sense of social normality (which is what he hopes to find on his return to Moscow). Shalamov in contrast to the boy and the father would seem to need the safety and reassurance of a settled family life in Moscow.

Shalamov illustrates a microcosm of the Russian people whose lives have been altered by their experiences. The lieutenant is a friendly drunkard, the nurse is a sad prostitute, and the happy criminal father is reformed. The businessman uses personal photographs and joviality to hide his business dealings. The 'saviour' has been reformed, and his power is no longer effective once he has left his sphere of influence. Shalamov has succeeded in transforming character traits that deviate from the expectations of the reader. In doing so, he has asked us to question our own preconceptions of these characters and to confront traditionally viewed 'characterisational motivations'.[120] Shalamov has blurred the boundaries defining the meaning of good and evil, especially when confronted with extreme conditions such as Kolyma.[121] All characters have been metamorphosed into displaying a 'good' side. Their actions are morally questionable, but Shalamov portrays them as 'living' again. They are trading, playing and loving without animosity towards others. The retreat away from Kolyma is the hero's 'first happiness, the unending happiness of "freedom"'.[122] The epilogue here as in *The Lawyers' Plot* makes no attempt to speculate on the future and is merely concerned with arrival. The hero has now fully awakened from his 'dream' and has returned to his previous life.

1.2.4 Setting

Shalamov's tales are remarkable for their use of brevity of information and setting motifs. As Toker puts it he 'rejected stylistic embellishments, landscapes for the sake of landscape, non-functional non-symbolic detail.'[123] The specific themes he employs in both *The Lawyers' Plot* and *The Train* are not exceptional in comparison with the rest of the tales, but what is particular to Shalamov is the way in which a theme is repeated and expanded in these tales. For example; food, memory and morality are common themes. Tomashevskii found that themes are motivated by a particular need or an idea, in order for the theme to be explicit. Shalamov explores the relationship between the hero and setting in many of the tales, but *The Train* and *The Lawyers' Plot* display a transient scene where the themes transcend their spatial placement. That is, the setting effectively takes the motif with it. For example, the idea of 'Moscow' moves with the hero from Irkutsk to Moscow itself. The setting therefore becomes necessarily dynamic, and transcends any fixed point in time and space.[124] Any travel is marked by an action motif and it is this motif that moves the tale along.[125] As well as the aforementioned dynamism, the setting in *The Train* is also static and it is the dénouement that separates these two setting styles: i.e. the station is static and the train dynamic. Yet, although the station is the main focus of the first half of the tale, the hero is able to wander in and around the station. Also, whilst the hero is in the train, paradoxically time and space become enclosed within the carriage. Unlike *The Lawyers' Plot*, whose motion is continuous with perceptible linear movement, *The Train* only achieves this in the first part of the tale. What becomes apparent in *The Train* is how sensual themes are used as a dominant feature of the hero's progress. The opening line has a light bulb illuminating the hero, under the control of the authorities. However, later in the complication it is used as a marker. That is, the light marked the hero's place on the station, but with his position occupied, the hero has no option but to move back into darkness. The light bulb therefore is used as a determining factor in order to highlight both the spatial position of the hero, and advance the story. Essentially the prologue portrays at close quarters a prisoner who is under the jurisdiction of the authorities and marks a return to the station where he had started his journey.

The exposition of the tale shifts the focus from the train station to recent memories of the hero's arrival at the first village, Yakutsk, where his comrades add the contextual necessity for him being there. The memory jumps forward to his present town, Irkutsk, before completing the jumps forward and back again. During this process the narration concentrates on sensory information in the hero's descriptions of the town and village. There is a contrast between the two places: Yakutsk is described as a town in fear with a dried-up river. It is a 'village' that metaphorically fears the return of the flood of Stalin's victims. Away from Kolyma, the narrator reports more life, human constructions, large buildings and the ability to buy items. Shalamov looks at the 'boiling green Angara River', touches the 'cold brown rail', smells 'gasoline fumes and dust' and sees 'hurrying pedestrians'.[126] All his senses are alive to a town that even in winter, displays the life and warmth of an urban embodiment. Irkutsk has come to represent a renewal of life and the hero comments 'I realised that the most precious time for man was when he was acquiring a homeland...'[127] The hero has undergone a rebirth, but he has yet to obtain a family or love and therefore Irkutsk represents his birth home. As he states in *Sententious*, love is the last emotion to return; therefore this town is the beginning of his new life.

The first complication finds the hero being led into the darkness and the images used in *On Tick* are repeated here, where Naumov is seen as coming into the light. Evil intentions are highlighted with the other convicts slowly following the first thief's lead. After this incident the thieves return to the darkness, and the hero metaphorically rids himself of the ghosts of his Kolyma past. Irkutsk is cold and bright, thus dispelling the darkness. The station itself is packed with nameless people, who like himself are in a state of 'constant movement'. The station is portrayed as a sea, with waves of people queuing at the ticket counter. The final complication marks a change from movement to one of a final stillness, within the noise and chaos of the carriage. The last statement that relates to movement not to the train itself; rather it is the 'barracks' that are moving away from the hero: '…the barracks [were] moving before my very eyes.'[128] The hero remarks that his 'prison car' has set out 'just as if [he] were beginning to fall asleep.'[129] Shalamov is reporting the hero's confusion via the incoherent thoughts one experiences between awake and sleep. The setting has transformed into a camp, and the hero has difficulty in believing that he is leaving this prison. External stations and stops punctuate the journey, but their presence does not interfere with the internal life of the carriage. Only by degrees does Shalamov allow the train's progress to interfere, when for example, 'the car lurched' and 'the train lurched'. This movement however, effects other passengers in the car, but the hero only observes these effects and does not experience them himself.

The division of social space in the carriage enhances its function as a microcosm of Russian society. Areas are designated to each passenger, yet they each create their own additional spot or re-create zones for their own individual pursuits. This does not apply to the father and son, who are able to transcend their specific area of occupancy. They move within the train's movement, up, down, left and right and well as back and forward. Their freedom seems to be reflected in this ability to move independently. The bunks are arranged in a vertical and horizontal way, which creates a hierarchy. The lieutenant is 'above' the hero, while the businessman is below and to the side. The train carriage is an open environment, yet there are enclosed places, where activities can be carried out in 'secrecy'. The prostitute is hidden away from the others, yet all the occupants are aware of her activities. All available space is used for any purpose possible; for example, the businessman's baskets fill up the gaps between bunks and people. No space is left unused, almost as if 'nature abhors a vacuum'. The last sense to be breached is hearing: the final audible noise of the train breaking 'surf' as it enters its final destination, Moscow. Thus, all senses have awoken along with psychological and physical faculties. The hero is now in a position to enter 'civilisation' along with the great ocean of people who have finally reached the welcome beachhead.

NOTES

[1] A traditional Russian proverb. In R. Jakobson, 'On Russian Fairy Tales', In *Selected Writings,* IV, Slavic Epic Studies, (Hague: Mouton, 1966), p. 93

[2] O'Toole, *Structure, Style and Interpretation in the Russian Short Story*, p. 11

[3] Loc. cit.

[4] Cited in various texts, including Andrew's Introduction to 'The Structural Analysis of Russian Narrative Fiction', pp. i-xxix and O'Toole, *Structure, Style and Interpretation in the Russian Short Story*, pp. 11-14

[5] Andrew, Introduction to 'The Structural Analysis of Russian Narrative Fiction', p. xii

[6] Aristotle first identified this simple fact, alongside his more technical analysis of plot in *Poetics*. Cited in O'Toole, *Structure, Style and Interpretation in the Russian Short Story*, p. 3

[7] Andrew, Introduction to 'The Structural Analysis of Russian Narrative Fiction' pp. xi-xii

[8] *The Lawyers' Plot* was written in 1962, and based on events in 1938. *The Train* was written in 1964 and was based on Shalamov's experiences in 1953.

[9] The first function of the hero according to Propp was to experience 'separation' from home, family, friends and loved ones. Therefore the hero would have to experience the unknown in order to complete his 'task'. This 'task' always contains a journey, whether physical or psychological. For an explanation of Propp's 31 functions and 7 functionaries, with a complete list of both see Shukman, 'The Legacy of Propp', pp. 82-94

[10] *The Lawyers' Plot* is based around events in 1938, yet the Doctors' Plot was in 1953. Shalamov is deliberately indicating that there are similarities between these two events. Beria's swift retaliatory measures against former persecutors (Yezhov especially) enabled the charges to be dropped against Shalamov. The doctors' plot in 1953 only ceased when Stalin died, and the persecution of Shalamov (from a penal perspective only) also ceased. Censorship and various forms of exile still dogged Shalamov for the rest of his life.

[11] However, *Sententious* can be regarded as an exception. An analysis of this tale is found later in this thesis.

[12] V. Shalamov, 'New Prose' (Novaia Proza), *Novyi Mir*, XII, 1989, pp. 3-71 as cited in V. Petrochenkov, 'State-sponsored Persecution as Violence: Varlam Shalamov's *Kolyma Tales*', in W. Wright & S. Kaplan., (eds) *The Image of Violence in Literature, the Media and Society*, (Pueblo, Colorado: University of Southern Colorado, 1995), pp. 491-7

[13] Bolshakova, p. 7

[14] *Kolyma Tales*, p. 131

[15] Ibid., p. 127

[16] P. Ricoeur, *Time and Narrative*, I, (Chicago: University of Chicago Press, 1983), p. 10

[17] *Kolyma Tales*, p. 127

[18] Ibid., p. 130

[19] Loc. cit.

[20] Ibid., p. 134

[21] Ibid., p. 136

[22] Ibid., p. 138

[23] Ibid., p. 143

[24] Ibid., p. 145

[25] P. Cobley, *Narrative*, (London: Routledge, 2001), p. 19

[26] *Kolyma Tales*, p. 126-7

[27] Examples of 'suspense' used to shape the story may be found in Pushkin's *Snowstorm* or Lermontov's *Taman*.

[28] B. Tomashevsky, 'Thematics', in Lemon & Reis, pp. 61-95

[29] Ibid., p. 70

[30] *Kolyma Tales*, p. 132

[31] See Solzhenitsyn's *First Circle* for a similar account of disorientation after Innokenty Volodin's arrest. A. Solzhenitsyn, *First Circle*, (London: William Collins, 1979), pp. 632-68

[32] *Kolyma Tales*, p. 145

[33] V. Propp, *Morphology of the Folktale*, (Austin & London: University of Texas Press, 1973), p. 62

[34] The hero is reminiscent of Bakhtin's description of the hero of a Greek adventure tale: a loner, with no links to anyone, society or country. Bakhtin, M, 'The Form of Time and the Chronotope in the Novel: From the Greek Novel to Modern Fiction', *PTL: A Journal for Descriptive Poetics and Theory of Literature*, III, 3, October 1978, pp. 493-528, (p. 513)

[35] Clark and Holquist describe 'Self-time [as] open, incomplete, whereas the others' time (secondary characters) can be defined as closed, finished.' Cited in Bolshakova, p. 5

[36] *Kolyma Tales*, p. 126

[37] Tomashevsky, in Lemon & Reis, p. 90

[38] *Kolyma Tales*, p. 127

[39] Loc. cit.

[40] Ibid., p. 126

[41] Ibid., p. 128

[42] Ibid., p. 129

[43] Ibid., p. 127

[44] Ibid., p. 129

[45] See *Captain Tolly's Love* in *Kolyma Tales*, pp. 325-36

[46] *Kolyma Tales*, p. 131

[47] This roadside conforms to Bakhtin's characterisation of the Greek *road novel*, where meetings are chance and where people from all social strata meet freely. Bakhtin in 'The Form of Time and the Chronotope in the Novel: From the Greek Novel to Modern Fiction', p. 516

[48] *Kolyma Tales*, p. 136

[49] Ibid., p. 140

[50] Loc. cit.

[51] V. Shalamov, in Toker, *Return from the Archipelago*, p. 281n

[52] V. V. Nabokov, cited in Dipple, p. 48

[53] I. H. Evans, *The Wordsworth Dictionary of Dictionary of Phrase and Fable*, (Ware: Wordsworth Editions, 1994), p. 1086

⁵⁴ *Kolyma Tales*, p. 146.This is an attack on Stalin's belief that common criminals were misguided and ignorant and therefore still 'friends of the people'. However, he believed political prisoners must know what they were doing and therefore were dangerous enemies. Kochan, & Keep, pp. 368-97

⁵⁵ To use Tomashevsky's opposition, in Lemon & Reis, p. 78

⁵⁶ 'Nowhere is there a description of a country as a whole with it peculiarities.' Bakhtin, 'The Form of Time and the Chronotope in the Novel: From the Greek Novel to Modern Fiction', p. 508. Shalamov uses brevity to pursue a point rather than panorama. The hero in this tale also has no need for sweeping statements about his journey as his interest is concerned only with survival.

⁵⁷ *Kolyma Tales*, p. 127

⁵⁸ Lice figure metaphorically here. Convicts were referred to as 'lice'; that is, irritating parasites who feed off their hosts and need to be eradicated. In the state's view, malingering or non-working prisoners were literally 'parasites' and the hero is in such a position.

⁵⁹ Joost van Baak, 'The House in Russian Avant-garde Prose: Chronotope and Archetype', *Essays in Poetics*, XV, 1, 1990, p. 3

⁶⁰ *Kolyma Tales,* p. 132

⁶¹ It is unlikely that Shalamov uses 17 kilometres by chance: his prison sentence totalled 17 years of futility and disorientation.

⁶² *Kolyma Tales*, p. 139

⁶³ Loc. cit.

⁶⁴ Van Baak likens the enclosure of a house to resemble the safety of the womb. See van Baak, 'The House in Russian Avant-garde Prose: Chronotope and Archetype', p. 3.

⁶⁵ V. Shklovsky, 'Art as Technique', in Lemon & Reis, pp. 3-24

⁶⁶ O'Toole, *Structure, Style and Interpretation in the Russian Short Story*, p. 13

⁶⁷ Loc. cit.

⁶⁸ *Kolyma Tales*, p. 392

⁶⁹ Loc. cit.

⁷⁰ Ibid., p. 132

⁷¹ Ibid., p. 393

⁷² Loc. cit.

⁷³ Loc. cit.

⁷⁴ Shalamov either projects these episodes forward to the time when he is writing them, i.e. after they have happened or he reinforces the notion that memory is crucial to reporting events. In *The Train*, the hero and consequently Shalamov is very much aware that to leave Kolyma and forget is easier than to remember these traumatic events.

⁷⁵ Shalamov has stated himself that there are 'contradictions etc.' in the tales. Also he does not claim that other tales, such as *Pugachov's Battle*, are literally true. He wrote the tale as a recreation of similar events in the camp, but he uses certain stylistic and artistic techniques to fictionalise a convict breakout.

⁷⁶ *Kolyma Tales*, p. 393

⁷⁷ Loc. cit.

⁷⁸ Ibid., p. 395

⁷⁹ Ibid., pp. 394-5

[80] Shalamov was well known to have had an almost photographic memory. In the camps, to recognise someone quickly gains you valuable thinking time to assess the possibility of a threat. Freud reputedly formulated the most basic of human reactions when meeting an anonymous person: 'can I eat it?' 'can it eat me?' or 'can I mate with it?'

[81] *Kolyma Tales*, p. 195

[82] This is one of many religious images that can be found in Shalamov's tales; yet paradoxically he steadfastly refused to belief in the Orthodox Church and its doctrines.

[83] Ibid., p. 196

[84] Loc. cit.

[85] Ibid., p. 197

[86] Loc. cit.

[87] Ibid., p. 398

[88] Ibid., p. 401

[89] Ibid., p. 402

[90] Culler (1981) in Martin, p. 127

[91] Barthes comments '...to use the Formalists terms which seem appropriate here – retardation devices can be either artistically or realistically motivated.' As cited in S. Rimmon-Kenan, *Narrative fiction: Contemporary Poetics*, (London: Methuen, 1988), p. 127

[92] *Kolyma Tales*, p. 394

[93] Loc. cit.

[94] Ibid., p. 393

[95] Cobley, p. 16

[96] It is almost certain that a prisoner would have taken the train for much of the journey to Kolyma. It is more likely that Shalamov wanted to express the fear of an ex-prisoner finding himself in a full train carriage again.

[97] *Kolyma Tales*, p. 397

[98] Ibid., p. 392

[99] Rimmon-Kenan, p. 15

[100] *Kolyma Tales*, p. 395

[101] Ibid., p. 398

[102] Ibid., p. 401

[103] Ricoeur, p. 3

[104] *Kolyma Tales*, p. 402

[105] Martin explains that closure exists in order to 'round off' a story, giving it a finished feel. Fairy and folk tales employ this technique very effectively, but Shalamov's tales form a large mosaic where each tale fits in around the others, evading closure in this way.

[106] *Kolyma Tales*, p. 392

[107] The colouring of the armbands could be suggestive of danger or the spilling of blood. In any case, although they are meant to be guardians, the guards are nevertheless regarded as a lethal threat to any convict on the platform.

[108] *Kolyma Tales*, p. 392

[109] Dipple argues that a reader will always look for a character trait that he will recognise, and therefore he will empathise with the character. In other words, a reader will warm to a character if he or she shares the same outlook or feeling. But the hero

is not 'one of us', and unless the reader had been in the same situation, she or he could not truly empathise with him. Shalamov is not trying to impress or disgust his readers; he is just reporting the facts as experienced. See Dipple, p. 23

[110] Post-Traumatic Stress Disorder is an infrequent but sustained reaction against previous trauma, but the body has methods to overcome his or her experiences. Self-induced memory loss and withdrawal are common symptoms. See R. S. Feldman, *Understanding Psychology*, (New York: McGraw-Hill, 1993), pp. 518-19. The hero in *The Train* fights to overcome his memory but continues with a camp survivalist strategy of maintaining a distance from others. Shalamov's post-Gulag years include both these paradoxical mental strategies; that is, he confronts his traumatic years by writing about them, yet retained a camp mentality and consequently he never established 'normal' relations with others. Towards the end of his life, Shalamov retreated into camp habits, thus never having escaped the Gulag grip.

[111] *Kolyma Tales*, p. 393

[112] Loc. cit.

[113] A function of characterisation is to create recognisable features common to a certain type of character the author wishes to portray. By exhibiting certain exaggerated attributes that the reader will recognise, the character will also take on certain expected psychological mannerisms. See the following text for more information on different characterisation techniques: Scholes & Kellogg, p. 86

[114] *Kolyma Tales*, p. 394

[115] The extended single fingernail was affected by convict bosses in the camps. It could also refer to the proverb 'Recognise the Devil by his nails'. Cited in Elena Mikhailik 'Varlam Shalamov: v prisutstvii d'iavola. Problema konteksta', *Russian Literature*, XLVII, II, 2000, pp. 199-219

[116] *Kolyma Tales*, p. 394

[117] Ibid., p. 397

[118] Ibid., p. 401

[119] Loc. cit.

[120] Scholes and Kellogg, p. 87. Shalamov's underlying viewpoint is that what 'we' would see as deplorable traits in a character are not necessarily bad or evil traits, but occur as a result of a system that has distanced any resemblance of 'normal' traits we would find in real or fictional characters.

[121] '...He (the author) makes us sympathise with what he presents as good and deplores what he presents as evil.' Tomashevsky in Lemon & Reis, p. 61

[122] *Kolyma Tales*, p. 402

[123] Toker, *Return from the Archipelago*, p. 150

[124] Tomashevsky in Lemon & Reis, p. 78

[125] Shalamov makes action the determining force behind travel in both these tales.

[126] *Kolyma Tales*, p. 394

[127] Loc. cit.

[128] Ibid., p. 397

[129] Loc. cit.

Chapter 2

Point of View

This chapter will examine how point of view is crucial to the construction of Shalamov's tales. While the narrative structure is said to constitute a refraction of the theme, O'Toole considers the narrative to be 'further refracted by the workings of point of view, and the particular pleasure reading provides seems to be due largely to the play with point of view.'[1] In Shalamov's case, the 'pleasure' of reading is not based on the subject matter of his stories, the content of which is simply described by Robert Young as 'heartbreaking'[2], but rather on the sophistication of their construction. Every piece of work can be construed as subjective because an author has moulded it, resulting in the conscious creation of a narratorial perspective. As Bakhtin comments 'We have two events – the event narrated in the work, and the event of the narration itself.'[3] Point of view is a 'trademark' of Shalamov's work and, as Toker puts it, 'it is the personality of Shalamov the narrator rather than of Shalamov the prisoner that dominates his tales.'[4] The most common perspective in *Kolyma Tales* is Shalamov's use of distance between text and author. He mostly places the narrator at close quarters to proceedings without involving the narrator/hero in the actual process of events. This gives the tales an observational slant, whilst retaining an intimate feeling. Indeed, '[t]he figure of the narrator is an unusually passive one. He is always the victim of the action, and almost never initiates any of his own.'[5] It is also usual for Shalamov to write a tale from a third-person omniscient viewpoint when he obviously could not have witnessed the original event. The effect Shalamov creates in employing an observational narrator is to produce a studied and neutral tone that falls somewhere between mimesis and diegesis in Genette's definition.[6] Where the tales involve a first person narrative, it is possible to detect Shalamov the author providing limited information on events. However, there is little subjective intrusion by the author, owing to Shalamov's particular style. The authorial voice is an exact replica of a hero in a state of exhaustion and indifference and the tone and mood of the text reflects this. Thus, what occurs in the tales is a dispassionate, yet powerful observation of events in Kolyma.[7]

Nevertheless, when Shalamov is indisputably the narrator, he is very aware of his involving presence and deliberately avoids preaching and keeps his commentary to a minimum.[8] However, where a narrator/hero makes deliberate comment on a situation or other characters, Shalamov ensures that there is a reason. For example, in *Sententious*, the hero makes many remarks on his awakening and his feelings towards others. This is 'acceptable' to Shalamov because the story is about a rediscovery of the 'self' and therefore about finding an individual voice. This new voice is going to be allowed to make comments, whereas in *The Lawyers' Plot*, the hero cannot comment on others as he has no 'voice'.

Point of view is not just 'voice' or 'voices' but a device for shaping the trajectory of a tale. A suspense tale written 'from the end backwards' has to employ a point of view that does not reveal the outcome before it occurs in the tale. *The Lawyers' Plot* is one such obvious case, because the hero is released unexpectedly, although his death had seemed the most likely outcome. However, all tales that relate prior events are written retrospectively and thus the author 'knows' how they end. The narratorial perspective therefore has to ensure that any deliberate 'suspense' is not compromised. Also, point of view can be an inclusion device whereby the reader is deliberately asked to think about events. It can also be an exclusion device to withhold information at crucial times in order to move the plot along. Knowledge of the hero's fate in *The Lawyers' Plot* uses this technique not only to move the story along, but to explicitly foreground the secrecy and mis-information in Soviet Russia during the purges. Toker describes *Kolyma Tales* as 'documentary prose' inasmuch as the fiction is based on real or imaginatively reconstructed events, as in *Cherry Brandy*. All the tales are re-creations of what Toker calls 'what-it-would-have-been-like'. She claims that camp authors such as Shalamov possess 'the ability to imagine certain situations, such as the death of a poet in the camp.' Thus, Shalamov's fictional situations are perhaps 'not impossible extensions of his own experience.'[9] Therefore, the narration in *Kolyma Tales* reflects this notion of fictionality based on real events. Each event is contextualised and given symbolic meaning, not specifically for the reader's benefit and understanding, but to show how irrational and unexpected events and especially death occurred in the camps.

The stories chosen for this chapter are *An Individual Assignment*, *Berries* and *Quiet*. Each tale is about the death of an individual, but Shalamov uses a different narratorial perspective in portraying events. Shalamov thought of the multitude of dead as an incomprehensible statistic, but he viewed the death of a single man as a tragedy.[10] Death occurred everywhere in the camps and on a day-to-day basis, and the theme of these tales concentrates on the circumstances surrounding each man's death. Point of view is mostly from the first person in all three tales; the narrator is present to witness events but is a passive participant. He does not instigate or cause the deaths, yet in a way makes himself responsible for reporting the events. Point of view is shown not to be a static tool, but a device that is able to attach itself to various characters. For example, in *An Individual Assignment*, Baranov's knowledge of future events is hinted at, and in *Berries*, Seroshapka's threatening words give emphasis to the death of the prisoner. Where the focus falls on a particular character it is reasonably safe to assume that he has a significant part to play in the death of a convict. Even so, Shalamov places great emphasis on disavowing individual responsibility for a convict's downfall. There are always many characters directly or indirectly involved in the death of a prisoner, whether fellow convicts or guards.[11] No character is introduced without a specific reason for his presence, and Shalamov utilises him in several ways; examples are, he is foregrounded or an observer of symbolic importance in the tale. Shalamov's use of brevity in settings and characterisation also relates to his employment of point of view. The narrative focus often shifts from character to character, but usually from the author/observer perspective. This creates an impression for the reader of a roving camera, taking in many different perspectives and points of view.[12] Shalamov forms opinions on characters by reading their body language or utilising prior knowledge to predict thoughts. Shalamov almost never acts as an omniscient narrator by attempting to 'read' the minds of his characters.[13] He 'merely' focuses on the physical results of their psychological processes and implies that certain thoughts are taking place. In this way Shalamov remains truthful to events, without the need to resort to embellishments. Unwarranted speculation does not appear in the tales, and therefore Shalamov might be said to be treating his readers with a certain respect.[14] Essentially, point of view is the interaction between the tale, the narrator and the reader and analysis of the following three tales will demonstrate this powerful feature of Shalamov's poetics.

2.1 *An Individual Assignment*

'A face that toils so close to stones is already stone itself'.[15]

An Individual Assignment differs from *Berries* or *Quiet* in its lack of participative first person narration and its use of the observational third person. The narrator is not an active participant in the tale, yet his tone suggests that he was privy to all the events. Andrew highlights this type of narration as '...where the narrator is clearly a witness to the events, but plays no part in the action, and is not even named.'[16] This form of narration is therefore from an informed third person perspective, and as such we have to rely on the narrator's reporting of proceedings to deduce events. It would be easy to conclude that this point of view is third-person omniscient, but that implies inner knowledge of the characters. Shalamov, as previously mentioned, does not generally attempt to read the minds of his characters; rather he infers mental states from physical actions or words. This process gives *An Individual Assignment* the feeling of an informed tale but also a sense of impartiality. The reader is aware that Dugaev has been marked out for special attention by the association with the 'individual assignment' and our understanding of events is governed by this fact. Point of view is refracted through this information, and we gain an insight into the processes surrounding Dugaev's, the overseer's and the foreman's actions after the death. Shalamov has made an attempt to link the real and fictional worlds in his tales and his method conforms to Scholes and Kellogg's analysis of this connection. Scholes and Kellogg suggest three factors which sustain an element of realism in fiction: 1. the recording of specific fact; 2. representation of what resembles specific fact, and 3. representation of generalised types of actuality.[17] *An Individual Assignment* conforms to the second factor, as is the case with most of the tales. Although the events described may not be completely 'true', they certainly seem to conform to a specific class of 'true' events. In effect Shalamov is just relating the necessary facts and allowing the reader to make up his/her own mind about events.

2.1.1 Narrative Structure

An Individual Assignment is a comparatively short tale, at just over a thousand words, and although there exists a narrative structure, it is not explicit or crucial to understanding, as is the case in other tales. According to several theorists on narrative structure, the basis or theme of a story can be deduced by pinpointing the peripeteia or transformation.[18] This 'change' could be arguably located in one of two places in *An Individual Assignment*: in the very first line or at the point at which the overseer confirms Dugaev's fate with 'Good luck!'[19] The reason why the peripeteia can be adjudged to be in the first line is that Dugaev's work and consequently his quota has already caught the overseer's attention. However, these events occurred outside the frame of the tale, and should not be included as a part of the narrative structure. The opening of the tale, although incorporating this structurally ambiguous first line, has a clear prologue. It is possible to define the first line as a specific prologue, which is then followed by a description of the secondary characters (general prologue) and then more detail on Dugaev. The first three paragraphs constitute a mixed prologue, rather than a complication or peripeteia and therefore set the scene for the rest of the tale. The introduction of several characters opens the possibility for other character structures. As O'Toole points out, there can be several parallel narrative structures based on one or more characters, but in *An Individual Assignment*, the focus on other characters is only in relation to Dugaev. Therefore, although it is possible to follow Baranov, the overseer or even the foreman and trace their narrative trajectory, the narration itself is firmly focused on Dugaev.[20]

The structure looks something like this:

Specific Prologue   - Dugaev's fate
General Prologue   - Presentation of secondary characters
Specific Prologue   - Short history of Dugaev
Exposition   - All convicts in Cafeteria
First complication   - Overseer allocates assignment
Second complication   - Narrator notes Dugaev's progress
Third complication   - Quota measured
Peripeteia   - Overseer reports findings

| Dénouement | - Dugaev is shot |
| Specific Epilogue | - Thoughts on Dugaev |

The minor details we obtain from the prologues and exposition do not mark out Dugaev as being particularly special, but rather as someone who was in the wrong place at the wrong time. The protagonist can be seen as representing one of countless young men, thrust into the extreme conditions of the camps. The narrator underlines his anonymity by stating 'No one would be concerned about the fact that Dugaev could not last a sixteen-hour working day.'[21] The specific and general prologues give the reader sufficient information to understand Dugaev's situation, without the need to expand on any of their individual pasts. The narrator briefly draws on secondary characters before reporting 'facts' about Dugaev. That is, the narrator has retreated from describing current events and addresses the reader directly. However, immediately afterwards, the tale resumes its presentation of the current situation. This concentration on 'events' occasionally adds extra information, which the reader may infer to be either 'informed' or simply the narrator's point of view. It is difficult to distinguish whether Dugaev has imparted his knowledge of convict 'rules' or ideas on friendship to the narrator or whether the narrator is hazarding an inference about Dugaev's beliefs. Again, it is Shalamov's attempt at the re-creation of a common event in camp life that colours the text with inferences. When the first and third complications occur, they are easy to distinguish, as Shalamov has included spoken words by the overseer. He is in control of Dugaev's fate and to this extent has all the life-changing words at his disposal. In the second complication the overseer is speechless and words are not deemed necessary. The peripeteia once again forms the overseer's speech, but from this point onwards his part has finished and he ceases to be heard. The narrator then fills in the necessary formalities of the execution, before finally assuming Dugaev's thoughts and comments: 'Dugaev regretted that he had worked for nothing.'[22] The narrator does not wait for the execution to take place, but correctly times the words before Dugaev's death. The narrator is intimating that this is most likely what Dugaev would have thought.

2.1.2 Fabula and Sujet

An Individual Assignment displays an interesting approach to fabula and sujet. The first sentence essentially sets a 'foreboding scene' based on the verbal statement by the overseer and the reaction by the foreman. The narrator informs us of the overseer's words and then refocuses on the foreman; as a result the reader becomes conscious of imminent changes. The fabula is essentially concerned with the presentation of the actions of a condemned man, who is unaware of his own fate. We therefore have a series of incidents which concern the 'ignorant' Dugaev, and here the sujet is presenting the reader with the reasons and facts behind actions which relate to his future death. The sujet is primarily the narrator's voice and the reader has to rely on his words for information. For example, after the opening scene, the narrator draws back from his observations to include a crucial fact concerning Dugaev. '...everything that he saw and heard here amazed more than surprised him.'[23] The sujet does not deviate in time and space from Dugaev's situation and remains firmly focused on the protagonist's plight. In this way, the fabula is never very far from the narrator and vice versa. The fabula also includes foreknowledge by the others of Dugaev's fate and indeed of Dugaev's ignorance. This binary relationship of knowledge and ignorance is tightly incorporated within the fabula, and is a major factor in the tale's theme. The sujet therefore is responsible for ensuring that both sides never 'meet' in the tale and the distance between them is kept clear.

There are several narratorial deviations during the course of the tale, all related to Dugaev, where the narrator digresses from current events. The narrator imparts to the reader several of Dugaev's 'thoughts', but in such a way as to make them part of camp psychology. The fabula is primarily about the fate of Dugaev, but the sujet interjects with comparative narratorial irony on the inherent mistrust and untruths within the camp. Firstly, the narrator elucidates the three physical facts of camp life - cold, hunger and sleeplessness - leading on to three psychological specifics: don't believe, don't fear, don't ask.[24] There is a direct relationship between these states: Shalamov points to the latter as a direct consequence of the former. Essentially, disbelief, fearlessness and an unquestioning stance, stem from a lack of basic physiological needs. Also, the human belief system has been distorted to such a degree that a denial of hope, is preferable to a belief in an unknown future.[25] Secondly, the narrator comments that 'yesterday's farmers did not have to know that Dugaev was new to this sort of work...'[26] This observation is Shalamov's way of foregrounding the terrible role reversal at play in the camps. He continues to correlate petty stealing with large-scale corruption, before significantly returning to Dugaev. The narrator therefore implies that it is not just the prisoners who are caught up in this network of deceit. Finally, the narrator manages to finish the tale with the biggest lie of all: his ironical statement that all prisoners 'believed' that the gunshots were tractors backfiring. Denial that this fatal event took place is morally unacceptable to Shalamov, but he is in the same position as everyone else. He is also culpable in denying that it took place, but in writing the tale he is able to share some of the blame and guilt for the event. Dugaev's non-appearance the next day would obviously be noticed and it would be improbable to infer any reason other than his execution.

Strict temporal order is observed in *An Individual Assignment*, and disruptions in linear time are relatively few. The only real diversion by the narrator is when he refers back to Dugaev's life as a student before entering the camps. He implies that he knew the student, by providing the reader with facts concerning his previous life. He continues to emphasise that Dugaev is just a young man, unskilled in hard labour and selfishness, who will lose his life in an environment where no one cares. There exists a sense of Shalamov's playing with time: Dugaev's sleep is almost non-existent, interspersed with vivid dreams of food. As with the dream images in *Condensed Milk*, there appears to be a link between Shalamov's reporting of these dreams and future events.[27] They seem to portend the future of the character, food equating to a release from camp life. Night exists very briefly, before Dugaev has to fulfil an even longer day than usual, thereby ensuring that his torment and subsequent regret are accentuated. By using evenings at strategic points in the tale, Shalamov conveys a sense of transition from one state to the next. Dugaev is identified on the first evening, assessed and convicted on the second and sentenced on the third. Thus the 'traditional' day has ceased to lead on to the closure of night. The barriers have been destroyed in order to emphasise the dismantling of normal day/night relations and the narrator concentrates on the effect that Soviet Reality has on the life of Dugaev.

2.1.3 Characterisation

Through the title of this tale Shalamov presents a message in two ways: Firstly, it suggests a special task, which not just anybody can undertake. In this way, Shalamov regards 'an individual assignment' as separate from the usual collective work. Secondly, Dugaev is named and as a consequence, he has ceased to be one of the nameless collective, thus regaining some sense of humanity. The irony, of course, is that this special consideration is a marker for his death. Shalamov is fully aware of the paradox whereby it is necessary to remain anonymous to avoid individualisation and consequently persecution: survival is conditional on the loss of a convict's identity.[28]

The narration remains focused on Dugaev and there are repeated statements about his physical debilitation leading up to death: 'I'm getting weaker'; 'He was already totally exhausted'; and 'There had been no reason for him to exhaust himself on this, his final day.'[29] The narrative perspective shifts from direct narration to focalising on Dugaev and back again. He only speaks openly once more: 'I hear you,'[30] in reply to the overseer's loaded statement. It is possible to infer that Dugaev is not ignorant of his fate, but he is just too exhausted to even care. This is a character theme that runs through many of Shalamov's works and Dugaev, like the exhausted Andreev in *The Lawyers' Plot*, is willing to allow events to occur around him. But it is true to say that Dugaev's subliminal awareness is not strong enough for consciousness and therefore he is not aware of his impending doom. Shalamov has merely invested Dugaev with what Hosking's calls 'spiritual calm'.[31] What Dugaev and Andreev have in common is a 'psychological awakening'. The change in Dugaev comes through the narrator, who after firmly stating that Dugaev was never surprised at anything, notes that Dugaev *is* 'surprised' at Baranov's offer of a cigarette. Also, after finding out that he had managed to complete twenty-five percent of the quota 'He was surprised at this figure.'[32] This narrative ensures that events are not normal for Dugaev. He has time to reflect on his last day and it is not anger, but regret at working for nothing that is dominant in the text. Toker comments on Dugaev: 'He has been no expert on camp semiotics; and by the time a key point is revealed to him, the knowledge is largely useless.'[33]

Baranov, Dugaev's work partner is the key to this tale, inasmuch as he is fully aware of what an individual assignment entails. The point of view focuses on Baranov as much as on Dugaev, and where Baranov is, there also is Dugaev. This binary relationship is important for an understanding of how 'comrades' react to each other. The offer of the cigarette can be universally recognised as a dying man's last wish and it is Baranov who is in the best position to make the offer.[34] Yet, he normalises this offer, by adding, '...but leave me some.'[35] It would certainly have raised Dugaev's suspicion without this proviso. Also it was Baranov who 'helped' with the overseer's measuring of the test pits and who was thus in a position to alter or distort the measurements and therefore 'help' Dugaev. But, if he had been caught, then it would have been Baranov who would have been shot. Shalamov stresses the unwanted roles that other convicts assume in keeping up their charade. Baranov spends the whole of the next day with Dugaev, but the narrative distances him from any input or actions. The text ensures that Baranov's knowledge and Dugaev's ignorance remain separate.

The foreman has a less involved role in the tale, but his sudden silence serves as an omen. His actions alert the reader, not Dugaev, to future events, and when he re-appears he merely orders Dugaev to wait for further instructions. In doing so, he is distancing himself from any personal responsibility. The most significant character as far as Dugaev is concerned is the overseer who measures and reports the work achieved by the convicts. There is more text time spent on measuring the work, than on the convicts' performance of it. The point of view therefore concentrates mostly on the results of the work. The narrator does not focus on any character's workload, except Dugaev's. His work is his best effort, yet it is still not enough to save him. The overseer measures the area for Dugaev before he starts, looks at it after lunch and then finally at the end of the day. The other characters who appear in the tale are massed and anonymous, merely a complementary background to the characters who matter. The narrative focuses on ordinary workers, such as farmers and carpenters who, by working in their profession highlight Dugaev's unsuitability for manual or skilled labour. The focus always shifts to individual characters, and the narrator always makes Dugaev one single man out of many, and as such he walks with them to work, returns with them and goes for food with them. It is only when an action is required, such as working or eating, a task that becomes individualised, that the focus shifts to a character. The workgang on his final day is again described as massed and never makes the transition from non-personal collective to specific characterisation.[36] The investigator is anonymous as are the soldiers who shoot Dugaev; thus the narration distances their part in his downfall, underlining the inevitability of his demise. As Todorov comments on Nazi guards and executioners, it is important to dehumanise the convicts first in order to execute them. Shalamov's narration distances their culpability from their actions, by keeping them anonymous and distancing them from the executed.[37] The system is also cruel in its ability to ensure that they have '[squeezed] the last pounds of gold-bearing sand out of the victims.'[38]

2.1.4 Setting

An Individual Assignment has its background located in the physical landscape and in the locale of food and sleep. The main action of the tale takes place outside at the work pits, but the consequences of physical work impact upon the psychological processes inside the kitchens and barracks. The focus of the tale on the first day moves from worksite to kitchens, and then finally to the barracks. This process is repeated the next day, with an important break for lunch, then back to work. In effect, the tale moves between locations chosen for their symbolic significance. Primarily, this is the effect of work on hunger, and hunger on the acquisition of food. Dugaev's preoccupation with food sustains him through work, and it is only the narrator's concentration on a single sentence, that marks the end for Dugaev: 'The sensation of hunger had long since left him.'[39] Although food is a psychological and physical necessity, its importance to the setting is crucial. Dugaev thinks about, sees and dreams about food to such an extent that unusually, rations have become his physical and mental world. In a sense, acquisition of food is his idea of reaching Heaven: a psychological setting that cures all ills. The physical need has modified his psychological perception of his environment to such an extent that it only includes work, sleep and food. Therefore, the settings of kitchen, barracks and work pits are his only physical environments, with food as the overriding Nirvana.[40] Interestingly enough, the purges produced a quick death for the prisoner, whereas a cut in rations created a slow but inevitable one. Shalamov therefore wanted to portray this cruel quota system with as much impact as possible.

The task to which Dugaev is assigned, both with Baranov and by himself, is to dig out test pits. Baranov is transformed into an undertaker measuring up Dugaev for his personalised coffin and Dugaev has in effect become his own gravedigger. His final words are enough to supply an epitaph: 'Well, I guess that's that.'[41] The grave is carefully marked out and Dugaev is almost enthusiastic about completing the task. This metaphor can be extended to the chasm, where the narrator detects that the barbed wire 'nearly blocked off a small ravine.'[42] The deliberate use of 'nearly' indicates that the ravine is not closed completely, but has a purpose for body disposal. This ravine will provide a collective burial pit and therefore Dugaev's individual pit will have been superseded. Even Dugaev's right to dig his own grave has been taken away, and his senseless labour has become an ironic symbol of his fruitless attempt to stay alive. He had been handed all the tools for the job: 'a shovel, pick, crowbar and wheelbarrow'.[43] The narrator uses a repetitive motif to describe his work. 'swung the pick, hauled, dumped...hauled and dumped...swinging his pick and dumping.'[44] The wheelbarrow going up the gangplank is the final item Dugaev remarks on: 'His calves ached, and his arms, shoulders, and head hurt from leaning into the wheelbarrow.'[45] All these facets of the work, described in great detail, serve to express just how difficult it is to accomplish. After lunch, the quartz marker was still a long way away, and the reader is forced to witness this failing attempt, blow by blow. The obvious analogy here is of Dugaev playing out the role of Sisyphus, where he has to roll the rock up the hill, before it rolls down again in order for him to repeat the process. The focus on this sequence reinforces the futility of this kind of work, which ultimately points the finger at the Soviet system: meaningless work culminating in death.

The hill at the beginning of the tale is one setting that Shalamov uses briefly, and the foreman 'stared at an evening star sparkling over the crest of the hill.'[46] This simple display exemplifies Shalamov's idea that the convict '...has no leisure to think of the psychological significance of landscape detours.'[47] However, this evening star could be thought of as the evening planet Mercury, which in Greek mythology is the god of thieves. Here, Mercury is glancing over the hill to pass judgement on the 'greatest' thief of all; Sisyphus or ironically Dugaev.[48] This is reinforced by the narrator's conviction that Dugaev did not possess the single most useful survival tool: 'He did not know how to steal.'[49] Shalamov, by using this analogy, brings all the might of the Soviet justice system to bear on one individual. This single focalising technique is essentially symbolic of the whole tale.

2.2 *Berries*

Berries describe one man's ambition to fill his cup with delicious berries in order to trade for some bread. This man's work partner narrates the events from a first person perspective. However, the theme of this tale does not relate specifically to Rybakov, but to the narrator himself, who knows where the boundaries for survival lie. His actions, from a beating to watching Rybakov being shot, all indicate that this man knows what is acceptable and what is not. It is understandable to be beaten for being unable to carry a log, but to trespass into an 'official' forbidden zone carries with it the ultimate punishment. The narrator fulfils the major part of telling a story, that is to furnish extra details that explain more than the events themselves. For example, when the narrator comments 'The marker should have been hanging from a tree which stood two yards farther away,'[50] he is explaining that he knows it has been moved for a reason. It is a deliberate attempt by the guards to tempt the narrator into moving beyond the boundary. Rybakov's instant death indicates that the guard or in this case a named guard, Seroshapka, was waiting for the narrator to make a move. His survival instinct ensures that temptation in this Garden of Eden does not extend to the sweetest and best berries. Rybakov or Adam, by transcending this barrier, has incurred the wrath of the ultimate power of the camps.[51] The narrative tone can be best described in one sentence of the text 'I had reached the stage of absolute indifference.'[52] This is of course, a major theme throughout Shalamov's works, and *Berries* combines it with his other themes of luck and chance (as necessary conditions for survival). In one sense the story is an observation of events that Shalamov witnessed, but it is also a story about chance. It is a first person testament to Rybakov and others like him who might have survived their imprisonment. Shalamov is acknowledging his own survival, inasmuch as he believes it could so easily have been himself who died.

2.2.1 Narrative Structure

The narrative structure in *Berries* is interesting in that the peripeteia focuses on the death of Rybakov, but the story is about the narrator. He dictates the flow of information and we follow him around, coming across Rybakov later in the tale. Importantly, the story begins with the beating of the narrator and only returns to him at the end of the tale. But it is his conduct that is important to the context of the tale, and the peripeteia reflects this. The death is an important warning to the narrator and as such is an integral part of the tale. The narrative structure is shown below:

Specific Prologue	- The narrator's beating
General Prologue	- Concern for work gang
Exposition	- Work practice
Complication	- Wants Berries
Peripeteia	- Rybakov is shot
Dénouement	- Seroshapka threatens the narrator

The story opens in a similar way to *An Individual Assignment*, in that a challenge confronts the protagonist. Rather than an assignment, the narrator/hero receives a beating and a threat to his future safety. Thus, this tale bases itself on an explicit warning to the protagonist, with the promise of a life-changing challenge to come. However, *An Individual Assignment* bases its plot on the characters' all knowing the consequences of this assignment. In *Berries*, there is at first nothing specific to relate the narrator's beating to Rybakov's death. The only link is the introduction of Seroshapka, who states 'Let me have a look at you, so I'll remember you,' which creates tension and in turn marks the narrator for future reference.[53] The focus therefore remains on the narrator, who will act as the important message carrier.

Shalamov uses direct and indirect narration to facilitate this role. Information relating to the narrator is in the form of internal monologues, and is used to motivate himself. He uses speech sparingly to focus attention on specific events and when he responds to Fadeev that, 'It's not me who's a fascist, it's you,'[54] he explains the reason for this outburst. This is a specific feature of Shalamov's tales, and it is made prominent in *Berries*. Speaking out loud and proclaiming one's thoughts to the world are not actions that increase life in the camps; rather they shorten it. Internalising one's thoughts stems from a prisoner's need to remain anonymous and not draw attention to himself. The dynamic and argumentative narrative here is necessary to reveal another theme running through the story. Although the narrator is 'absolutely indifferent' to consequences, there is still a small flame of self-preservation and physiological reaction that prevents him from sacrificing his life. This is further reinforced by Shalamov's recurrent premise that nobody will help anybody else, whatever the circumstances. For Baranov, in *An Individual Assignment*, the primary rule is not to interfere with others and in *Berries*, the narrator's work gang are angry and amused by his beating. Therefore, Shalamov is always keen to point out the distance between persecuted characters and the rest. An unwritten rule, aptly demonstrated in *My First Tooth*, is not to get involved with persecuted convicts.[55] However, in *Berries*, the narrator 'helps' Rybakov, by pointing out the markers. Yet, this is not a purely altruistic act, rather it is the narrator's attempt to distance himself from a dangerous situation. The exposition deals with the setting up of the camp and auxiliary information surrounding the prisoners' work detail. The tale adopts a documentary style and the narrator takes in both general and specific details. He informs us of firewood collection by the convicts, but juxtaposes it with the fact that only guards can have fires. He then focuses on what is to be the major subject matter of *Berries*. He waxes lyrical about the different varieties of berries, before eventually bringing in Rybakov and his own berry collecting. From this point on, all but one of the important stages of the narrative are marked by direct speech: 1) 'Look at that...' 2) The gunshot (a symbolic utterance), 3) 'Leave him there...' 4) 'I wanted to get you...'[56] These utterances are interspersed with the narrator's own thoughts. These thoughts fulfil a major concern of Shalamov's, that is, he always finds a good with a bad, a bonus where one expects all to be gloom. It is his way of accurately depicting how cause and effect have been twisted in the camps, where once again nothing is as it seems. The narrator now has a 'chance' to get more bread for himself, after Rybakov's half-full can rolls towards him. This cup is not overflowing, but has just the correct amount of berries.

2.2.2 Fabula and Sujet

Shalamov uses a similar approach to that taken in *An Individual Assignment* in arranging the chronology and cause and effect of *Berries*. Seroshapka has been marked for future reference by promising to remember the narrator in the future. This technique therefore creates a link between the start and end of the tale. However, there are no predictions of the future or retarding reminiscences; rather Shalamov uses the narratorial voice to expand or explain certain details. The tale displays a textual linearity, with the narrator reporting facts and details consecutively. The narratorial commentary also coincides with the time of the action and is not a retrospective reportage from a later point. It is hard to distinguish the future from the present in *Berries*, as the narrator interweaves action with secondary facts. For example, he describes himself lying in the snow with a log, and explains that all convicts carried a log to take home and all were tired. His beating is holding up this return to the barracks and he repeats himself with 'But I was lying in the snow,'[57] to acknowledge that he is the cause of the hold-up. What follows is the narrator interspersing action with segments of information: Information – action – information – action – information. The narrator clarifies all the information thus presenting the fabula and sujet in an alternating pattern:

Use of Formal address (sujet)
Narrator and Fadeev's exchange (fabula)
Explanation for his reaction (sujet)
Introduction of Seroshapka and beating (fabula)
Explanation for fellow convicts shouting (sujet)

The fabula and sujet do not always follow this binary pattern and the narrator's description of the berries falls under both fabula and sujet. The reader is informed of the delights of the berries, with reference made to both the consumption and to Rybakov's. No speech is reported until the narrator finds the boundary markers. Prior to this, the narrator almost, but not quite, reports from a future state. He states

'...I ate the berries myself, carefully and greedily pressing each one against the roof of my mouth with my tongue.'[58] This description is in the past tense, as if in remembrance, yet the narrator moves on to the present where 'Rybakov's can was filling slowly, and we were finding fewer and fewer berries.'[59] This is another of Shalamov's devices, where he takes 'literary' time out to focus on an event. That is, the author dissociates himself from Rybakov and berry picking, but time is still flowing in the tale. This is a common feature of his tales where Shalamov the author is speaking to the reader directly, while remaining in touch with events in the tale. It is where the boundary between author and narrator becomes blurred, but essentially it does not affect the fabula as his reporting merely adds detail to the story. However, this authorial interlude has a subtle function. It is possible to make out the author 'hypothetically' eating the berries whilst writing, as the descriptions are so vivid. The two different approaches to berry collecting offered by Rybakov and the narrator also come under fabula and sujet. Rybakov will trade his berries, thus projecting his immediate goal to a near future, while the narrator satisfies his craving for instant enjoyment. Thus, two philosophical approaches to camp life are adopted by Shalamov; the fallacy of planning for the future is highlighted and the 'now' is much easier to satisfy. Shalamov seems to favour immediate enjoyment over planning for the future, probably because of his belief in the fallacy of hope.[60]

The narrative returns to the present tense just prior to the narrator's warning and it is the fabula that becomes dominant, though punctuated by the sujet. Three explanations are offered to mark three consecutive actions: firstly, the reader is informed that the markers have moved; secondly, an explanation is offered for the second shot and finally the narrator becomes aware of the dangerous environment in which he finds himself. These narrative 'digressions' enable the reader to follow precisely the chain of events and this leads up to the final statement: "I wanted to get you,' he said, 'but you wouldn't cross the line, you bastard!" [61] It is fitting for this tale to end with the fabula and reported speech. This mirrors the first line and brings the presentation of facts to a close. The sujet merely makes one interjection, by adding the word 'calmly' to Seroshapka, thus negating any return to a state of normality.

2.2.3 Characterisation

Characterisation in *Berries* concentrates on singular, rather than groups of characters. Shalamov also utilises different techniques to portray their characteristics. The narrator reports speech where it is necessary, but treats Rybakov to a richer characterisation than any other character, while not giving him a voice. The narrator, whilst possessing a voice, also has his physical position portrayed. His prone position on the ground is characteristic of Shalamov's use of the up-down dichotomy.[62] A convict falling or lying on the ground is a sure sign of death, as Kline notes 'in terms of...the numerous references to it in the text.'[63] However, this time the prone figure is not going to die, but prefigures the death of another: Rybakov. Shalamov also makes use of the technique of 'giver' and 'receiver' as a major character binary.[64] This *modus operandi* is prevalent in all character exchanges, and the narrator informs the reader of where and how these exchanges take place. Moreover, each character can be identified as falling into both categories. Point of view is relevant to the reader's perception of this binary and crucial to our understanding of these exchanges. In the opening line Fadeev addresses an anonymous person or persons: 'Wait, let me talk to him,'[65] but the narrator brings in his own character and the binary is complete. Fadeev as 'giver' is then superseded by the introduction of Seroshapka. Seroshapka himself changes to receiver, when the foreman makes a fire for him. Rybakov is also a receiver of the berries and of the bullet from Seroshapka, when eventually the narrator becomes receiver in picking up the can of berries. This sequence of give and take is Shalamov's way of highlighting the fact that to give or to receive is a continuous alternating process. It also follows that to give is not necessarily a good thing, nor to receive a bad thing, and vice versa. It is altogether more preferable for a convict to exist in a neutral position, where he is neither indebted nor a creditor to anyone. The narrator does not offer to help Rybakov and remains neutral, thus saving his own life. Propp's analysis of folklore (according to Doležel) suggests that no exchanges are altruistic and the same can be argued for *Kolyma Tales*.[66] Where both parties are equal in an exchange, it is primarily out of self-interest. This is what Doležel names an 'interactional motif' and as such, Shalamov's approach to exchange always reflects the concept of loss and gain. Any character who trades loses something in transaction, but should gain something equal to it. There is rarely an instance where the item received is better than the item given, but sometimes it is even possible to withhold your 'item'. This is illustrated in *Condensed Milk*, where the hero understands that Shestakov's gifts in return for an escape attempt are not altruistic in any way. He takes the milk but declines the offer of participating in the escape attempt, and later hears of the death of all the escapees. Altruism and trade in Kolyma are therefore not without their dangers.

The narrator refers to Rybakov always in the third person and because of this, apart from his name and the nature of his berry collecting, no personal character details are provided. The narrator deliberately distances himself from alluding to a close personal bond with Rybakov. However, the limited information he imparts reveals a lot about the narrator and character relations in the camp. Similarly, in *An Individual Assignment*, the characters do not rely on each other, but form a loose bonding, based on necessity and ultimately on the extreme shortness of a convict's life.[67] The narrator comments 'I never even considered helping Rybakov in his gathering, and he himself would not have desired such aid...'[68] There exists a metaphorical and physical distance between the narrator and Rybakov and this is needed for the shot to make its mark. Rybakov can be seen rather as an unfortunate scapegoat in the larger picture of events. He dared to cross the barrier and paid the price, when it is the narrator who was destined to be shot.[69] The narrator reports the smallness of his body amongst the hummocks and makes a correlation between here and the beginning of the tale, when it was the narrator who was grounded.

Whereas *An Individual Assignment* can be considered a philosophical story, *Berries* is more moral. It pinpoints exactly how both sides of the prison system have to abide by an obscure set of moral guidelines. There are rules to be obeyed and Shalamov has a unique angle on any rule, whether written, unwritten or moral. Rybakov has crossed the boundary, metaphorically and physically, and has paid the price, yet the narrator and importantly Seroshapka have not. Seroshapka respects the arbitrary line indicated by the markers and also formally fulfils the camp rule of a warning shot first, by firing a second time. Yet, he waits patiently for Rybakov to cross the line before shooting him. He has waited until this moment, yet it would have been perfectly feasible to shoot him first and move him beyond the line later.[70] This also begs the question why he didn't shoot the narrator and move him forward or even move the 'line' back to place him outside the limits. In the middle of a forest with no prisoner daring to question his guards, he could have shot the narrator without any consequences. Yet he didn't and interestingly enough, he even warns the narrator not to move forward. The narrator has drawn in the rest of the work detail by stating: '*We* knew what this second shot meant. Seroshapka also knew. [Italics mine]'[71] The significance of two shots has been recognised by the rest of the work party and the narrator is keen to acknowledge this fact to the reader. Seroshapka's last comment reveals some tension between the evil intent of the guard and his adherence to the rules. He could have 'got' him, and he also could have made threats for the narrator's future, but he did neither. He merely 'touches' his shoulder with the rifle barrel, without dealing out a beating. This is perhaps symbolic of the state's potential for committing more violence in the future. The past tense used in the sentence indicates a finish to events, an ending of the threat. He has had his kill, and must be satisfied with it.

The other convicts are presented by the narrator in two ways. He reports their plight objectively and also their treatment of his character. This tale places the author in a sympathetic light, in comparison with his fellow convicts. He is treated with disdain and abuse by the work gang, but magnanimously comments 'The cold had gotten to them while I was being beaten.'[72] This capacity for forgiveness does rather seem to put the narrator/author in a favourable position. They are the crowd baying for his blood, and this image immediately evokes a Christ figure. The narrator doesn't necessarily distance himself from the others, because they are all carrying a metaphorical 'cross' on their shoulders. They are all carrying their 'sins' on their backs in various sizes. Fadeev's remark: 'It's not even a log – just a stick'[73] might just suggest that the narrator is not carrying a big enough cross for his sins. The narrator thinks his log is too big for him to pick up and rejoin his comrades. The image depicted is one of a long column of people descending the mountain carrying their 'crosses'.[74]

2.2.4 Setting

Point of view in *Berries* impinges on setting as much it does in *An Individual Assignment*. There is a lack of superfluous imagery or details and the narrative concentrates only on the bare facts. In an environment as hostile as Siberia, shades of colour, sounds, taste and smell are limited; therefore when the author has observed a sensory delight, he deliberately makes use of its distinctiveness and in this tale, the colours and taste of the berries are lavishly described. The basis for this explosion of sensory information stems from a seasonal thaw. The landscape has receded to make way for these images. The narrator is in awe of nature's fruits and he uses a variety of superlatives to describe the assault on the senses: 'extraordinary', 'more delicious' and 'indescribably delicious'.[75] They are almost good enough to die for, and for Rybakov, this proves to be the case. In contrast to the fresh and alive berries, the convicts' work involves dead natural features: tree stumps are being uprooted, relics from the previous year. In other words, every possible use is made of the surrounding area in order to survive. The tree stumps also suggest an analogy with the prisoners, who have been stunted by the system. In *Sententious* reference is also made to the tree stumps, but here not even the stumps survive. There is thus the additional analogy of the state taking away the life of a man just as they take away the life of a tree. When the narrator refers to the vastness of the environment, he comments 'God only knew how many people could be killed and buried among the hummocks along these mountain paths.'[76] He is asking a rhetorical question but there is a deeper one too. Are humans replacing the trees? The holes left by the uprooted trees are being filled by bodies, thus creating a macabre exchange of a life for a life.

2.3 *Quiet*

'Ours is a worker's government and the constitution states that "he who does not work shall not eat."'[77]

This longer tale from Shalamov is again about the presentation of the death of a fellow convict. The narrative technique differs from that of the other tales in its viewpoint. The narrator in the other two tales either take up an observational stance outside the text or adopt a remote individual viewpoint within the text. In *Quiet*, the tale is also in the first person, but frequently expands to include the inclusive 'we' or 'us'. This pronominal perspective changes the whole tone of the tale and the author/narrator or protagonist is now a part of a group. As Toker sees it, it is a *focaliser*, as distinct from a particular narrator, who is important in defining who is speaking and when. Toker's observations are worth quoting in full:

> Here the attitude of the memoirist as the narrating voice is different from the attitude of the memoirist as the focal character of the text, the prisoner who has witnessed the events and situations described: the focaliser was a sharer of the common lot, yet the retrospective narrating voice belongs to a concrete historical individual with his or her private memory, antecedents and affiliations.[78]

Shalamov uses an element of distancing in both *An Individual Assignment* and *Berries*. In the former, Dugaev is isolated from his workgang by the narrator. In the latter, it is the narrator who distances himself from the cheering crowd. The narrator in *Quiet* takes a different approach and positions himself firmly on the side of the majority. He is on the other side, watching events, but can be described as neither wholly distanced nor properly included with them. The sectarian and the narrator in *Quiet* could almost be doubles for Rybakov and the narrator in *Berries*. They could also double for Dugaev and Baranov respectively in *An Individual Assignment*. These pairings are based on a link between one character who dies and another who witnesses the death. The narrators in *Quiet* and *Berries* both fulfil the latter role. The narrator in *Quiet* can therefore represent Baranov in *An Individual Assignment*, where he also is the witness, not to the actual death but to the circumstances surrounding it.

The narration in *Quiet* is more assertive and angry than in the previous two tales. Shalamov emphasises the strength of a collective unit of cold and hungry men. They fight for warmth, silence and food and the narrator does not stand apart from this. There is a definite sense of narratorial grievance and anger at one's lot and this is reflected in the narrator's comments on people, food, work and of course the sectarian, Dmitriev: '[He] got on everyone's nerves in the barracks.'[79] The tone therefore differs from the previous tales and the narrator imparts a totally different impression of events. This expression of grievance, coupled with his exhaustion and hunger, makes him an unreliable authority in reporting events, but this is specifically Shalamov's point. You cannot create a completely objective account, because you have to recreate the situation in which the narrator/hero finds himself at the time. The hero's own physical and mental limitations are therefore evident in the re-telling of this tale.[80]

2.3.1 Narrative Structure

Quiet, as one of Shalamov's longer stories, has a definable structure, with a clearly demarcated beginning, middle and end. Again, like the previous two stories, *Quiet* begins not with a clear *status quo*, but with an apparent complication and this structural device is of symbolic significance. It is Shalamov's way of ridding the tale of the convention of having a 'normal' beginning and introducing complications at a later date. The common theme that runs through the tales therefore is that there are no 'normal' circumstances to base the tale on. Also, an early 'complication' and an opening which is arguably *in medias res*, fit in with Shalamov's idea that there is no 'closure' and therefore there is no 'beginning' either. This applies to *Kolyma Tales* as a whole: the events in the tales exist independently from one another and reflect different stages of his camp experience without suggesting chronological progression.[81] *Quiet* then, begins with an apparent complication which nevertheless functions as the introduction to the tale and thus can be classed as the general prologue. The narrator's use of the first person perspective has the effect of precluding a specific prologue: the change of person from plural to singular which might signal a transition to the specific prologue never takes place. The narrator always remains in some way a part of the convicts and consequently distant from the protagonist Dmitriev. Nevertheless, the narrator ensures that the content of his words retains a personal perspective distinct from his comrades' opinions. The narrative structure is thus based primarily around the narrator's version of events. The structure is as follows:

General Prologue   - The convicts awaiting their food

Exposition   - Naming of various comrades, including the sectarian

Complication	- New food regime
Peripeteia	- Sectarian shot
Dénouement	- Public berating of the educator
Specific epilogue	- New work partner
General epilogue	- A change reported amongst the men

The narrator's reportage begins with the convicts waiting for their food with a 'mixture of surprise, suspicion, caution and fear.'[82] He continues in this collective vein by describing the way in which all the prisoners were treated as 'human trash'. The general prologue concludes with the narrator emphasising the importance of food and outlining the convicts' position in the camps.

The exposition starts with the inclusive 'we', but quickly reverts to the personal 'I'. The narrator, although distancing himself, never fully excludes himself from his comrades. 'I moved together with these lumps in pea coats...'[83] He continues to mention several names, job positions and even interjects a comment about a fellow convict. The exposition's function is to set the scene, and in *Quiet*, it clearly fulfils this role. The scene is of a 'Doomed Brigade' of society's worst 'enemies of the state'. But to the narrator, his fellow convicts and the guards, the worst criminal in the brigade is the sectarian. Whilst bringing forward the main protagonist, and declaring that '[he] got on everyone's nerves in the barracks'[84], the exposition moves on to more physical deprivations, specifically lack of food and warmth. Yet the narrator is quick to return to the sectarian and assure the reader that Dmitriev is the most hated figure in the brigade. The sectarian, indeed, can be thought of as the narrator's 'nemesis', because while he is one of the main characters in the tale, he also plays an important part in the narrator's personal life. There is an underlying sympathy for the sectarian, and in Freudian terms the narrator overcompensates for this by demonising him. There is no room for sympathy in the Gulag and to confirm this, the narrator accentuates the hardships all the convicts have to go through (himself included) before returning to the present situation.

Shalamov ensures that the complication is underplayed and includes polarising incidents to negate an exciting or devastating interruption to the day or a man's life. It is the narrator's strong belief that the announcement of the new food regime can only be good news, since

'There is a certain point beyond which anything is an improvement.'[85] There are similarities between the acquisition of hot food and Akakii Akakevich's new coat in *The Overcoat*. In both cases, possession of these items is treated by the receivers as something better, but both lead to a downfall. The new rationing instructions are a complication in the lives of the convicts. If it were not for the hot food (or new coat in Akakii's case) the convicts' situation would have remained the same. As it is, the blessing is short-lived and expensive, especially for the sectarian. The educator and the area chief debate whether to continue with the experiment and this argument creates tension for the convicts. All the convicts pray to their chosen God for a favourable result, and the narrator specifically singles out the sectarian as possessing a different god from the rest of the gang. The narrator reports the conversations between the foreman, educator and area chief, also filling in any gaps. The complication is an argument between the state's requirements to fulfil the quotas and the human cost of the actions. The narrator reports the debate and fills in the essential arguments for and against the extra ration. The narrator is speaking from the table, eating as much as he can, whilst listening and repeating these arguments. He places himself with the other convicts and states: 'The collective will of twenty men strained itself...and the educator had his way.'[86] The narrator returns to the collective 'we' and once again the sectarian is distanced from the group. The narrator and his comrades are collective witnesses to the death of Dmitriev, but it is the educator and the area chief who remark on the death; their arguments carry the tale from the peripeteia through the dénouement right up to the specific epilogue. The narrator returns to the personal 'I', before finally settling on the collective 'we'. 'It was the same work that the sectarian and *I* used to do...Later *we* returned along the same road. [Italics mine]'[87] The tale's journey, then, takes in the death of the narrator's partner and his need to find a new one, before the workgang are returned to work. The tone of the tale changes at the peripeteia, but the narrator ensures he keeps his distance. He is only narrating the tale, and is not a part of the specific events. There is a kind of closure to the tale, when the narrator expresses his gladness that 'I was even happy that it was finally quiet.'[88] However, a change has come about because of the (albeit temporary) unlimited food ration. There has been a fleeting alteration in their perception of their lives and the narrator comments: 'Later we returned along the same road, as usual not having met our quota, but not caring about it either.'[89] Their small gain in strength and temporary happiness clouds over the issue of death, and in the camps where death is too common a situation to trouble with, the group is able to enjoy a blissful peace.

2.3.2 Fabula and Sujet

As in *An Individual Assignment* and *Berries*, the focalising prism ensures a fairly linear tale, with Shalamov's focaliser filling in any necessary gaps. The fabula is therefore presented in three stages: expectant prisoners, fulfilment of experiment and consequences of the experiment. The focaliser is important in re-creating the events and he adds depth and a qualitative understanding of 'why' the experiment takes place.[90] The sujet therefore is entirely the focaliser's presentation of events and we thus have to rely on his opinions. The arrangement of presented information is similar to *Berries*, where a scene is set, an alteration occurs and then the focaliser adds additional information to clarify events. The reader is placed in the dining hall ready for a delayed dinner and an element of suspense is used to heighten the mystery. What follows from this 'waiting' by the convicts is a staged performance enacted by the educator and the area chief. The convicts have become an audience, waiting for the main production. This image is reinforced by Shalamov's use of circles of men around a stove, again suggestive of a group of listeners. The stove appears firstly during the focaliser's tale and secondly when he and his comrades are without the sectarian at the conclusion. The arguments for and against the extra food also resemble a pantomime, in which the audience is particularly involved. Their survival depends on the food, and the situation would be farcical if it were not so deadly. The audience moves outside to witness the next performance; the end of the main protagonist, Dmitriev. The fabula remains foregrounded and as usual for Shalamov, he limits any unnecessary words or pronouncements: 'The sectarian…stood up and walked past the guard into the fog, into the sky…'[91] In the final three paragraphs the sujet imposes itself, and the focaliser begins to reflect on events. When he comments 'He [the sectarian] needed that extra portion of kasha to make up his mind to die,'[92] a distance can be discerned between the storyteller and the convict narrator. He is telling the reader what he believes, yet it is possible for the reader to work this out for himself. Essentially, Shalamov has foregrounded his convict-self as witness, whilst retaining the story-teller function. The focaliser is not reiterating the tale from a future state, from the viewpoint of Shalamov the author, but rather it is Shalamov the prisoner who imparts information. He keeps the reason for the 'suicide' until the penultimate paragraph, thus delaying the reader's understanding for the death. This is typical of Shalamov's ability to retain the element of suspense in the tale, without revealing the crucial facts. The tale concludes with the focaliser returning as one of the audience and they are waiting for the third performance to begin. The sujet and fabula have come full circle to be reunited as the men circle the stove. However, there is no final performance by the educator, area chief or the sectarian and the tale finishes.

2.3.3 Characterisation

Shalamov's aim in *Quiet* is to present an array of anonymous men, with ill-defined but specific attributes and their relationship with the narrator and the sectarian. The narrator ensures that he and the rest of the work gang are presented, ironically not as completely anonymous, but as a special group worthy of special treatment. By being 'the weakest, the worst and the hungriest,'[93] their status is the most precarious both for themselves and also for the camp authorities. They are a drain on resources offering little in return for their food and board. Consequently, they are hidden away and treated as rejects, but still fed the same as nearly everyone else. The exceptions were the best work gangs, who received the 'thick' part of the soup.[94] The narrator describes his fellow workers objectively, yet ensures that he is also included in these descriptions. The events in *Quiet* did not happen independently, to his comrades only, but also to himself. However, Shalamov 'always keeps a certain distance from his characters, even from those through whose eyes he is conducting the narration.'[95]

The narrator ensures that any physical descriptions of the workers emphasise their anonymity. 'I moved together with these lumps in pea coats, cloth hats that covered the ears.'[96] This depiction typifies Shalamov's limited use of facial description, which assigns the convicts to a nameless mass, and makes one man representative of the many. Yet, a little later in the tale, the narrator identifies the red face of the Tartar, Mutalov and his persecutor Efremov. The narrator, filling in the audience between arriving at the table and serving of the rations, names several of the convicts and even adds comment on a former head of the secret police; 'Listening to you, I don't know whether to laugh or spit in your face.'[97] It is one of few occasions where Shalamov as prisoner intervenes in the text and talks within the tale's time and not from an observational position. The narrator is therefore speaking in real-time and not from the author's position in the future. This ensures that the tale does not diverge from the actual scene, but remains focused on events. In his naming of several members of the brigade, he fills in necessary background information and the reader is suddenly aware of the diversity of men in this brigade. There is a propaganda official, an assistant prosecutor, a train engineer, a head of the secret police and one of his 'wards'. Finally there is Dmitriev, the sectarian. All these men represent how anyone can become a victim of the system.[98] Yet, because of the power of the party line, to be disgraced and sent to the camps does not necessarily mean that a man questions the reason for his being there. He accepts his fate, precisely because he believes that the system is always right and he should be there. The secret police agent in the brigade still believes that it is not the system that is at fault, but people whom he prosecuted. He comments 'It's because of insects like you that I got fifteen years.'[99] This fallacious belief is proof of a system that imposes falsity at the expense of truth to enforce a tyrannical control and alter man's perception of good and evil. As O'Toole puts it: 'humanity depends on man's individual awareness of truth and inhumanity grows out of truth produced by corrupt public institutions.'[100] This brigade is not a cohesive and group minded set, but a loose collection of self-serving individuals. The narrator informs the reader of a group hierarchy, based on an ill-defined pecking order: '…someone with the right to shout or even beat us would jump out and drive the hungry workers from the stove with oaths and kicks.'[101] He also makes speculations about other members of the group, asking whether they are 'Generals? Heroes of the Spanish War? Russian writers? Collective-farm workers from Volokolamsk?'[102] The brigade has become a representation of all Soviet Russia, and is a metaphor of how the system makes no differentiation between one group of people and another. To the system, their lives are literally worth their weight in gold, and when one is no longer convertible into gold, then one is to be disposed of. They are alchemists, in a way, turning stones into gold for the state.

The narrator depicts the sectarian in several lights, but his harsh comments create a first and lasting impression for the reader.[103] He is the most hated figure in the brigade and even the narrator has a personal dislike of him. Yet, he calmly explains how, why and what the sectarian sings. He provides the reason for the singing in the sectarian's own words and there is an element of sympathy for him. The narrator never shouts at him, even though he spends all day with these psalms and hymns. The sectarian is harmless, but only in the physical sense. He has to be physically moved around and placed in line by his work companions. He is helpless, but has others running around him, therefore gaining a certain amount of respect. The sectarian does not respond to his name, but ironically his attempt at anonymity increases his individuality. Precisely because of this paradox, the sectarian's life expectancy decreases. In effect, adopting a special role in the camps, like Dugaev in *An Individual Assignment*, is signing your own death warrant. Rybakov's challenge to the system in *Berries* also marked him out for attention. The sectarian is not a bad man, but is treated as such. He is unwittingly torturing the men psychologically and they torture him back physically. The narrator comments on the sectarian: 'The other members of the section rested from the singing while working, but I didn't have even that relief.'[104] The enclosed barracks is a place of torture for the men, but outside is a retreat from the sectarian and his psalms. However, the narrator does not even have this privilege. The narrator allows the sectarian one chance to defend himself and the reader finds the man on the verge of death. For all the sectarian's vocalisation, the narrator reports only these words: 'I don't ask God for death. He sees everything himself.'[105] The narrator's remarks on the sectarian's quietness after the meal seem to conform to a transitional period, between life and death. The songs are no longer needed, no prayers to God, just sufficient strength to perform his last feat. The meal is metaphorically his last supper, with the rest of the apostles sitting around the table. As Toker comments, it is Shalamov's attempt to provide a pre-death wake. The silence after the meal is therefore an ironic yet fitting tribute to the sectarian. No one is singing around this (empty) fireplace.[106]

The narrator presents the area chief and educator through direct speech, in order for the reader to hear exactly what was said. However, the reader is only able to form judgements on what is presented, and not on other probable communication that occurred at the time although the narrator always reports any speech directed at himself or the workers. Direct speech is important to the immediacy of the tale, and is a means whereby Shalamov draws the reader back from general discussion to the present situation. 'Speech' in this sense includes shouting at the sectarian and the exchange between the chief and the educator. What is important about these speeches is that they represent a change of tone, from that of a relatively impartial narrator to the making of strong forceful points. The educator is transformed into a magician for his audience and his words: 'Now it's up to you to answer by working, and only by working,' is almost a religious exhortation. He is asking them to 'believe' in his magic power, but when this fails his coaxing and praise simply results in 'Loafer[s]!'[107] Essentially, throughout *Quiet*, the narrator keeps a roving eye on events, reporting pertinent characters and conversation. Although the educator and the area chief possess most of the dialogue, the sectarian and, most significantly, the guard utter just one line each.[108] It is they who play out the final performance, thereby ensuring that all are participants in a much larger show. It is the narrator's role to present this performance to the reader.

2.3.4 Setting

Physical setting in *Quiet* is divided between two locations: the work pits and the dining barracks. Travel between these two is conducted on a daily basis, with a journey from the outside in to the dining hall and then a return to the exterior. With this in mind, Shalamov creates consequences for the external setting based on occurrences inside. The interior and exterior conform in important ways to van Baak's spatial model. The interior hall is a place of human interaction, with decisions being made and the results of these decisions being transferred to the world of work outside.[109] The interior is safe according to van Baak's theory, and this is true for the workgang in *Quiet*. The narrator is among known comrades and before him is the life-saving food. The sticky tables represent safety in familiarity, but as the maxim states, 'familiarity breeds contempt'. The narrator is bored, his comrades are wary, but the enclosed environment is keeping them safe. There is nothing the authorities can do in here to make their lives any more miserable. Outside, the cold, fog and hard work all strive to kill the men, but it is not these factors that directly kill the sectarian. The metaphorical freedom of outside with all its deadly trappings is the psychological arena where the sectarian can take his own life without any physical restraints. In effect, the release of the sectarian from his physiological restraints, i.e. from his debilitating condition, has lent him psychological strength. This in turn leads him to explore the external world, unaided, and be rewarded with his desire to die.

When the convicts leave the food barracks, they are enclosed in fog and frost. The narrator, in true Shalamov style plays down the 'miracle'. Firstly he states: 'The frost didn't seem too bad to us – but only at first. It was too cold to be ignored.'[110] The narrator ensures that the reader does not become too overwhelmed with the importance of the meal, and although this was a good day, tomorrow follows and brings with it still same work, cold and lack of food. The narrator makes a curious point, referring to the sectarian's progress, not into the fog, but 'into the sky'. There is thus a visible yet moveable boundary, as in *Berries*, but here the guard uses the 'legal' way to shoot someone. He fires a warning shot, then an aimed shot. The sectarian did not cross this invisible barrier to commit suicide, but according to Toker it was an act of defiance based upon implicit narrative and not from the focaliser.[111] The reader fills in this intellectualisation of the situation, based on their knowledge of camps and their own intelligence. The reader has already pieced together the death, when he/she reads that the sectarian has defied the guard and walked purposely away from the shouted orders. Conceivably, there may have been another reason for the sectarian to walk slowly away, but as the focaliser alone provides us with information, we have to rely on his testament alone. The testimony of the setting is minimal and is compensated for in other areas, such as characterisation. The fundamental reason for this is the nature of the teller. He is in no position to explore scenic views or extramural details, because of his exhaustion. In effect, this is one of the reasons why there does not exist much scenic description in *Kolyma Tales*. The stove, the sticky table and the empty fireplace are the only areas for discussion. Heat, food and rest are all represented, but in true Shalamov style. All three are fatally flawed and none fulfil their function. The table lacks (nonsticky) food, the stove fails to heat and the after-dinner singing around the fireplace does not involve a comradely fire. Kline argues that 'The campfire replaces not only the sun, but religion, as it alone has the power to save in a universe in which physical needs have displaced spiritual ones.'[112] Here, un-wanted spiritual needs are discarded and the tangible fog pervades everything. No other physical environment is necessary, as it is only these three factors that matter to the narrator. He expresses no surprise at their fallibility.

NOTES

[1] O'Toole, *Structure, Style and Interpretation in the Russian Short Story*, p. 37

[2] R. Young, 'Shalamov, Tragedy and Poetry',
http://www.litkicks.com/beatPages/page.jsp?what=VarlamShalamov&who=youngrobert

[3] Bakhtin, 'The Form of Time and the Chronotope in the Novel: From the Greek Novel to Modern Fiction', p. 525

[4] Toker, *Return from the Archipelago*, p. 78

[5] Glad, 'Art out of Hell: Shalamov of Kolyma', p. 48

[6] I.e. a minimum amount of intrusion with a maximum amount of information [mimesis] and also a maximum amount of intrusion with a minimum amount of information [diegesis]. Cited in O'Toole, *Structure, Style and Interpretation in the Russian Short Story*, p. 65.

[7] *Kolyma Tales* also conforms to Genette's description of discourse, because of the narrator's tight control of narratorial proceedings. However, the tales cannot be described as 'pure' discourse, because of the narrator's tendency to jump from narrating events in real-time to narrating events outside time. In this way, each tale is a mixture of both causal-chronological sequences and temporal irregularities. For a full discussion of definitions see D. Baguley, 'A Theory of Narrative Modes', *Essays in Poetics*, VI, 2, September 1981, p. 7

[8] For example, unlike the authorial voices in Tolstoi or Solzhenitsyn.

[9] Toker, *Return from the Archipelago*, p. 151

[10] This is of course a reference to Stalin's comments to Churchill at the 1945 Potsdam conference. In the camps, one death became like another and numbers ceased to matter.

[11] His message in the tales is always that the system is ultimately accountable for any deaths. The exceptions are the common prisoners, whom he holds fully accountable for their actions.

[12] See Chapter 4, (The Structures of Narrative: Narration) of S. Cohan, & L. M. Shires, *Telling Stories: A Theoretical Analysis of Narrative Fiction*, (London: Routledge, 1988) for comparisons between narrator and focaliser and the focus of a film's camera. The latter implies the use of different camera angles to create a specific perspective. Shalamov's narrator as it were, is the camera operator, whereas the reader only gets to see the object of the camera's focus.

[13] However, *Major Pugachov's Last Battle* is an exception to the rule, being strictly from an omniscient perspective: Shalamov speculates on Pugachov's thoughts, though having not been with him at any point during these events.

[14] Shalamov seems sensitive to the author-reader relationship, and in a way, he is talking directly to the reader. Bakhtin refers to the author-reader relationship as '[A] literary work is directed outside itself to the listener-reader and in some measure anticipating his possible reactions.' Bakhtin in 'The Form of Time and the Chronotope in the Novel: From the Greek Novel to Modern Fiction', p. 527

[15] A. Camus, *The Myth of Sisyphus*, (Harmondsworth: Penguin, 1980), p. 108

[16] Andrew, Introduction to 'The Structural Analysis of Russian Narrative Fiction', p. xv

[17] Scholes & Kellogg, p. 87

[18] Andrew, Introduction to 'The Structural Analysis of Russian Narrative Fiction', p. xii

[19] The latter conforms to Shklovskii's conventional linear exposition, and the former to a form of experimental prose. Linear exposition conforms to a beginning, middle and end, and experimental prose alters the order of these three stages. Shklovsky, V. *Theory of Prose*, ibid., pp. x-xi

[20] O'Toole's analysis of Gogol's *The Overcoat*, demonstrates that both Akakii and the 'Person of Consequence' exist independently from each other in the narrative. Thus, the reader is able to follow two different journeys through the tale. O'Toole, *Structure, Style and Interpretation in the Russian Short Story*, pp. 20-34

[21] *Kolyma Tales*, p. 23

[22] Ibid., p. 24

[23] Ibid., p. 21

[24] Loc. cit.

[25] That is, where there exists hope, there exists belief, and in Kolyma, hope is a terrible fallacy, usually resulting in death. The mind can withstand only so much failure, and the resignation that follows results in an early death.

[26] *Kolyma Tales*, p. 23

[27] In *Condensed Milk*, the hero is in a quandary about whether to accept the offer to escape in exchange for the sugar-rich milk.

[28] In the *Night*, for instance, is dedicated to the need to forget any sense of personal identity in order to perform terrible immoral acts.

[29] *Kolyma Tales*, pp. 22-4

[30] Ibid., p. 23

[31] Hosking, 'The Chekhov of the Camps', p. 1163

[32] *Kolyma Tales*, p. 23

[33] Toker, *Return from the Archipelago*, p. 152

[34] Ibid. This is in the absence of an officially selected executioner who would traditionally make the offer.

[35] *Kolyma Tales*, p. 21

[36] The three days taken by the action are perhaps suggestive of Jesus' resurrection. That is, Dugaev's metaphorical release is comparable to Christ's rebirth on the third day.

[37] See the chapter on depersonalisation for dehumanisation methods used by the German camp personnel in the concentration camps. T. Todorov, *Facing the Extreme: Moral Life in the Concentration Camps*, (London: Weidenfeld, 1999), pp. 158-77

[38] Toker, *Return from the Archipelago,* p. 152

[39] *Kolyma Tales*, pp. 23-4

[40] Individual assignments are given to convicts who are failing to fulfil their set quotas. This tale is based on work assignments which Shalamov had to endure later on in his sentence. For Shalamov, not fulfilling the work assignment 'merely' resulted in a drop in rations. However, *An Individual Assignment* refers to an earlier time (1938-39), when execution was the norm. In Toker, *Return from the Archipelago*, pp. 151-2

[41] *Kolyma Tales*, p. 24. As if nothing could be done. It is also possible to view the nameless overseer, as Pontius Pilate, handing over the prisoner to the people for trial; moreover the people surrounding Dugaev have already condemned him. In the

Gospels the masses too have already made up their minds to free Barabas and send Christ to execution.

42 Loc. cit.
43 *Kolyma Tales*, p. 23
44 Loc. cit.
45 Loc. cit.
46 Ibid., p. 21
47 Toker, *Return from the Archipelago*, p. 278
48 Camus, p. 107
49 *Kolyma Tales*, p. 23
50 Ibid., p. 59
51 This authority does not stop at the camp, but is projected back to Stalin. The guards assume Stalin's power and pass judgement on Stalin's behalf.
52 *Kolyma Tales*, p. 57
53 Ibid., p. 58
54 Ibid., p. 57
55 This tale describes Shalamov's rude introduction to the camps, when he loses a tooth defending a fellow prisoner.
56 *Kolyma Tales*, p. 59-60
57 Ibid., p. 57
58 Ibid., p. 59
59 Loc. cit.
60 As previously mentioned in *An Individual Assignment*. The protagonist in Solzhenitsyn's *One Day in the Life of Ivan Denisovich*, eats his bread ration continually through his workday. This simple contrast would therefore highlight the main difference between the two writers: Solzhenitsyn's optimism to Shalamov's pessimism.
61 *Kolyma Tales*, p. 60
62 On this structural opposition see J. J. van Baak, 'The Place of Space in Narration: A Semiotic Approach to the Problem of Literary Space. With an Analysis of the Role of Space in I. E. Babel's Konarmija', *Studies in Slavic Literature and Poetics*, III, Amsterdam, Rodopi, 1983, p. 55-60
63 Kline, p. 389-90
64 Propp, V. in L. Doležel, 'Narrative Semantics and Motif Theory', *Essays in Poetics*, III, 1, 1978, pp. 47-56
65 *Kolyma Tales*, p. 57
66 Doležel, p. 51-2. To receive a gift or instruction was not without a benefit for the 'creditor', and in a way this is a reflection of human nature. In every gift, no matter how altruistic in nature the intention of the giver, there is an unconscious benefit to the latter in the form of moral satisfaction. Shalamov seems to subscribe to this viewpoint in that when a 'good' act is reported, he is suspicious of the motive. The trouble attendant on the receipt of a gift outweighs its benefits.
67 To form a close friendship is a mistake, when the friend can disappear at any time, as was especially the case during the purges. Also, physical deterioration was so rife after arrival in the camp, that life expectancy was reported to be between two weeks and three months. In L. Toker, 'Varlam Shalamov's Kolyma', in G. Diment, & Y. Slezkine, *Between Heaven and Hell: The Myth of Siberia in Russian Culture*, (New York: St. Martin's Press, 1993), p. 155

[68]   *Kolyma Tales*, p. 59
[69]   This crossing the line is reminiscent of Raskolnikov's breach of moral and social boundaries in *Crime and Punishment* and he was punished accordingly. Camp society creates boundaries, whether physical or artificial and these are enforced by various officials, who are also responsible for ensuring they too stay within these boundaries. Seroshapka as an instrument of the state, although enforcing these laws, is also bound by them. However, the Soviet system has corrupted these laws to such an extent, that there does not exist a definable and comfortable boundary system to work within.
[70]   Toker, *Return from the Archipelago*, p. 181
[71]   *Kolyma Tales*, p. 60
[72]   Ibid., p. 58
[73]   Ibid., p. 57
[74]   This image, to take the analogy further, is the reverse of the biblical walk to Calvary.
[75]   *Kolyma Tales*, pp. 58-9
[76]   Ibid., p. 60
[77]   A. S. Marakenko, 'Lectures to Parents: Lecture 6 – Work Education' http://www.marxists.org/reference/archive/makarenko/works/lectures/lec06.html
[78]   Toker, *Return from the Archipelago*, p. 77
[79]   *Kolyma Tales*, p. 436
[80]   Scholes & Kellogg question the reliability of a narrator, where narratorial bias or forcefulness can lead a reader to form the author's desired conclusions. Shalamov is scrupulous in his narratorial creations and his narrators are never fully informed in reporting events. An answer to the question of the narrator's limitations would be the usual camp phrase: 'If you don't believe it, call it a fairy tale.' See Scholes & Kellogg on the authority of the narrator. pp. 256-73
[81]   There are often clues as to when a tale's events took place (such as during the purges or upon arrival at the camp,) but it is not Shalamov's wish to group the stories in such an obvious way. Toker calls Shalamov's ordering of his works as 'veridical fiction'; that is, the dominant theme and all events are either fiction based on facts, or are artistically reconstructed to lay bare a certain theme. The tales cannot conform to a set chronological order because the reported events did not occur just once, but were repeated several times through his camp years. Cited in Toker *Return from the Archipelago*, p. 141
[82]   *Kolyma Tales*, p. 435
[83]   Loc. cit.
[84]   Ibid., p. 436
[85]   Ibid., p. 438. In fairness to the narrator, this remark is a truism, inasmuch as the system did not operate in an honest and open way. If the system issued fatal or dangerous instructions to the prisoners, then it was always without actually mentioning any lethal results that might have occurred. For example, Dugaev did not know that failure to achieve the necessary quota in his individual assignment would result in death. Also the hero in *The Lawyers' Plot* is never told about the nature of his summons until it is almost too late.
[86]   Ibid., p. 440
[87]   Ibid., p. 442
[88]   Loc. cit.
[89]   Loc. cit.

[90] That is, there must exist a state of affairs in which an experiment is introduced in order to change or challenge it: i.e. The food rations are distributed according to work production; the most productive brigade receives the most food, and the educator challenges this ration system.

[91] *Kolyma Tales*, p. 441

[92] Loc. cit.

[93] *Kolyma Tales*, p. 435

[94] The thin part consisted of a few nutrients, proteins and carbohydrates and therefore did not constitute enough energy to sustain a convict's labour. The consequences for the convict are then obvious.

[95] Hosking, 'The Chekhov of the Camps', p. 1163

[96] *Kolyma Tales*, p. 435

[97] Ibid., p. 436

[98] Achieving a high position in the Party is dependent upon absolute faith in the party line and ability to obey orders without question. A statement by a higher official is a statement by Stalin's proxy and therefore cannot be wrong. There were many cases of Government officials who accepted that they must have done something wrong in order to be sent to the camps, because Stalin believed they had.

[99] *Kolyma Tales*, p. 436

[100] O'Toole, *Structure, Style and Interpretation in the Russian Short Story*, p. 20

[101] *Kolyma Tales*, p. 437

[102] Loc. cit.

[103] Genette in *Narrative Discourse* stresses the importance of first impressions in characterisation. A text will reinforce a reader's perception of a character by constantly referring to a particular trait. Therefore, if a character is initially wronged, then the reader will judge the character only on that first image. The narrator's initial and continuous attack on the sectarian only reinforces a negative reader reaction. In Rimmon-Kenan, p. 120

[104] *Kolyma Tales*, p. 437

[105] Ibid., p. 437

[106] Toker, *Return from the Archipelago*, p. 283

[107] *Kolyma Tales*, pp. 441-2

[108] The guard calls 'Halt! Halt!' before shooting the sectarian. Ibid., p. 441

[109] See van Baak, 'The House in Russian Avant-garde Prose', p.3. Shalamov may be indicating in *Quiet*, that for all the political and ideological wrangling in the safety of the workroom barracks, the work reality is very different.

[110] *Kolyma Tales*, p. 441

[111] Toker, *Return from the Archipelago*, p. 176

[112] Kline, p. 404

Chapter 3

Fabula and Sujet

'How can time exist if the past is no longer, if the future is not yet, and if the present is not always?'[1]

'Plot is only the indispensable skeleton which, fleshed out with character and incident, provides the necessary clay into which life may be breathed.'[2]

The purpose of this chapter is to identify the relationships between the motifs in *Kolyma Tales* and the form in which they are presented. According to Formalist theory, the former reveals the *fabula* and the latter, the *sujet*. Tomashevskii wrote: 'The story [fabula] is the aggregate of motifs in their logical, causal-chronological order; the plot [sujet] is the aggregate of those same motifs but having the relevance and the order which they had in the original work.'[3] The fabula is really the story, or 'what happened', whereas the sujet is how the story is relayed to the reader.[4] The reader either consciously or unconsciously pinpoints the fabula in each story he/she reads and at its simplest level it can be easily summarised by a few short sentences.[5] However, a story that presents itself in a simplistic way is not intrinsically satisfying, and therefore the role of the sujet is to creatively disrupt the 'natural' order of events. Tomashevskii sees 'the story as a background against which elements of the plot are studied.'[6] Ricoeur argues that the fabula is identified by its ordering and 'brings about [plot] completeness and its wholeness.'[7] The fabula may develop in a simple linear fashion, with a 'central conflict or intrigue' to disrupt the storyline, but it is the play with time and perspective of the narrator that governs the presentation of information.[8] Presentation of time by the narrator involves several different approaches; for example, actual times and dates may be given, the duration of events may be recorded or an impression of duration may be created. The sujet gives the reader the causal motivations for the plot and therefore a logical sequence of events can be identified. The plot is a combination of smaller motifs or motivations, a coherence that draws all the strands of a story together to form a unifying element. For Tomashevskii, 'The aesthetic function of a plot is [the] bringing together [of] the arrangement of motifs to the attention of the reader.'[9]

The way in which all the motifs occur and are presented create a particular plot structure. For instance, withholding vital information would ensure a suspense story, whilst the introduction of various dissimilar characters could create a 'road' story.[10] Sujet, like fabula is affected by the use of time techniques and this ensures that the story has depth. There is a relationship between the reader and the fabula and sujet binary. Inherent in the latter is the need to disguise motivations, alter perceptions and create tensions, with the aim of disrupting reader judgements. Aristotle wrote that 'the crucial elements of plot structure are recognition (involving ignorance and knowledge) and reversal (of intention, or of situation).'[11] Therefore, every plot will incorporate techniques that aim to mislead or hide the true motives from a discerning reader.

Contemporary discussions on fabula and sujet do not follow traditional Formalist analysis, as authors have introduced certain modifications to the arguments. A useful example is that of Ann Shukman's analysis of the short story. She rejects the fabula and sujet binary and replaces it with narration time (the level of the signifier) and event time (the level of the signified).[12] However, there is still an argument for their continued use, because every story contains a challenge for the reader to identify how and why it has been created. There is a distinction between fabula and sujet simply because 'there exists a distinct chronological set of facts that existed before the tale itself.'[13] The reader will always find the plot, as mentioned before, but with experimental literature, new ways of presenting a work and challenging the reader will always need to be analysed. The recognition of the sujet is reliant on the reader's ability to recognise cause and effect, that is, the reader makes links and assumptions as to why and how events occur. An author can suppress, mix up or reverse the placement of cause and effect in a work and conversely remove it from the text. As O'Toole comments '…he [the author] is still playing with our assumptions regarding cause and effect: a negative case is still a case.'[14] Temporality impacts on plot construction and motives are placed and identified at specific times to create an understandable and logical sequence of events. For example, the narrator enlightens the reader about the near death of Merzlakov in *Shock Therapy*. He is willing to undergo all kinds of tests just to remain alive, and the reader is fully aware of why he puts himself through these trials. The simple linearity of the plot, allows the reader to understand this, but in other tales, this linearity is not clear-cut. How one understands a story is also linked to the narratorial perspective. Andrew argues that there may be different narrators or perspectives in the course of a work, thus creating a mixed fabula, with no overall perspective from which the story derives.[15] This would heavily influence both the fabula and sujet, in that it would be difficult to identify the original story and the causal nature of the work. However, Shalamov's works have a tendency to rely on the first person and/or single person perspective. This unifying narrator consequently affects a single sujet that has a direct relevance to the fabula. It is then possible to analyse temporal deviations and plot markers in relation to each other, without the need to analyse them separately.

The stories chosen for this chapter are *Sententious* and *A Piece of Meat*. Both tales represents two different ways of presenting the fabula and sujet and play around with the presentation of time and the narratorial perspective. In fact, both of these tales possess a particular Shalamovian approach to memory. Memory is probably the mental function that Shalamov insists on reporting most frequently and both tales tackle the question of memory recall in extreme circumstances. Following his release, Shalamov was proud to be able to recall as much as he could, but within the camps, possessing a memory was dangerous. An exception to this, analysed here, is to be found in *Sententious*. The focaliser's life is saved by his awareness of the link between life and memory whereas ordinarily memory of one's previous life proves to be a burden. It could also be argued that memories are not consciously created in the camps, but are stored for recall at a later date. Only instinctive and life-saving memorial experiences are useful within the camp and any non-lifesaving experiences are disregarded. Consequently, it is only after Shalamov has left the camps that he avails himself of the luxury of remembering his experiences.

One of the side effects of Gulag existence is a physiological reaction to the psychological strain. Memory ceases to function as a reliable utility, and this is not necessarily a negative experience. Shalamov often reports of the necessity of forgetting one's past in order to fulfil an unpleasant or morally abhorrent task. Grave-robbing in *In The Night* is one example; the hero is only able to steal items from a corpse because he valiantly forgets his previous occupation as a doctor. Lack of sufficient glucose and vitamins are also physiological determinants for memory loss, which are precipitated by the body's reaction to stress.[16] The convicts endure extreme traumatic experiences and the brain conserves physical energy by shutting down advanced memorial functions. This allows the body to cope with current events by refusing to allow the consciousness to fully focus on past conditions.[17] This means that the vast majority of Shalamov's characters are portrayed as merely concentrating on basic aspects of survival: 'It [memory] was more expendable than lungs or hands. In fact you did not need it at all'[18] notes one commentator. The mind, therefore, is limited solely to fulfilling the three basic human survival necessities: food, warmth and sleep. These two stories represent what it is to lose, utilise and regain memory functions. However, possession of memory does not amount to longevity in the Gulag and there appears to be no definitive proof that memory is either a blessing or a curse. Memory is linked with time, due to its unique function of reporting events after they have occurred. The fabula constitutes the events in a particular order, but in both tales, the memory of the narrator is crucial to the presentation of the tale. The sujet therefore is the how, why and where of remembered events: Shalamov shows how memory is crucial for survival in *A Piece of Meat*; *Sententious* is Shalamov's study of memorial awakening. The sujet deals with the confusing and often troubled nature of memory, and in both tales, affects the reader's understanding of the work. *Sententious*, for example, is almost wholly sujet, without any recognisable temporal marking. *A Piece of Meat* however, provides mnemonic flashbacks to aid the convict's life. These stories both represent the necessity of memory and consequently foreground the existence of the sujet. Indeed, according to Chvany, foregrounding of a particular factor is identified with 'sequentiality or plot-line'.[19] Memory, as a major part of the literary make-up of the tales is this driving force and *raison d'être*.[20] Another factor that Shalamov foregrounds is the concept of Soviet Reality. Although, as discussed in Chapter 1, it is a vital part of the sujet presentation. Without any or little sense of temporal flow, Shalamov's stories indicate the disorientation effect, which the camps had on the lives of the convicts. Day and night are unimportant as markers; indeed, a number of tales seem to exist a-temporally. The reader therefore, is presented with a series of tales that sometimes indicate a vague date or time, but usually exists in some ill-defined temporality. These two tales are Shalamov's testament to the disorientating nature of his experience and this chapter will attempt to discover the temporal ordering and causality of the tales. However, it will also take into account Shalamov's specific desire for the tales to remain as stand-alone testaments with, as such, no formal link between them. This concept precludes any large-scale fabula and sujet analysis of the tales, but does allow analysis of individual works.

3.1 *Sententious*

Sententious[21] is dedicated to Nadezhda Mandelshtam, the wife of the poet Osip, who tragically died in the camps. He famously wrote: 'The word that I have forgotten that I have meant to say.'[22] It is a tale about the process of Shalamov's re-awakening from near death to near life, and yet it is perhaps one of the most negative in the Kolyma collection. The tale is a travel journal as much as anything else, but it is a mental journey, rather than a physical. The body slowly heals, yet it is the mind and memory that are the objects of the tale. Recovery of the latter leads to a re-development of the former. Shalamov does not portray his character as completely rejuvenated; rather he slowly introduces memorial developments linked to physical recovery. His physical recovery is never complete at any stage, indeed, neither is his psychological awakening.[23] The title of this story can be thought of as one aphorism amongst many. The most powerful is 'Little flesh was left on my bones, just enough for bitterness – the last human emotion; it was closer to the bone.'[24] The tone of *Sententious* reflects this feeling and throughout the work, the narratorial voice is one of *zloba*. Hosking asks: 'What is its meaning? Is it a kind of final manifestation of the will to live?'[25] There are no adages or maxims for camp life because as Kline puts it, there are 'no eternal truths which govern the laws of behavior there.'[26] There are no higher philosophical truths or meanings in the Gulag system, because the convicts exist in an organised chaos.

3.1.1 Narrative Structure

The peripeteia of *Sententious* is the most striking and focal feature of the tale. 'Sententious! Sententious!' the hero shouts.[27] This exclamation marks the turning point of the hero's awakening, but it is not what might be considered conventional or appropriate. Yet this is the point Shalamov wants to make. A word represents language, and 'thus personality, humanity and the return to life.'[28] The focaliser has awoken, and of course, Shalamov ensures that this return is stifled. Someone shouts 'Idiot!' but a change has occurred. The strength of this word and its implicit meaning leads the hero from near-death towards some sort of life. Events leading up to the peripeteia and the consequences fit neatly into a logical narrative structure. The inclusion of this turning point creates a plot, which *prima facie,* indicates a life without words.[29] There is a descent from near living to near death, then a swift return to life. Post-peripeteia, the focaliser gives the reader one natural metaphor of his return to life, with the ability of the river to burst its banks. Also, he marks a recognisably human invention, music. The structure of *Sententious* is as follows:

General/Specific Prologue   - The focaliser and the flow of fellow
                                 convicts
Exposition   - The focaliser in a state of near death
Complication   - Indifference followed by fear of
                                 death
Peripeteia   - Sententious! Sententious!
Dénouement   - Metaphor of water as life
General/ Specific Prologue   - Cross-section of the camp gathered
                                 together

The prologue in *Sententious,* as in *An Individual Assignment* is a mixture of the general and the specific. This reflects Shalamov's underlying philosophy of one convict being part of a whole in which the other convicts are all linked to the focaliser in some way. It is arguable that the first paragraph is story, and that what follows is memorial information. That is, Shalamov has set the physical scene and introduced his philosophical ideas on bitterness from a narratorial point in the future. A binary pattern, like that in *Berries,* with the fabula followed by the sujet could be applied here. However, the temporal markers do not make for a purely logical reading. It is possible to re-arrange several fabulaic sections of the text into a different order. For example: 'I ate indifferently, stuffing into my mouth anything that seemed edible,'[30] and 'My frostbitten fingers and toes ached, hummed from the pain.'[31] These events occurred extra-temporally, but the reader knows that they occurred inside the frame of the tale. The events obviously occurred before the peripeteia, but there is no logical reason for them to have taken place in that order. The second paragraph, highlights the narrator's beliefs about himself, and interjects this with physical labour and scenery. There is a logical order where the narrator is boiling water, and we are informed of the end results, but after this, the narrator suddenly begins talking about grouse. The tale, until the peripeteia, is purely sujet and always from the narrator's point of view. The complication is also sujet, where it takes the form of reminiscence: 'Once at night I suddenly realised that I heard groans and wheezing.'[32] This is not the focaliser, but the narrator writing from the future. He follows this up with 'Later, as I recollected this moment of amazement, I understood that the need for sleep, forgetfulness, unconsciousness had lessened.'[33] After the complication, the narrator continues on the theme of love, specifically love for animals. The fabula almost breaks through when the focaliser argues with the topographer. There is direct speech, but the narrator immediately reports the conclusion of the argument from his future position: 'But the topographer didn't want to quarrel and didn't report the incident.'[34] This event illustrates the narrator's point, but this incident like every other is a single instance of the sujet explaining away the fabula. This event also possesses a kind of closure, when the bird is allowed to escape.[35] What one gets therefore is a collection of incidents, seemingly unrelated, but which taken together form the reasons behind the peripeteia. Immediately prior to his outburst, the narrator finally comments on language. He states that his own language was 'crude...and it was impoverished as the emotions that lived near the bones.'[36] This explains his outburst, or at least his surprise at this 'new' word. All these events and their explanations, therefore, go some way to create the sujet. The reader can find the cause and effect of these events; however, there still does not exist a definite temporal link between them. A clue regarding this is obviously the narrator, who is in charge of relaying events. (This will be explained fully in the next section.) The dénouement brings with it a feeling of temporal linearity. Days and weeks occur, and at last there exists a temporality within the text. These references to days are also akin to the focaliser's words, in that they occurred spasmodically and without warning.

The focaliser marks the concluding part of the tale with 'Then came the day...'[37] This event becomes a unifying feature for the fabula and sujet. This does not represent a finale to the tale as such, but merely allows the focaliser to re-enter the camp proper. From here, the narrator seems to be saying, 'I can recover or return to near-death'. However, as the narrator is speaking from the future, we know that the focaliser will go on living. The tale does not possess a conclusive closure, but a kind of tableau is performed. Toker explains that the ending of *Sententious* can be both a 'memorable finale and [an] open-ended half-promise of a sequel.'[38] It can also be neither. The tale does not require extra furnishing, nor indeed is it an ending. This is Shalamov's idea of the continuation of Kolyma life. With his strength regained, it is likely that the focaliser/narrator was returned to a hard labour camp to begin the process of physical and mental degeneration again. It is therefore also conceivable that he might have returned once more to the situation in which we find him at the start of the story. Shalamov is indicating that life in Kolyma is cyclic in nature and unless a man escapes these circles, he will always return to the point of near-death.[39]

3.1.2 Point of View

Brewer offers a sound analysis of the narrative technique in *Kolyma Tales*, and makes important observations about *Sententious*: 'Nearly all of Shalamov's stories are told through the eyes of a zek, but with the hindsight and bitter memory of an ex-zek, temporally and spatially removed from the narrative events.'[40] This narrator seeks to influence proceedings and it is the narrator's voice that is dominant. There is the narrator as convict, but his voice is limited to events within the tale. The fabula would therefore appear to be represented by the focaliser's voice. He provides details on events and reports dialogue, but this is strictly rationed. The sujet is dominant and it is the narrator's 'future' voice that controls this. He provides all the emotional and physical motivations for the convict's human state. It is the narrator's bitter memories that colour the focaliser's return from the dead, when he utters the word 'sententious'.[41] Also, it is interesting to note that it is the narrator and not the focaliser who is using aphorisms in the text: 'There is an old Arab saying: "He who asks no questions will be told no lies."'[42] This cannot be the focaliser, because he is in a state of near death and without words, let alone aphorisms. Prior to the peripeteia, the narrator explains that the focaliser's language is reduced to basic, almost inhuman grunting and expletives. This is a sound technique by Shalamov to ensure that the impact of the focaliser's outburst is maximised. The narrator also relays his own future beliefs in the text. Commenting on the return of emotions, he (the narrator) still cannot be reconciled with love for fellow human beings: 'Love didn't return to me.'[43] Events in the text are thus refracted by two points of view: the author as focaliser and the author as narrator. It is difficult to distinguish who is relaying the information, but a clue to finding out is how the narrator projects an end state from a rhetorical question. For example, the narrator asks the question: 'What remained with me until the very end?' and answers 'Bitterness.'[44] The narrator then immediately directs his thoughts onto the focaliser and the reader is returned to the focaliser's position: 'But death, just recently so near, began to ease away little by little.' The narrator then continues in his documentary style, but there follows a deliberate series of switches between the narrator's future and the focaliser. This in turn creates the tension between narrator and focaliser thus disturbing the logical ordering of the tale.

The main indication of the fabula's presence is direct speech. These limited dialogic exchanges between the focaliser and the topographer, and the focaliser and his fellow prisoners are reported as they were spoken. They provide a definite distance between the focaliser and narrator, but the focaliser is still the narrator's mouthpiece. Shalamov has ensured that speech is only reported as the focaliser gains strength. The narrator comments on this unexpected vocalisation: 'I realised that something important had returned to me.'[45] The focaliser then embarks on a mission to assert himself and breaks Shalamov's own belief: to ask for something. Upon Vronsky's question, 'A foreigner?' and its dangerous implications for the focaliser, the narrator thinks 'But I couldn't care less about Vronsky's question.'[46] The narrator distinguishes himself from the focaliser and 'true' events are reported verbatim.

The real question to be asked is, whether the events in the tale are causally linked or merely instances that fill in gaps. There is a series of events, not directly linked to his awakening, which show how near death the focaliser is. The return of long forgotten words is a reflection of his return to life, yet it is not the focaliser's viewpoint that is dominant, but the narrator's. It is his own story of how he recovered from near death. It is almost as if the focaliser is merely an actor for the narrator to manoeuvre and control for his own benefit. The tale is mostly one long sujet of narratorial remembrance and not a 'real' tale. The events undoubtedly occurred but they have been coloured by the spatial and temporal distance of a future author/narrator.

3.1.3 Characterisation

The first question to ask is, who is the main character? The narrator or the focaliser? As previously mentioned, the text is narrator-driven and the focaliser merely plays the part of actant in the proceedings. Yet, both 'characters' must be taken into account, whether as separate or shared entities. The narrator focuses on his focaliser who then in turn reflects the narrator's views and actions. It is also important to remember that the narrator is an older version of the focaliser and as such is not a completely separate character. This relationship is not only crucial to the fabula and sujet; it has in fact created it. If the tale's perspective was only the focaliser's, then a completely different tale would emerge. As it is, the refraction through the focaliser gives cause, effect and a unique temporal linearity. The focaliser is needed for contrast with the future narrator. The reader is with the focaliser, but primarily gets his/her information from the narrator. Therefore, character analysis will acknowledge a split in 'personality', but will focus on character action in the tale and the narrator's viewpoint.

The focaliser is in a state of near death, and the narrator reports on his physical and mental debilitation. The narrator sets the scene for the focaliser to die, by creating a sense of fatality. The focaliser is transferring his own death-like state onto others and the narrator states '...I would think my neighbour was dead and be surprised that he would rise...'[47] The focaliser is waiting for death, and indifference is the key philosophical attribute both he and his fellow prisoners possess. He does not boil the water, but this does not matter. 'We were totally indifferent about the dialectic leap of quantity into quality.'[48] The narrator's philosophical statement on this matter re-enforces the difference between what is presented in the tale and what actually occurred. The cause of this aphorism stems from this seemingly innocuous act by the focaliser. The narrator gives the quality of heated water strength to represent the quality of the focaliser's life. To paraphrase Toker, the little quantity of flesh on the focaliser is directly related to his sparse memory and consequently his language.[49] When the focaliser regains his flesh, his memory returns. The fabula can only return once this quantity of flesh returns to the focaliser. Kermode in *Genesis of Secrecy* explains that to develop a character signifies more narration, and to develop a plot means to enrich a character.[50] The plot becomes enriched when the focaliser awakens. Consequently, the narrator defers his opinions in favour of the focaliser's, once the latter's life is restored. It is the narrator who makes philosophical aphorisms not the focaliser. Basic life survival strategies are more important to the focaliser, until the very end of the tale. He may remember words, but to create aphorisms is an impossible feat whilst still in the camps. The return of his language is not a sudden occurrence, but as the narrator comments 'Each returned alone, unaccompanied by the watchful guards of familiar words.'[51] The return of words is unbidden and dangerous to the focaliser. It is as if the focaliser is speaking the language of tongues and this 'religious' awakening is only later analysed in the mind. His memory is now storing these words to be used later by the narrator for this story.

Shalamov's use of anonymous characters is markedly evident in *Sententious*. At the beginning of the tale, the focaliser and the other convicts are in much the same position as later in the text. The narrator lists a stream of convicts occupying whatever bunks they can and expresses surprise when convicts reawaken the next morning. They appear spasmodically throughout the tale, almost as shadows of the focaliser. The narrator reports 'groans, snoring, wheezing, coughing, and the mindless swearing of sleeping men.'[52] The characters have a vocal life that rivals the focaliser's muteness. It is not only the focaliser who returns from the dead at the end. The focaliser can now walk and climb to get to the clearing, the other prisoners also are able to do this. However, their recovery rate is quicker and they arrive before him. The narrator does not focalise on these other prisoners, but then they are always used as a yardstick from which to base the focaliser's strength. This relationship between the other anonymous prisoners and the focaliser is again a reminder of Shalamov's distancing between his main and secondary characters. The narratorial focus may briefly follow the latter, but always returns to concentrate on the former. In another sense, these secondary characters are not deserving of Shalamov's attention as he insists on only reporting intellectual or powerful figures. The only named characters in the tale are Moses Kuznetsov the blacksmith and Vronsky. The narrator makes a curious point concerning the former. He refers to him as a 'blacksmith and a clever, intelligent man.'[53] A blacksmith is a craftsman, and indeed 'clever', who transforms metals. Therefore the narrator seems to be referring to his ability to make intelligent comments: 'I'd woken up, as Moses Kuznetsov used to say.'[54] Words and aphorisms are at a premium in the camps and this seems likely to be an attempt by the narrator (indeed Shalamov) to pinpoint a fellow thinker or linguist.[55] Moses is in strong contrast to Vronsky the informer, who, given his powerful position in the camp could have immediately denounced the focaliser. Vronsky deals in words, he questions and analyses them. He represents the paranoia of Soviet Reality, and although the focaliser has been brought back to life, it is cruelly ironical that his life could be taken away again.

The two remaining foregrounded characters consist of the topographer and the chief. The former is an ex-prisoner, but now has the power of life and death over escaped prisoners and, as the tale demonstrates, birds. It is a symptom of the focaliser's return to life that he is willing to save the bird from death. Another symptom is that his new-found strength is not challenged. The topographer represents a defeated bully, who does not inspire respect from his underlings. Conversely, the chief commands a great deal of respect from the surrounding audience. Indeed, Kline likens the chief to a conductor, co-ordinating proceedings with a 'heft hand'.[56] The narrator imposes his own interpretation on the chief by noting that 'the expression on his face was such that he seemed to have written the music for us, for our desolate sojourn in the taiga.'[57] The focaliser, in his awakening, has returned from the dead to rejoin the rest of the listening crowd. The isolation and loneliness of a near dead man is replaced with a sense of community and mental faculties to match. He is able to appreciate this momentous event. This event does not specifically represent the climax to the focaliser's awakening; rather it is the narrator's aphoristic belief that this event is a turning point for the focaliser (namely himself).

3.1.4 Setting

The setting in *Sententious* is varied and it is therefore interesting that he makes use of wider scenery in this tale. The focaliser is neither stationary nor consistently on the move; his resurrection brings him into contact with a variety of environments. The world around the focaliser has symbolic meaning for the narrator. The enclosed environment of the tent is where the tale starts. The focaliser is rooted to the bed, only able to watch the constant stream of convicts come and go. The narrator has 'taken over' the focaliser's eyes, and reports movements through this focal world. There is no stability to this world and the focaliser's perspective is severely restricted. His perspective has been narrowed to tunnel vision and he is unable to recognise other convicts around him. When the focaliser moves from his bed, his world expands to 200 yards. The work area is in a little village that was 'like an island in the world of the taiga.'[58] Thus, the narrator has created a concentric world:

bed → tent→ village→ taiga

As this world expands, the focaliser finds it difficult to reach the outer limits. However, the sujet keeps the outer world close to hand. The focaliser takes strength from natural elements; for example, he drinks the elixir of water to face 'the path of death'[59] The grouse did not figure in his eating, but the more natural 'berries, the roots of the grass, the rations.'[60] This natural environment is also his undoing. The narrator describes it as 'cold red sun, bare mountaintops, where the rocks, the turns of the river, the trees were all sharp and unfriendly.'[61] However, the narrator makes the comparison between the focaliser's current life and his previous one in the mines and this marks a change in the focaliser's beliefs. He is not willing to die just yet and the setting marks a change in the narrator's perspective. The sujet jumps back to the mine and in making the comparison returns to the focaliser's current life. The only sensory input for the focaliser is this natural environment and, in a way, he must learn to accept it as preferable to complex human creations: 'I hadn't seen newspapers or books for years, and I had long since trained myself not to regret the loss.'[62]

As Toker notes, the focaliser's rebirth leads the narrator to remark on mystical insights regarding the natural environment.[63] With a new sense of being and sensory perception, stones cease to be merely stones, but become animate objects. The grass, the trees and the river also become as animated as the focaliser himself. The ice-cold water he drank and later boiled is now 'not only the incarnation of life, not just a symbol of life, but life itself.'[64] Thus, the river reflects the narrator's comparison between language and life. Shalamov suggests that when a man suffers loss of language, it is only temporary, and an unpredictable force will always return to give that man his voice again. This voice is the language of survival, both for the river and the focaliser. The sujet has treated the tale as a dried river waiting for the first rain to release its flow. The final scene is the setting's concluding impact on the sujet. The return of the focaliser's memory marks the re-commencement of time. The narrator offers one final aphorism, and likens memory to the record that 'spun and hissed.'[65] Memory does not disappear, but as Toker contends, it is contained within the grooves of the mind, ready for a mental record player to replay memorial thoughts.[66] The tree stump is also an enormous memory bank that has stored 300 years of memories, all within a spring like formation. The focaliser has metaphorically and physically escaped the lower part of the spring in order to begin creating more memorial grooves.

3.2 *A Piece of Meat*

For a tale to be fully understood, it must incorporate information capable of explaining cause/effect and motives. The sujet provides this information whether it is in the form of flashback, projection or textual devices within the tale. *A Piece of Meat* is completely dependent upon Shalamov's play with the sujet, where flashbacks provide not only the reasons for Golubev to have an operation, but his need to remember the dangerous convict's past.[67] Memory is the key to *A Piece of Meat*, inasmuch as Golubev's life depends on it. The narrator is also fundamental to the presentation of the fabula and sujet combination. He creates the scenario and unlike the narrator in *Berries*, reverses the order of the events and explanations in the tale. In *A Piece of Meat,* the narrator explains background information, before applying it to the hero, Golubev. The narrator conveys the whole procedure for the year-end camp reshuffles and Golubev is the recipient of this information. Causes are applied prior to events, in order for the tale to make sense. The plot therefore is easily recognised, but without the retardations and memory recalls by the narrator, the fabula would be difficult to pick out. This is especially true for Kononenko/Kazakov, whose history is important not only for Golubev, but for our understanding of the tale. The narrator therefore is dominant, if not omniscient, and as such, his information and presentation of facts allows the tale to be fully understood.

3.2.1 Narrative Structure

A Piece of Meat is one of several stories that provide an epilogue at the beginning of the work. The *appendix* operation is something of an irony in view of the work's ambiguity. The epilogue has become an *appendix* to the tale, offering aphoristic meanings for such a simple and routine operation. This first paragraph is an unusual device for Shalamov, in that he has provided an explanation for the rest of the tale. This literary technique alters the narrative structure, and in turn affects the presentation of the rest of the tale. The sujet has in effect been written first, and the fabula has been written around this fact. The sujet can be broken down into bite-sized chunks and the narrator fills in the specific and general effects they have on Golubev:

Sujet	Fabula
Reasons for the operation	
Explanation on end of year inspections	Golubev is on 'black' list
Last year's inspection and surgeon's friend	Golubev hears a way to avoid this for himself. Acts on it.
Intends to use this knowledge	Intro. of Kononenko
Kononenko's past explained	Implications for Golubev
Situation gets worse	'Kazakov' introduced
Kononenko decided not to kill Golubev	The new instructions reported to Golubev

This can be translated into the following narrative structure:

Epilogue/Prologue	- Reasons for the operation
Exposition	- End of year inspections
Complication	- Implications for Golubev
Peripeteia	- Instructions are related to Golubev
Dénouement	- Golubev's new knowledge gives him strength

The epilogue has all the marks of a prologue, but it is retrospective in nature. Golubev has been introduced and his sacrifice has become a necessity to save his own life. This play with the temporal ordering informs the reader that Golubev survived the operation, but not why. Once again, Shalamov has differentiated between the how and why of events in a tale. The exposition gradually builds up reasons for this operation, but Golubev is not mentioned until the end of the exposition. The exposition is a series of events in a documentary style that outlines the process of appointments/demotions in the camps. Only when Golubev is reintroduced does the reader become re-apprised of these events and their implications for Golubev. Consequently, Golubev's plan to act on his thoughts is inevitable. His memory serves him well both for remembering his last spell in the hospital and also for prolonging his symptoms. It is important for the fabula to shift to the sujet in order to clarify reasons for entering and prolonging his stay in the hospital. What is interesting here is the placement of thoughts assigned by the narrator to both Golubev and Kononenko. The reader has Kononenko's knowledge withheld from him, and it is only when this information is released that the reader is becomes fully aware of how close Golubev was to death. 'And I would have "fixed" you, sent you to the moon. And I wouldn't have hesitated.'[68] Essentially, the sujet has created even more suspense than the reader has been aware of. Kononenko was going to kill Golubev before he (and the reader) knew of this fact. The dénouement clarifies this situation and the fabula is left to follow its natural course to the end. The epilogue is better placed where it is, because of the ordering of events. Golubev may have sacrificed his appendix, but he was very close to losing his life. The epilogue explains this fact, without mentioning Kononenko's presence, but it is not the criminal's actions that are important here, but Golubev's self-preservation methods.

3.2.2 Point of View

The narrator in *A Piece of Meat* is crucial to the ordering and interpretation of the plot. His dominant and omniscient approach to telling the tale shapes the reader's understanding of events. He is also in a position to withhold information and organise the linearity. Indeed, the tale is dominated by temporal binarity. We know that the first paragraph of the tale occurs after Golubev's operation and subsequent brush with the criminal. It can be regarded as a foreshadowing of events, whereby the results are known before the tale starts.[69] What we do not know is when this paragraph takes place. In one sense it occurs just after the end of the tale, but most importantly, it is the narrator who focalises these thoughts at an unspecified point in the future. Another and most probable explanation is that the narrator utters these extra-temporally. This gives us a clue about the narrator's position and also about how the tale is narratively organised. The reference to Shakespeare gives a clue to his identity. He seems to be acting the part of a Puck, a chorus or court jester, informing the audience of future events and making philosophical aphorisms. 'The rudimentary organ turned out to be not rudimentary at all, but essential, functional, life-saving.'[70] The Shakespearian 'narrator' is independent and knowledgeable and is often able to transcend temporal limitations. Shalamov's narrator also possesses the very Shakespearean irony: 'And, of course, conditions of absolute sterility were observed in offering the bloody sacrifice...'[71]

After this opening paragraph, the narrator fulfils a more conventional role and he is very similar in style and approach to the narrator in *Sententious*. However, the difference lies in his almost exclusively third person approach. Golubev is never reported in the first person, but the narrator does possess insights into Golubev's inner processes. This is one of the few instances where a narrator in *Kolyma Tales* reports thoughts. Therefore, the narrator is writing from an omniscient perspective and has full access to Golubev's mind. However, the narrator mainly reports his actions, and not his thoughts. This technique provides a deeper understanding of the fabula and especially the sujet forces at work in the text. We are able to deduce events from Golubev's thoughts and the reason for his operation becomes clear. Sujet information also works against the reader. For example, while Kononenko has already worked out who Golubev is, the latter is still trying to work out who Kononenko is. The reader, guided by Golubev's thoughts, is therefore taken aback by Kononenko's knowledge of Golubev. The narrator thus is in complete control and the reader must be careful about trusting him. Conversely, the narrator is crucial in providing much needed information for understanding the plot. Kline notes that '[He] moves away from his characters temporarily in order to provide background information for the reader: information that the character is aware of but would not naturally think about at the time being depicted in the story.'[72]

3.2.3 Characterisation

The opening paragraph makes reference to a ritual played out in the camps. Indeed, the Shakespearian works mentioned in the tale all require a sacrifice from the protagonist. The narrator's comparison is of Golubev acting out a part in making a sacrifice to 'the almighty god of the camps.'[73] In this case, it is possible to identify Stalin as the god-like figure. Shalamov has shaped this tale to include the theme of self-sacrifice as the central act for the main character. This then raises an interesting idea as to the time structure of *A Piece of Meat*. The characters in this tale are not individuals, but conform to universal psychological types. Shalamov mentions Lady Macbeth, Richard III and King Claudius. All these characters are the epitome of evil, and it is only the setting that differentiates them. This setting is the hospital and the evil character is Kononenko. He has killed and will kill again to achieve his aims. All these characters are but 'individuals in a mimetic world acting out the pattern of their mythic destinies.'[74] For Tomashevskii: The more significant and long lasting the theme, the better guarantee of the life of the work.'[75] Accordingly, the characters play out a pre-determined role, where their motives, causes and effects can be identified. Scholes & Kellogg wrote 'Insofar as a character, or any other element in narrative, becomes dynamic, it is a part of the plot.'[76] Time exists in this tale, but it only has a limited function, as these events will undoubtedly recur in the future. The flashbacks and memorial recalls by the doctor, Golubev and indeed Kononenko aid understanding of the tale and also inject an individual feel for the reader. The reader knows that next December the black raven will re-appear, and it will be different characters that are involved.[77] In effect, the tale has already been written and it is only the use of additional characters combined with delaying techniques that impart depth and understanding to this tale of sacrifice.

Familiar power relationships are exhibited in this tale, but the ubiquitous threat affects all levels in the camps. Higher authority does not discriminate between lower or higher ranks. The privileged positions are most at risk, but even a doctor can be carried away. The narrator continually refers back to a list of prisoners in good positions and camp heads. The reader's understanding of the tale relies on the precarious situation of all involved. The information on good, bad or indifferent camp heads (all anonymous) is specifically related to Golubev's position. The reader can discern that the camp head is of the 'good' variety, someone who waits for the commission to make its changes. Yet, this information is related in a documentary style and exists outside of the focaliser's situation.[78] This explicit information affects the surgeon and every member of the prison staff. The current head is not named at any point, nor does the narrator comment on what his managerial approach would be regarding his treatment of prisoners. Despite all the information supplied on the commission raids and the officers involved, the tale withholds specific information relating to Golubev. He is as much in the dark as the reader; Golubev only reveals an understanding of this situation when 'someone' runs up to him. He does not however think or speak his thoughts, but merely replies to the duty officer's demand: 'Right away.'[79] It is important to note that no other convict prisoner is named prior to the commission raids and presumably this is to ensure that the narrative focus remains on only those characters important to the plot.

Golubev is depicted in two triangular relationships. Firstly, he observes the activities of the surgeon and the surgeon's assistant and secondly he is the object of Kononenko's wrath with Podosenov as the unwilling observer. The power relations between the two groups revolves around Golubev, but he also passes through five triangular sub-relations. In these five, Golubev is illustrated at the apex, the object of attention. He passes between two orderlies, two surgeons, surgeon and nurse, surgeon and assistant surgeon, and finally between two orderlies. In the last scene Kononenko/Kazakov occupies the apex of the triangle with the two lower and vulnerable convicts at his mercy. In this figure, it is clear that there is a direct linear progression from a state of relative safety to extreme danger. He has metaphorically and physically moved from one state to another. The fabulaic element of the tale progresses alongside Golubev's movement. His state of mind also progresses with the body. This typical Shalamovian approach ensures that Golubev does not meet safety, rather the reverse. 'For good to turn to bad and vice versa,' writes Ricoeur, 'it is temporal. A reversal takes time, but it is the work's time, not the time of events in the world.'[80] The transitional period of the operation is accelerated within the text, and the bad (carried away) turns to good (life-saving operation) turns to bad (Kononenko) extremely quickly. Yet, although the operation is 'fast' it corresponds roughly to narration time.[81] Shalamov employs this summary/scene dialogic relationship to emphasise the transition. The scenes prior to the hospital and after the operation are summaries of past events and are quick descriptions of longer periods of time. In effect, Shalamov has given the impression that the operation is faster than the preceding parts, but the reverse is true. Also, the scene of reminiscence just after the operation is longer than the time spent with Kononenko. The surgeons, nurse and orderlies form a significant part of this structure. The surgeons provide the cause for the tale, with the secondary characters providing the fabulaic elements.

3.2.4 Setting

Physical setting in *A Piece of Meat* is restricted to the hospital, but some allusion is made to areas outside the hospital. The yard and the porch in the camp play an important role in the presentation of facts. The narrator's reminiscences of the previous year include all the vital physical and symbolic material for Golubev to embark on the operation. The 'black raven' is crucial in creating a terrible foreboding for Golubev. It swoops in and carries away the 'trapped, snared, unmasked convicts' as if they are animals caught in a trap.[82] The yard is in a state of turmoil, with senior officers scurrying around like defenceless chickens. The scene has become a farmyard, with the farmer deciding what to choose for the dinner table. The surgeon and Golubev are witnesses to this and this duality of experience gives the tale a firm link between the past and the present. The physical setting with its deportation process is replayed not once, but twice by Golubev. The memory is replayed to himself: 'the firm eyes of the surgeon, the bus cloaked in a cloud of dust… ' Then after approaching the surgeon, Golubev comments on the distant look in the former's eyes, 'perhaps it was the cloud of dust that enveloped the bus,'[83] This is what Genette calls 'repeating anachrony' or 'narrating n times what happened once.'[84] Shalamov uses this technique to create a causal link between why the surgeon should believe Golubev's complaint and why he subsequently operates on him. Shalamov uses a typical masking technique to hide the final consequences from the reader. It would be possible for most of Shalamov's tales to include the phrase 'he died' or 'dead' or some other explicit reference to death. It is not necessary of course: the reader knows full well what occurs. Symbols of death are used to take its place, and in *A Piece of Meat* there are two instances of this. Firstly an all-covering dust envelops the bus and secondly the narrator describes the bus crawling away 'to disappear in a mountain ravine.'[85] Shalamov also uses a third grammatical device, ellipsis to denote that someone/thing is physically and metaphorically lost every time the bus leaves.[86] This device is not particularly usual for Shalamov, but it is employed in place of the ravine. The future for the captives not only extends into an infinite future, but also into a certain past. The third and final mention of the bus finishes with 'that took the other surgeon away for ever.' Thus, Shalamov has finished each reference to the bus with a different, but vitally important causal datum.

The porch is also vital to the continuation of the tale because it represents a transitional point in this story. Golubev does not cross the porch line and neither does the doctor, but this halfway house leads Golubev in another direction, to the hospital. The third physical location exists outside the limits of the camp, and is situated some distance away nearer the vast taiga. Kline describes hospitals in *Kolyma Tales* as 'represent[ing] the most desirable physical space in the work,' though they are 'spatially restricted.'[87] There is a certain mystique to the hospital, yet there is a dual function to its role. In one sense hospitals are life-saving places, but in another they return a broken convict back from the dead to resume his place in a cruel regime.[88] However, for a convict to experience a period in hospital is more than a physical reprieve: 'As Shalamov's world-view hinges on an understanding of the irrevocable interconnectedness of the physical and the spiritual, the hospital can be seen as a church and the doctors as priests who, by resurrecting the body, have the ability to resurrect the soul.'[89] The hospital in *A Piece of Meat* does not fulfil this ideal for Golubev. It has become a supremely dangerous place for the convict, with no guards or foremen to control the inmates. The building exists outside of time, with no indication of day or night. Golubev refers to a future time by delaying his release, but with time effectively ceasing, Shalamov has organised the text to preclude any future. By using reminiscence and extra-temporal narration, Shalamov places Golubev in a period of timeless reverie. Enter Kononenko and with him, the typical Shalamovian device of destroying any pre-conceived ideas of personal safety. As Kline correctly notes,'[I]f the hospital in *Kolymskie rasskazy* is a place of resurrection, it still has only a minimal sense of order, being vulnerable to the laws of chaos and absurdity that govern all aspects of the camps.'[90] Indeed, chaos has infiltrated Golubev's reverie and the hospital has ceased to be a place of resurrection, but is on the contrary, deadly.

In Kline's view Shalamov's use of space is incompatible with any fixed dichotomous relationship. Van Baak's concept of 'open-closed' space tends to conform in a human context to 'free-unfree'. In Shalamov's tales, this comparison does not materialise. Kline argues that for Shalamov 'open-closed' implies 'unfree-unfree'. 'Free' open space does not exist in the text.'[91] Consequently, any movement within a tale, as demonstrated in *A Piece of Meat*, does not lead a convict from an un-free space to a free space. The promise of a 'free' hospital cannot materialise and Glebov finds himself in a confined closed space instead. The location of the hospital is also at odds with van Baak's open-closed/free-unfree dichotomy.[92] The hospital, though located away from the closed space of the camp, nevertheless 'shares the spatial constrictedness so characteristic of closed space.'[93] The chaos from lying on the periphery has intervened making the 'subspace' of the hospital dangerous. The fabulaic pre-conception of unsafe→safe in relation to securing a stay in hospital is overturned.[94] The sujet inverts this concept, whereby safe→unsafe or in Glebov's case, unsafe→unsafe exists.

NOTES

[1] Augustine in Ricoeur, p. 7

[2] Scholes & Kellogg, p. 239

[3] Tomashevsky in Lemon & Reis, p. 68

[4] Andrew, Introduction to 'The Structural Analysis of Russian Narrative Fiction', p. ix

[5] For example, boy meets girl, boy loses girl, boy sets out to find girl and finally boy gets girl. There is also an element of the fairy or children's tale, where the listeners easily identify the fabula.

[6] Tomashevsky in Lemon & Reis, p. 61

[7] Ricoeur, p. 47

[8] Andrew, Introduction to 'The Structural Analysis of Russian Narrative Fiction', p. ix

[9] Tomashevsky in Lemon & Reis, p. 68

[10] For example, in *The Lawyers' Plot*, when the hero confronts many different characters in different settings.

[11] Martin, p. 117

[12] A. Shukman, 'The Russian Short Story, Theory, Analysis, Interpretation', *Essays in Poetics*, II, 2, September 1977, pp. 27-95

[13] Martin, p. 109

[14] O'Toole, *Structure, Style and Interpretation in the Russian Short Story*, p. 113

[15] Andrew, Introduction to 'The Structural Analysis of Russian Narrative Fiction', p. xv

[16] See Toker, in *Return from the Archipelago*, p. 96

[17] In extreme fight or flight situations the brain shuts down non-essential functions in order to keep the heart and lungs functioning. The result of this is memory loss and mental fatigue. See on-line journal http://www.trauma-pages.com for more information. Specifically, Bessel van der Kolk's article 'The Body Keeps the Score: Memory and the Evolving Psychobiology of Post-traumatic Stress.' http://www.trauma-pages.com/vanderk4.htm

[18] C. Thubron, *In Siberia*, (London: Penguin, 2000), pp. 273-4

[19] C. V. Chvany, 'Foregrounding, Transitivity, Saliency (in sequential and non-sequential prose)', *Essays in Poetics*, X, 2, 1985, pp. 1-27

[20] Foregrounding has also been linked with causation in the sense of explaining causes: a function of sujet). Where, in these tales, memory has a dominant function, the reader is given a causal reason for its presence. Memory causes the hero to shout out his new/old word in *Sententious* (p. 289) and the life-saving advice by the doctor causes Golubev to avoid the round up in *A Piece of Meat*.

[21] The *Oxford English Dictionary* gives several meanings: 1. Pompously moralising. 2. Affectedly formal. 3. Using maxims. J. A. Simpson, (ed.) *Oxford English Dictionary*, (Oxford: Clarendon Press, 1989)

[22] Quoted in Toker, *Return from the Archipelago*, p. 172

[23] Neither will be recovered until the convict has physically left the camp. In Shalamov's case, he never fully recovered from his ordeal.

[24] *Kolyma Tales*, p. 284

[25] G. Hosking, 'The Ultimate Circle of the Stalinist Inferno', *NUQ*, Spring, 1980, pp. 161-8

[26] Kline, p. 308

[27] *Kolyma Tales*, p. 289

[28] Brewer, '"Authorial," Lyric and Narrative Voices in Varlam Shalamov's *Kolymskie rasskazy*: A Close Reading of Sententsiia', http://www.pitt.edu/~mmbst35/shalamov. html, p. 2

[29] Without this peripeteia, there would not exist a plot, or a reason for this event to occur and subsequent events to follow. According to Rimmon-Kenan a plot must have a reason or else it remains a simple story. Rimmon-Kenan, p. 17

[30] *Kolyma Tales*, p. 285

[31] Ibid., p. 286

[32] Loc. cit.

[33] Loc. cit.

[34] *Kolyma Tales*, p. 288

[35] The bullfinch or 'bird of the snow' (*snegir'*) in Russian folklore represents the power of life to exist when all around is metaphorical death. This bird is able to live in such extreme conditions, and like the robin is associated with winter. To preserve the bird's life is to further the focaliser's own life. An interesting old proverb (kindly located by R. Reid) goes as such: 'When the bullfinch chirrups under the window, it means a thaw.' In Vladimir Dal', *Tolkovyi slovar, zhivago velikorusskago iazyka*, IV, St. Petersburg, 1882, (Reprinted Moscow, 1978-80), p. 250

[36] *Kolyma Tales*, p. 288

[37] Ibid., p. 290

[38] Toker, *Return from the Archipelago*, p. 165

[39] This tale is based on Shalamov's posting to a relatively lax coal mine at Chernoe Ozero. However, because the coal prospecting was unsuccessful, the camp was closed, and the prisoners were dispersed. Shalamov therefore returned to the rigours of hard labour. In Kline, p. 82

[40] M. Brewer, "Authorial," Lyric and Narrative Voices in Varlam *Shalamov's Kolymskie rasskazy*: A Close Reading of Sententsiia', p. 1

[41] Loc. cit.

[42] *Kolyma Tales*, p. 284

[43] Ibid., p. 287

[44] Ibid., p. 284-5

[45] Ibid., p. 288

[46] Ibid., p. 290

[47] *Kolyma Tales*, p. 284

[48] Ibid., p. 285. This stems from Marxist thinking that everything is in a state of flux. The water will always change into ice or into steam; the only constant is change itself.

[49] Toker, in *Return from the Archipelago*, p. 173

[50] F. Kermode, *The Genesis of Secrecy on the Interpretation of Narrative*, (Cambridge: Harvard University Press, 1979), p. 77

[51] *Kolyma Tales*, p. 290

[52] Ibid., p. 286

[53] *Kolyma Tales*, p. 287

[54] Loc. cit.

55 Shalamov possibly makes this reference to a kindred spirit, in order to distance himself from uneducated fellow convicts. Kline reports that Shalamov conducted research in the coal excavating camps, into which 19th Russian poets were most popular with the convicts. The ability to conduct this sort of research indicates the return of non-essential faculties. Therefore, this period can only have been favourable for Shalamov's health. In Kline, p. 82.

56 Ibid., p. 171

57 *Kolyma Tales*, p. 291

58 Ibid., p. 285

59 Loc. cit.

60 Ibid., p. 286

61 Loc. cit.

62 Ibid., p. 288

63 Toker, *Return from the Archipelago*, p. 172

64 *Kolyma Tales*, p. 290

65 Ibid., p. 291

66 Toker, *Return from the Archipelago*, p. 172

67 However, Golubev's knowledge is inconsequential to his own survival.

68 *Kolyma Tales*, p. 231

69 Foreshadowing in its broadest form is where essential knowledge is gleaned before the actions occur. Crime fiction (Dostoevskii's *Crime and Punishment* or Columbo, for instance) uses this technique to great effect, where the reader knows who the murderer is, but follows the detective in deducing the facts to catch him. Tomashevsky, in Lemon & Reis, p. 75

70 *Kolyma Tales*, p. 222

71 Loc. cit.

72 Kline, p. 416

73 *Kolyma Tales*, p. 222

74 Scholes & Kellogg, p. 230

75 Tomashevsky in Lemon & Reis, p. 64

76 Scholes & Kellogg, p. 207.

77 The appearance of a raven is commonly linked with imminent death. See Mark, Schwan, 'Raven: The Northern Bird of Paradox', http://www.state.ak.us/local/akpages /FISH.GAME/wildlife/geninfo/ birds/raven.htm

78 It is possible that Shalamov wants to portray these events as impartially as possible and by using this type of story telling, he furnishes the reader with explanations of specific day-to-day occurrences. This technique, whilst providing useful information to the reader, is also the basis of delivering the tale's meaning or importance.

79 *Kolyma Tales*, p. 225

80 Ricoeur, p. 39

81 According to Shukman, narration time is the literal time taken to read a passage, paragraph or book. Its binary counterpart is event time; that is, time duration described in the same passage. There is always variation between these two, but occasionally they coincide and the reader reads events at exactly the same rate as they happen in the text. Shukman links narration time and event time to scene and summary. A 'pure' scene would read at 'something like the pace at which [events] would have occurred.' Summary uses phrases such as 'many years passed' to denote a

temporal difference. See Shukman's 'The Russian Short Story: Theory, Analysis, Interpretation.' pp. 32-45

[82] *Kolyma Tales*, p. 224
[83] Ibid., p. 225
[84] Genette, p. 115
[85] *Kolyma Tales*, p. 225
[86] According to Rimmon-Kenan, the ellipsis gives the maximum textual speed. p.121
[87] Kline, p. 358
[88] See *Shock Therapy* for the inhuman lengths doctors will go to in order to 'resurrect' a patient and send him back to work.
[89] Kline, p. 386
[90] Ibid., p. 309
[91] Ibid., p. 382
[92] Van Baak, 'The Place of Space in Narration', p. 68
[93] Kline, p. 387
[94] This pre-conception, of course, applies only to a reader who is unfamiliar with conditions in the Gulag.

Chapter 4

Characterisation

'Death is common to all men. Its inevitability makes Achilles a man as well as a hero.'[1]

'Now, if the Russian fairy tale is really to do with order and individual liberty, then one can only comment that so too, at a certain level of generality, is every story anywhere that has a specified hero.'[2]

This chapter will contribute to the analysis of Shalamov's use of character in *Kolyma Tales*. Character is one of the main areas, as O'Toole puts it: 'where everyone has some contribution to make.'[3] Early schooling, fairy tales and bedtime stories all contribute to a child's and later an adult's perception of character. We can distinguish the good characters from the bad, without necessarily needing to know how the process occurs. The 'wicked' witch and the 'handsome' knight automatically engender particular images and physically recognisable characteristics. This recognition is the basis for the interaction between the writer and reader, with the former including particular and recognisable traits in his characters to be recognised by the latter. It is arguable that any character is a social creation (albeit fictional), but dominant features, such as love and hate are universally recognised. Also, it is primarily the reader who decides which character he or she likes, dislikes or empathises with. This final point is one of the most essential reasons why anyone reads fiction. The act of reading brings readers into contact with characters they want to love or hate and consequently they react as they would if they were real people.

A purely Structuralist approach would identify types of characters and categorise them in several ways.[4] Mudrick argues that characters do not exist at all and are only part of the images and events in a text: '…to discuss them as if they are real human beings is a sentimental misunderstanding of the nature of literature.'[5] However, this author feels that this singular approach would unnecessarily objectify the characters into inanimate objects. Certainly elements of Propp's functions are discernible in *Kolyma Tales*, but they do not tell the whole story. Herman describes Propp's analysis of character as a reductionist approach wherein Propp has subordinated the character merely to action.[6] According to such a view definition of character would be limited to sender-receiver, object-subject binary relations.[7] It is indeed true to say that characters are defined by their actions, and these actions give rise to the plot. However, without characters and their deeds, there would not exist a plot and hence a tale to tell. For O'Toole 'character and event are indivisible'[8], simply because of a character's presence in a story. Where a character appears, he or she plays a role or functions either explicitly or implicitly, that is ultimately significant to the story's meaning. Indeed, Bolshakova in 'The Theory of The Author: Bakhtin and Vinogradov', argues that the plot is dominant over characters because each character is important to the plot.[9] Shalamov's characters have individual stories, but for most of them it is only Shalamov who is able to tell it. Analysis of character usually stresses one or all of the following four functions for each character:

1. Importance of naming
2. Physical description, with physical mannerisms or gestures
3. Their locale as defining a character, for example, guard in guardroom
4. Psychological characteristics, biography, actions and speech

This type of approach provides a fuller understanding of character, whilst also highlighting the importance of the reader response. We can determine whether a character is 'flat' or 'round'[10] and on this basis define his/her function in the tale. The only drawback to this approach is that short stories are often lacking in complete characterisation, owing to the limited length of the medium. However, it is possible to identify universal character traits, without the need for a full characterisation.

Russia has a great tradition of producing memorable characters in her novels and short stories. Raskolnikov, Anna Karenina and Akakii Akakevich produce a reader response, in which understanding, sympathy or ridicule may be dominant reactions. However, what is also transparent is that these characters and many others evoke a host of other feelings. There are certainly undeveloped characters who are present mainly for plot advancement, symbolism or as part of the setting; however protagonists or heroines are never straightforward and easily understood. The same can be argued for Shalamov's characters: '[The stories] are vivid accounts of individual moments in the lives of individual men, for only in the particular can we begin to comprehend the horror of the whole.'[11] He occasionally evokes sympathy for a character, such as Dugaev in *An Individual Assignment* and also hate for non-political prisoners. However, the majority of characters are portrayed as victims who, although deserving of sympathy from the reader, also display a fallible humanity. They cannot be categorised as all good or all bad, but are creations of both Shalamov's memory and, hypothetically, the Soviet system. Shalamov has made each character as 'human' as possible, but it is a humanity developed from years of mistreatment in the Gulags. In Hollosi's words: 'All this is done by Shalamov very deliberately, because the people whom he describes are not part of normal life, and they had to create a special state of existence.'[12] It is also possible to observe characters whose role is functional but modified. Some of the 'traditional' characters in *The Train* have already been noted for their alternative lifestyles and functions.

The tales chosen for this analysis are *In the Night* and *Major Pugachov's Last Battle*. The characters in *In The Night* do not conform to the roles bestowed on them. Grave robbing is a deliberate inversion of the reader's expectation of what a doctor should perform. The characters in *Major Pugachov's Last Battle* are not stereotyped, though they do not wholly depart from this idea. The main twelve seem to fulfil an adventure tale of an escape and chase variety.[13] The difference lies jointly in their ability to change roles several times during the tale and also to modify the meaning of the hero function. Therefore, whilst conducting this analysis, each character has to be treated with the impartiality that Shalamov originally intended. This will be attained by treating each character as a function of the plot, his symbolised presence and his psychological/physiological being. *In the Night* presents the characters as symbols of an altered morality, and in *Major Pugachov*, the main character and title of the work are symbolic of rebellion. Both tales, coincidentally, have death either as the theme or as a part of the plot. Indeed, death was always close at hand in the Gulags and therefore for this to be included in some way is not surprising. Finally, this analysis will attempt to focus on how and why Shalamov includes particular characters and consider to what extent they are recognisable literary types.

4.1 *In The Night*

There are only three characters in *In the Night*, of which one is dead. Yet this occupant of yet another Gulag grave is treated to a full description, fuller indeed than the other two. This is not surprising however, given the fact that his possessions, which the two convicts are stealing, are the main interest of the story. This tale is in two senses character-led: firstly, it highlights the depths to which man will go in order to survive. Secondly, the reader is asked to follow the two men's foray into the hills and discover the reason for their journey. In some ways this tale follows the pattern of an adventure story, in that the characters overcome all odds to discover a hidden treasure. This is reminiscent of a mythological quest to steal treasure from the gods and bring it back to the mortals. The treasure is, in typical Shalamovian spirit, the offerings of a dead man. Shalamov does not follow a highly moral course, where the hero is obliged to obey moral concerns and still gain the prize. The treasure must be taken regardless of the means for gaining it. The protagonists are not moral guardians, nor do they adhere to the unspoken law against grave robbing. Yet, in order for this tale to possess as much force as it does, there has to exist the moral precedent that grave robbing is wrong. Therefore, the tale implicitly concerns itself with the morality of men in the Gulags: 'All the most desperate goners in Shalamov's tales are characterised by their lack of humanity.'[14] Shalamov's concern is not so much the reader's response to the morality of the situation, but 'why' the convicts have to perform this act. The textual markers and essential character actions point towards the reasons for grave robbing. Kline refers to an intrinsic quality of man, whereby physical well-being is needed to maintain moral good health. When avoiding starvation becomes primary, then morality has to be placed second. Kline therefore can sum up this tale as 'the needs of the body, the house of the soul, ironically [taking] precedence over the needs of the soul, outlasting that which it was designed to protect.'[15]

4.1.1 Narrative Structure

This tale manages to squeeze a narrative structure into three pages of text. It has a definite beginning, middle and end, with an interesting peripeteia. This could be identified as a crisis of conscience on the part of Glebov, who answers Bagretsov's instruction to wear the underwear: 'No, I don't want to.'[16] The tale begins with the pathetic meal and ends in the projection of an after-dinner cigarette. There is no prologue, but the tale begins in the food-hall and moves swiftly towards the complication, in the form of a quest. Once the quest has been resolved, the tale ceases. This continuous narrative reflects Shalamov's need to portray the single-mindedness of the two protagonists. Other concerns become subservient to the need to acquire food. Thus the full impact of the grave-robbing becomes apparent, not only to Glebov, but to the reader. However, this is short-lived, as Glebov is 'assimilated' with the underwear and he assumes a dreamlike demeanour. The tale possesses several retardation techniques, but they do not ultimately interfere with the quest.

The structure is as below:

Exposition   – Meagre dinner
Complication   – Hunt for the body
Peripeteia   – Mini-crisis of conscience
Dénouement   – 'Assimilation' of new clothes
Prologue?   – Projection of future plans

There is a 'leader/follower' binary, which is re-enforced throughout the tale. Bagretsov assumes the leadership role and remains in the ascendancy through all stages of the tale. This can be seen in the figure below:

Initiates the complication/action by declaring 'It's time'
Provides tension by stating 'Get down or they'll see us'
Finds the body: 'Here he is'
Challenges Glebov to hide the clothes: 'Better to wear it'
Provides salve to Glebov's conscience: 'Tomorrow you'll get your smoke'

At all stages of progression, Glebov is not essentially portrayed as an unwilling partner to this quest; rather he is content for Bagretsov to lead him. This binary relationship recalls the Hamlet/Don Quixote model, formulated by Turgenev.[17] Bagretsov is certainly the doer, and Glebov is portrayed as the thinker. However, Shalamov does not force any dominant psychological characteristics, as the convict's human psychology is stunted.[18] The camps have destroyed any legitimate moral feelings and instinct for brash action. The characters are therefore muted in their actions and reactions to their quest. The tale draws out Glebov's past as it has a direct bearing on the morality of the action, but thinking (and consequently memories) are muted: 'The time when he had been a doctor seemed very far away.'[19] The tale's progression relies on a series of conflicts, whether physical or emotional, to ensure essential details are filtered through to the reader. We can recognise the causes of the tale in its ability to provide pertinent thoughts about unrelated facts, which when taken together lead to the grave-robbing itself.

4.1.2 Point of View

The narrator in this tale operates from an omniscient perspective, but is extremely active in changing his position in the tale. However, he remains firmly within its frame. Given the limited number of characters, the narrator operates from two positions only: Glebov as focaliser and complete omniscience. As Kline correctly observes '[t]he narrator's mobility in these stories, albeit limited, allows him to see the character he is attached to from the outside and to present background information.'[20] For example, at the beginning of the tale, the 'narrator leaves Glebov...in order to provide the psychological motivation for his participation in grave robbing.'[21] The narrator moves to Bagretsov and fills in the second half of the binary relationship. However, the narrator only ever reports Bagretsov's facial expressions and direct speeches, whereas he reports the words, expressions and thoughts of Glebov.[22] What is common to both characters is the narrator's use of indirect rather than direct presentation. He reports action, speech and external appearance, but refrains from making direct comments about either of them.[23] This mode of narrating sets up a character bias that forces the reader to focus on Glebov, rather than on Bagretsov. Glebov is not completely innocent, but neither is Bagretsov completely guilty of the act. In forcing us to be privy to Glebov's thoughts Shalamov ensures that we are naturally governed by them and consequently take sides with Glebov. Therefore, if we are asked to say who is the main protagonist, we naturally reply Glebov, but it is Bagretsov who occupies most of the textual space. Furthermore, the narrator's style of withholding information creates a barrier between the reader and the characters. They 'know' what they are doing, but the narrator refuses to impart this to the reader. He therefore controls both the characters' thoughts and words, and only releases casual information. This tight control of information maintains not only the reader's focus of attention, but also that of the characters. Kline has written on exactly this point and merits full quotation:

> In this case the process of eating, Glebov's inability to fathom his pre-camp life, and his ignorance about the people around him are emphasised, whereas what would seem to the "layman" to be the more important details, those relating to the grave robbing, are related at a quicker pace in the past perfective which draws less attention to itself. This is because for the prisoner the details of the grave robbing are unimportant; his need to eat overrides all other considerations, including the need for social interaction or concern about the morality or gruesome nature of his actions.[24]

The narrator is also relaying this tale as he sees it, or as Kline observes 'events which are taking place for Glebov are in the narrator's past.'[25] Unlike in *A Piece of Meat*, the narrator does not emphasise his role or place any emphasis on the future. He always remains within the time frame of the tale. Indeed, it is not possible to place the narrator anywhere but within this frame. He adopts Glebov's temporal perspective and as Kline puts it 'counts time as Glebov counts it.'[26] The tale's perspective therefore always remains either Glebov's or the narrator's. In both cases, the work is located in the present and hence no future perspective is detected. The past is also affected by this synchronicity. When Glebov tries to remember that he was once a doctor, his past is revealed by the narrator as 'unreal'. The narrating voice then assumes Glebov's thoughts and states 'He never guessed further, nor did he have the strength to guess.' The narrative voice expands this idea to include his 'own' thoughts on the other convicts: 'Nor did anyone else.'[27] The narrating voice therefore foregrounds Glebov's position in the tale, while also asserting his own narratorial authority. The tale, then, never transcends its own time-frame, even with a 'roving' narrator. This is Shalamov's *tour de force*, with respect to the narratorial viewpoint. Essentially, he wants the reader to remain firmly within the temporal and spatial frame of the tale. When Glebov eats the crumbs and Bagretsov cuts his finger, time slows down to take in the deliberate nature of these acts. The reader becomes closely involved with these events and can almost taste the crumbs and feel the blood loss. Kline remarks that this is due to an imperfective narrative. A result of this technique is that it 'slows the flow of time in the narrative, making story time closer to discourse time, thereby foregrounding certain parts of the narrative.'[28] Thus, the crumbs and blood are dominant narrative features while the act of robbing the grave is cursorily described. The narrator has full control of what important information he feels necessary to impart. Grave robbing is less important to the convict and consequently in the tale, than individual trials. This also leads the reader to the psychology of the narrator. Skirting over such an obviously gruesome act is arguably suggestive of the Freudian notion of denial. The foregrounding of and emphasis on a particular event, such as the flogging in Dostoevskii's *House of the Dead*, reinforces the brutality of the event. The narratorial conscience is clear in portraying this. Shalamov has a tendency to flinch from explicitly describing such a scene and robbing the grave is one such instance. The reader's attention is drawn towards physical aspects of the corpse where the narrator even 'praises' its healthiness. The tone of the robbing is light-hearted, interjected with gruesome actions: 'Together the two of them dragged the corpse from the grave.'[29] Writing from a future point and never having come to terms with his camp existence, it is certainly possible to ask whether Shalamov ever came to terms with what he saw and acts he committed within the camps. Drawing away from particular events, is perhaps symptomatic of psychological denial on the part of the author.[30]

4.1.3 Fabula and Sujet

This tale works for the reader by deliberately obscuring the object of the characters' quest. Their final destination is unknown until they actually arrive. The simple fabula of grave-robbing has been coloured by the sujet. The point of this tale and indeed the characters' quest is withheld by the sujet. Although, the progression of the tale is largely linear, the sujet holds back necessary details of the quest. Specific information and a reason are given at the very start of the tale. The first line 'Supper was over'[31] indicates the cessation of one action, and therefore points to the beginning of further action. Shalamov gives the reader intense detail about the crumbs of food and information on the power that food has over the lives of the convicts. Food, therefore, has an authority of its own, and its meaning for the convict is directly relevant to this tale. Shalamov deliberately portrays Glebov and his fellow prisoners agonising over the last crumbs because this miniscule amount has become the *raison d'être* for the prisoners and 'the very possibility that anyone might ever share anything, never occurs to him or his comrades.'[32] Mere crumbs exert more power over a convict than no crumbs at all. This power is the 'realistic motivation'[33] for the quest, and Glebov, led by Bagretsov, now has to search for more and larger amounts of food. This 'food' does not exist in the literal sense, but in the form of a substitute. The search is the determining factor and consequently the sujet of the tale. However, this information is not gleaned until later, and the tale merely relies on the travel sequences to forward the plot. Indeed, until the object of the search is known, the tale does not possess a particular plot structure. The reader is not explicitly told of the reason for the quest and once again, it is only through retrospective reading that one grasps the plot. What occurs instead is a 'traditional' search, but without an explicit object-related goal. This secrecy is again Shalamov's nod towards Soviet Reality; it is important not to reveal anything of importance, in case of listening ears. This notion extends also to the reader. The two characters share information, known only to themselves, but this is withheld from the reader. Bagretsov is suspicious of Glebov, as a convict, and their partnership is not equal. Bagretsov deliberately makes the point that this quest could be handled alone, but importantly indicates that their friendship is secondary to making the job easier: 'I could have handled this myself...but it's more cheerful work if there are two of us. Then, too, I figured you were an old friend...'[34] The progress of the tale is often halted by character complications, and intriguing information is passed to the reader about the condition of the protagonists. We are informed that Glebov was a doctor, which emphasises the extent to which he must have changed in order to perform this act. Shalamov has deliberately exploited the stereotypical characteristic of doctors as lifesavers.[35] This aspect of the sujet also reveals a general principle for both Glebov and Bagretsov and a general truth about the camps emerges. The narrator comments '...if tomorrow Bagretsov were to declare himself a doctor of philosophy...Glebov would really believe him without a second thought.'[36] A convict's belief system has corroded into merely simple objectives, and Glebov's maxim restricts the object of the tale to just 'one goal only, that of removing the stones as quickly as possible.'[37] Once the causes for this quest (food) and the reason behind the cause (moral disintegration) are established then the tale can proceed with the act itself. Howe expands on the dangers of memories: 'Experienced prisoners apparently learn that to surrender oneself to such memories is to risk losing the discipline of survival.'[38] The introduction of the third character brings out interesting ` characterisational relationships between life and death. He is contrasted with the two protagonists in several ways, yet with a typical Shalamovian slant. His newly dead corpse is the reason for the quest, and it possesses qualities to rival the men. They are ill and tired, but he is young, soft and fuller in size: 'He's so big and healthy.'[39] Shalamov depicts the corpse as a great treasure for the two convicts. Acquisition of his clothing has made the quest worth completing and once the robbing is completed the two men depart. The journey is complete and closure is attained. The sujet therefore only makes simple demands on this tale. That is, starvation and moral loss combine to provide the motives for the tale. The fabula is dominant and in a sense the tale could exist without causal information. Shalamov does not excuse the convicts for their actions, but neither does he press the point of the causal relationship between their condition and the robbing. The mood of the tale does not allow for either moral disgust or great joy at their gains. Rather, the mood remains neutral as befitting men in an appalling physical condition.

4.1.4 Setting

In the Night demonstrates varied settings that enhance the nature and purpose of the tale. As discussed in the previous chapter, setting is sometimes modelled on the indoors/outdoors dichotomy. Setting in this tale is also defined by the transition between the safety of indoors to the chaos of outside. It has already been established that Shalamov finds chaos and uncertainty in both locations, but it is merely a matter of degree that differentiates them. The food hall setting at the beginning of *In the Night*, is not actually described, but attention is drawn to an external temporal pointer, the 'large orange moon crawling out on to the sky.'[40] This is a repeating motif, used by Shalamov, to suggest a guiding light for the task ahead and it also functions as a temporal marker. The moon here, as in other tales is not friendly, but tainted with blood, furthering the idea of imminent death. This moon draws Bagretsov's attention and thus its presence acts as a beacon or flare to begin events. The exterior remains enclosed and another repeating pattern, which Shalamov uses, is that of never letting the outside take on a larger perspective than required. The two convicts are forced to negotiate a narrow path towards a small terrace. As Kline suggests this diminished space is a metaphor for freedom, but 'free open space as such is never present in the text. Rather open and closed space are unfree.'[41] The two men are forcing their way towards the summit, but are hampered by their own physical difficulties as well as physical barriers: 'Although the sun had just set, cold had already settled into the rocks…'[42] The air and rocks have also 'died' and take on the coldness of death. Symbolically, these negative connotations subliminally insinuate the forthcoming deed to the two convicts. Shalamov has narrowed their spatial perspective to include only the destination. Kline notes that '[t]his constricted perspective broadens only rarely, and then only to provide insight into the psychology of the oppressors or to present the tragic events of camp life on a larger but equally disorienting and disturbing scale.'[43] The latter takes place only to question Glebov's past. The focus remains firmly on the characters, but the setting draws out their physical details: 'Whereas eyes and faces are usually windows to the soul, in *Kolymskie rasskazy* it is clothes, hands, feet and skin that reveal pertinent information about the characters.'[44] This fact is very important when the body is revealed. The shallow burial is marked by the big toe sticking out.[45] This physical detail acts as another beacon, albeit gruesome in nature. The toe is lit up by the moon, thereby accentuating the relationship between the moon and this quest. No other part of the body or indeed landscape is named. The focus therefore falls directly on to the object of their quest.[46] The quest is thus revealed to the reader, but the body has transformed into a 'grim reflection of the traditional mythological concept of treasure hidden in the mountains'[47] Of interest here is the function of verticality in the setting.[48] The two men fulfil their quest by working uphill and gaining the life enhancing treasure located above. Lotman reports three levels of verticality; heaven, earth and underworld.[49] The two men seem to find themselves drawn to the first, but ultimately dig down and arrive at the last state. Also, the process of crawling between heaven and the underworld is suggestive of submission to the will of a 'higher' power and as already noted, lying down is commonly linked with death.[50] The men have to lie down to avoid being seen, but this also relates symbolically to their working with death. The body lies just below ground, but with its single toe rising through the earth, it is demonstrating that it has not quite 'died', but retains a semblance of life. The body is lifted out of the ground, thus seeming to regain life temporarily, but once the desecration has finished, it is returned to the ground. This brief resurrection is all that is needed for the men and when the rocks cover the body once more the quest has been fulfilled. The moon re-appears; however this time the whole scene is illuminated. The character focus shifts from the quest to the 'scant forest of the taiga, revealing each projecting rock, each tree in a peculiar fashion.'[51] The moon has taken on a second face, that is, it has become personified, just as the men have been transformed. They also acquire a different face, one of happiness at their find and at finishing the quest. The moon, once just rising, has now filled the sky and the landscape.

4.2 *Major Pugachov's Last Battle*[52]

'Tales are myths in miniature.'[53]

'Myth interprets the state of the world, a tale describes the progress of a hero.'[54]

This story can be said to be character-led where the story's title and consequently the protagonist are the major focus for events. An interesting aspect of Shalamov's works, is that he often includes information on a man's occupation before he arrived in the camps. Shalamov's aim is to contrast a man's current life with his former, and in so doing he reveals a particular function, metaphor or other device. Glebov's position as doctor in *In the Night* is clearly an irony, but Pugachov's military position is significantly more pertinent to the character. Shalamov is aware of the difference between these two occupations and also the purpose of a convict's former profession. A soldier is more likely to repulse danger than a doctor. That is not say that a doctor does not have resolve or strength of 'character', but a soldier's role by definition is to attack and if necessary kill, whereas a doctor's role is to save lives. The Gulag system snuffs out any vestige of utilitarian impulses and with it any concept of self-sacrifice to achieve the greatest good for the greatest number. Yet, *Major Pugachov's Last Battle* achieves this aim, if only in a spiritual sense. Every man dies, but they have accomplished a death brought about by their own actions. These soldiers have retained their former status, thus fulfilling a metaphorical aim of Shalamov's. Their former lives have not been extinguished; far from it: their prior roles have helped them to create a major disturbance in the running of the camps. Shalamov ensures that the breakout is not solely focused on the soldiers but on every single member of staff, guards and civilians. It is therefore not surprising that Stalin turned on the returning prisoners of war.[55] They had the strength, organisation and determination to challenge the system.

As they all stand together and fight for the last time, they are challenging the system and, as Pugachov furtively declares 'we're preparing a concert that all Kolyma will talk about.'[56] The tale obviously alludes to Pushkin's famous *History of Pugachev*[57], thus ensuring that the metaphor of this tale transcends temporal barriers. Shalamov has made room for heroes, men who are brave enough to challenge the system, just as Pugachov was depicted in Pushkin's works. He is a romantic hero in the folkloric sense, but Shalamov moves the romantic aspects aside and concentrates only on the reality of a Gulag break-out: a generally hopeless endeavour and one always ending in death.[58] Shalamov has cast the tale as an adventure and re-enforces any folk-hero aspects. Major Pugachov, like his namesake, will achieve a notoriety that will develop into a myth. Truth and fiction in time will blend into a Kolyma folktale. This tale therefore, is Shalamov's attempt to help this process along.[59] This fictional creation, like Pushkin's, reinforces the folkloric elements of events and in turn re-establishes the myth: 'Fictional plots have a way of establishing themselves as myths just as myths have a way of becoming fictionalised.'[60]

4.2.1 Narrative Structure

Major Pugachov's Last Battle is a particularly suitable story for an analysis of narrative structure. Most elements of structure are in place and in the standard linear order. At every juncture of the tale a character or characters appear to progress the tale further. Their introduction is calculated to give the story a feeling of non-stop adventure. There are no mini-complications to regress the tale, and it proceeds seamlessly. Even the detection of the soldiers does not detract from the action of the tale. Indeed, the shoot-out resembles a Western film, but in this case it is not known who are the 'goodies' and who are the 'baddies'. Shalamov has ensured a blurring of this boundary, and essentially both the escapees and the chasers are guilty of a crime: the former of escaping and the latter of not preventing this from happening. The narrator drives the story, and he does not simply concentrate on the fugitives, but on the impact a break-out has on others. Shalamov also does not moralise on the consequences of a breakout and subsequent death of many soldiers and prisoners. What he does, however, is supply a considerable quantity of reasons (in the context of the tale) why this breakout should have occurred. Firstly, we are acquainted with the protagonist, then we are shown how he fits in with other new arrivals in the camps. His (Pugachov's) background and determination make him an ideal candidate for escape, and when placed in the context of the thirties purges, he stands out in contrast to his fellow prisoners: 'The professors, union officials, soldiers, and workers who filled the prisons to overflowing at that period had nothing to defend themselves with except, perhaps, personal honesty and naïveté.'[61] This factor coupled with immediate starvation and hard labour destroys a man's ability not only to fight back but also to know where to direct the attack. It is fitting for Pugachov to rise above forced apathy and for the narrator to declare on his behalf 'Major Pugachov clearly realised that they had been delivered to their deaths.'[62] Pugachov fulfils Frye's dictum on leadership: 'If superior in degree to other men, but not to his natural environment, the hero is a leader.'[63]

In fact, Pugachov's character is continually dwarfed by his environment, whilst retaining the obedience of his comrades. The tale progresses with an integrated plan of attack, involving recruitment, better job placements and a long wait until spring. Thus, a seasonal thaw arrives and with this metaphorical 'new' start to the year, the collected twelve can start living their lives again, albeit temporarily. Each character of the escape gang has a designated task to fulfil, including murder, subterfuge, acquisition of food, weapons and transport. They work as a clearly organised team and Pugachov ensures that nothing goes wrong during this period. Their quest intrinsically relies on teamwork and co-operation, where none would ordinarily exist in the camps. Shalamov's emphasis on character detail and forwarding techniques enhance the sense of a seamless operation.

Once the escapees have been detected the men split into two groups thus providing two military fronts. This split is metaphorical and indeed prophetic and one by one each man dies. Pugachov survives the military onslaught and hides away in a bear cave to take his own life. Whilst these events are occurring, several members of the camps are either aware of movement by the men or become involved as information filters through which the reader receives additional information. Shalamov has ensured that any relevant characters are drawn in temporarily as events unfold. With this in mind, it is possible to include other structures based on several of the guards, officers, and, curiously, doctors. The latter play a major role in this tale as a part of the clear-up operation, but their actional roles are limited. Although, for example, Braude is mentioned early on, his character is not introduced until he is needed for surgery work. He, like the rest of the guards and officers is limited to functional characterisation, and therefore does not occupy a great part of the text. The structure is predominantly based on Pugachov's beliefs and his leadership function, thereby earning him a greater share of narratorial discourse. The narrative structure is shown below:

Specific Prologue	– Introduction of Pugachov
General Prologue	– Introduction of prisoners and authority figures
Exposition	– Implementation of escape plan
Complication	– Detection by soldiers
Peripeteia	– Pugachov's temporary escape
Dénouement	– Shoots himself

4.2.2 Point of View

The narrator in *Major Pugachov's Last Battle* has a dominant presence, who frequently offers his own opinions on events. He is assuming the role of a traditional storyteller who possesses a certain omniscience and additional knowledge of all characters and events. He resembles a God in his own universe: 'everywhere present but nowhere apparent.'[64] He narrates from a future point, as the first paragraph informs the reader: 'A lot of time must have passed between the beginning and the end of these events....'[65] Here, once again, is Shalamov's use of a distinction between the narrator in the text and a future narrator. That is, the narrator's voice becomes distinct from the author's and he resembles a focaliser of the author's thoughts. The character becomes a medium through which to reveal information. Shalamov's employment of a knowledgeable narrator is in contrast to the limited speech and actions of the secondary characters. As in *In the Night,* the narrator concentrates only on the thoughts of Pugachov. The tale therefore divides the perspective between the overarching narrator and Pugachov's thoughts. The narrator follows Pugachov around the tale like a shadow and always reports any significant changes, details or action. What we do not see is anything of the author. Glad explains: 'The figure of Major Pugachov who leads the escape attempt is lionized, but this path of action remains a fantasy for the author himself.'[66] Shalamov has distanced himself completely from events, and the story always remains a third person narrative.[67] However, the narrator does move within the frame of the tale to include certain other characters. When the focus falls on a particular character he then becomes central.[68] The narrator follows Braude, the chief surgeon, and makes an attempt to read his thoughts: 'Braude didn't try to guess what might have happened and quickly set out as directed in a beat-up one-and-a-half-ton hospital truck.'[69] Similarly, the narrator reads his mind again to set up a mini-tale about 3000 deaths several years previously: 'Yes, Braude knew that things like that had happened before.'[70] Shalamov exploits the difference between Braude's thoughts and Pugachov's: "How quickly it's all ended,' thought Pugachov. 'They'll bring dogs and find me."[71] The narrator has inferred Braude's thoughts, but reports Pugachov's thoughts directly. The narrator does not transcend his position as Pugachov's familiar, but he has used Braude and others to make assumptions and fill in related information. The similarity between Braude and Soldatov is in sequence of thoughts and action. The thinking part is always qualified by an action. Braude 'didn't try to guess what might have happened...' and gets on the truck. 'Soldatov felt a burning sensation in both legs...'[72] and the head of the dead Ivashenko falls on his shoulder. This is a typical Shalamovian device to ensure that the narrator does not transcend his position. Yet, this literary construct begs the question, why does Pugachov receive special narratorial attention? Pugachov's and the other escapees' deaths preclude any sort of link between Shalamov as Pugachov's confessor at a later date. It is possible to reconstruct events from other witnesses: the wife of the guard, the tied-up guards, Braude and the pursuing guards. This still does not answer the question. A possible answer is provided when the work is read in the spirit of a daring adventure tale. These tales need a hero, a particular individual who challenges the system against all odds.[73] The focus of the tale will then naturally fall on Pugachov as leader and object of most attention. Any contact the narrator makes with secondary characters is usually in relation to Pugachov. It is possible to make assumptions concerning other characters simply because of the fact that Pugachov was able to view or hear them. The narrator's role then is to harness Pugachov's senses to reveal as much as he can of the hero's sensual world. The narrative also uses understatement in revealing details. The battle is short-lived and bloody, with traces of ironic humour. When the officer offers the escapees' the possibility of surrender, Ivashenko shouts 'OK, come and get the weapons.'[74] Scholes and Kellogg argue that understatement 'produc[es] an ironic tension between the cool narrative tone and the violence which the reader imagines within the minds of the characters.'[75] The narrator only reports relevant details and this is in line with Shalamov's need to keep the focus sharp.

Good oral narrative has the ability to create a believable world where minute details provide substance. The narrator knows exactly what he is doing in telling this tale. His provision of extra information to pad out the story, united with minute character details, allows the reader to follow events without the need for filling in any gaps. The narrator therefore guides the reader in both the events of the story and his own way of thinking. It is the narrator's words and actions that make a story. A fireside storyteller uses his own knowledgeable influence and voice to sway the listeners. He may use pregnant pauses or delay vital parts of information, but his main purpose is to ensure that his heroes are believable. Lévi-Strauss considered the reader's role in re-creating a myth. The reader is able to break down and understand all aspects of a tale and organise them into a form of reality.[76] The reader can understand the determination and fighting spirit of Pugachov, especially the idea that he has been wronged. The reader therefore contributes towards the tale in looking to see if he [Pugachov] can right those wrongs. This story is being transformed into a myth as the narrator unfolds events to the reader. He remarks that 'It [Kolyma] is a land of hopes and therefore of rumours, guesses, suppositions, and hypothesising.'[77] He is telling the reader not to believe anything he says and furthermore remarks that Pugachov's words are not to be believed either. Again the zek's statement: 'If you don't believe it, take it as a fairytale,' has never been so apt.[78]

4.2.3 Fabula and Sujet

An interesting feature, already investigated in the last section, is how far the narrator governs the presentation of facts and events. He provides motives, theories and the effects of the convicts' breakout and these facts obviously impact on the plot and linearity of the story. There are a greater number of flashbacks and regressions than is usual for Shalamov, but each is necessary for understanding the story. Indeed, the story revolves around the dissemination of information and the narrator's need to provide motives and causes. The story contains an orientation binary, in that the focus of the tale concentrates on both past events and their meaning for the future quest.[79] The focus of the tale is mostly concerned with 'what happens next?' but relies on past information to support the forward trajectory. However, what the reader must be aware of is the narrator's allusion to myth creation. This then is the basis of any analysis of the fabula and sujet of this story. The narrator is asking the reader to regard events with some scepticism. For example, he suggests that 'We could begin the story straightaway with the report of Braude...we could begin with the letter of Yasha...Or we could begin with the story of Dr. Potalina who saw nothing, heard nothing and was gone when all the unusual events took place.'[80] The reader is drawn into the process of determining possible sujets, but ultimately the narrator governs which sujet to apply.[81] The fabula or story proper does not begin until the reliability of events and background information is established. This information is reported in a documentary style, but crucially Pugachov's comrades are mentioned, though not by name. Any individual characterisation is withheld until later in the text, and the narrator merely provides military occupations: 'There were officers and soldiers, fliers and scouts...'[82] The beginning of the tale has thus revealed Pugachov, his comrades and most importantly, what awaits them. The narrator crucially distinguishes between the fighters and the defeated, thus flagging a soldier's ability to challenge his situation: 'But not all of the newcomers shook their heads in contempt and walked away.'[83] Shalamov is referring to the convicts who were sent to the camps after the end of the war. According to Hosking '[t]he *zeks* of the late forties were very different from those of the thirties, no longer bewildered, passive, disunited and well disposed to the Soviet state.'[84] Ultimately then, the narrator foreshadows events, by stating: 'It was virtually the only conspiracy in twenty years, and its web was spun all winter.'[85] The characters are thus pre-created and un-dynamic; that is, they do not develop or change within the frame of the tale. Rather, their roles are only pertinent to their place in a particular part of the tale. They follow exactly what Shalamov requires them to do, and character dynamism is not required.

Arguably, the real tale begins when the protagonists escape the camp. Thus, the subsequent sequence of events is the reported fabula interjected with additional information and characters (for example, Braude [twice] and the military personnel caught up in the escape). These other characters occupy positions related to the escape, but from a different perspective. They initially lie outside the centrality of action, but are drawn in as events unfold. It is also possible that Shalamov is trying to define prior events and the aftermath as pertinent but secondary aspects to the 'true' story. He seems to be playing on the readers' prior knowledge of Pugachov as a historical character and a consequent assumption that the escape attempt would fail, as did the historical Pugachev's campaign. Shalamov employs flashbacks to pad out any characters. For example, the guard entrusted with the keys is given a short history of his ten years service and double pay. This relatively comfortable position has reduced him to complacency and he 'had given the keys to the cooks thousands of times.'[86] Shalamov provides relevant cause and effect in his tales and *Major Pugachov's Last Battle* provides plenty of instances. He often employs a causal flag at the very beginning of the text, before fulfilling the effect at the very end.[87] He also includes unexpected plot diversions: for example, he assures us that '[e]verything was proceeding according to Major Pugachov's schedule,' before dashing the smooth flow of predicted events with 'Suddenly the wife of the second guard appeared.'[88] Shalamov does not as a rule include immediate markers, such as 'suddenly', but this timing marker quickens the tempo of the story time.[89] This is in keeping with the nature of this story and is added to keep the readership guessing as to what will happen next. He employs this technique when all the escapees hijack the lorry. In three lines, the good fortune of riding a lorry takes a particular 'right turn' to 'We're out of gas!'[90] The (unknown) distance covered is not reported, but we are to infer physical movement. The narrator does not feel the need to define this travel in time or space, but concentrates on reactions and consequences. The fourth line inevitably brings in Pugachov's reaction to the bad news, but it is the narrator who provides this response. He simply reports: 'Pugachov cursed.'[91] Shalamov has provided a humanistic impression of events and the escapees not only perform actions but also have thoughts distinct from the task at hand: Ashot and Malinin's argument over Adam's expulsion from Heaven. This passage does not allow a period of reflection on their escape as would be expected. There is no mention of the future, nor of the past and Pugachov instigates another temporal gap by ordering his comrades to sleep. What follows is Pugachov's remembrance of how he came to be in the camps. Information on his eleven comrades is also provided. Shalamov has made this phase Pugachov's period of reflection, whilst all action has ceased and most of the escapees are asleep. Soldatov is the only other man awake, adopting a sentinel position. His figure is a reassurance to Pugachov, who can then enjoy a safe reverie. The sujet is narrated at some length and starts from Pugachov's present. The past years and months are replayed but 'with unbelievable speed.'[92] The temporal order of narrated events is present – past – future. This can also be understood as consolidating – reconciling – confidence.[93] Pugachov needed to secure his emotional position, and is helped with Soldatov's gesture of reassurance. Secondly, he has to question why he has taken the correct and necessary steps to reach this position. He ponders Vlasov's[94] emissaries, but finds security in the knowledge that it was not only he who was caught out by the state's renunciation of returning prisoners of war: 'Captain Khrustalyov, a flier whose fate was similar to Pugachov's: his plane shot down by the Germans, captivity, hunger, escape, and a military tribunal and the force-labour camp.'[95] Finally, he can now look forward to the future with confidence. "No one betrayed us,' thought Pugachov...This knowledge reconciled Pugachov with life.'[96] Little text time is used to describe these events and is in direct contrast to the following gun battle where textual time is close to event-time.

All Pugachov's comrades are named. He also makes judgements on his men, although these are refracted through the narrator: '[Soldatov], a good man!' 'They're good men.'[97] The narrator does not report individual awakenings, and this reinforces the idea of a collective identity. That is, everyone is working together, whether consciously or unconsciously to forward the quest. No details of group activities are therefore provided as the group conforms to, ironically, a communistic ideal. Each man has his role and fulfils it with vigour and dedication, not for himself but for the cause. The introduction of Kushen is made precisely when he is needed. By using this technique, Shalamov ensures that no additional information interferes with the momentum of events. Interestingly, Soldatov occupies a dominant position in the text. He is present at several temporal markers. He was the first to suggest an escape attempt. Secondly, he marks Pugachov's reminiscence as the sentinel. Thirdly, his knowledge as a hunter in Siberia helps the escapees' progress. Fourthly, when he loses consciousness, the focus of the tale shifts to Braude who fixes up Soldatov. Finally, his ultimate demise represents the failure of the escape attempt. The final action is pure fabula: Pugachov's last battle. He has metaphorically laid out his comrades for burial and lists them. He even remembers the missing name, thus completing the process. Glad notices a common feature that affects and disrupts the flow of events: 'I believed a person could consider himself a human being as long as he felt totally prepared to kill himself, to interfere in his own biography. It was this awareness that provided the will to live.'[98] Pugachov interferes with a death against his will, either by a bullet or by natural forces. He concludes events, but also forces a major, if not short-lived character change. Pugachov is able to influence proceedings solely on his terms. He may 'finish' as an actional figure in events, but there is a continuation of action beyond his death. His escape attempt impacts on other people's histories and thus this story has continued beyond the pages. The fabula does not reach any kind of closure, as the focus of events extends beyond the specific to the general. Thus, the story of Pugachov extends over space and time and into the future, but the sujet limits the extent to which events are reported.[99]

4.2.4 Setting

The nature of this story and its purpose of fulfilling a quest, by definition involve pertinent and variable settings. *Major Pugachov's*

Last Battle contains a variety of settings, but they are not encountered in a strict linear fashion. The major movement in this story is between the camp and the taiga. The quest is short-lived because there exist several obstacles that retard the escapees' progress: the necessity of tying up the guard's wife, the truck running out of petrol and the sudden incursion of the soldiers. Each action involves a delay that inevitably proves costly. There is a sense that the escapees are on a piece of elastic that keeps drawing them back and the further they stretch the elastic, the stronger is the pull. This elastic does not 'stretch' merely through their escape attempt, but is taut before the escape begins. There are elements in the tale that suggest that everyone involved is also attached to this elastic which is in the hands of the state. The soldiers are just a few of many thousand, indeed millions who are being controlled by the state and at no point will the state allow one single person to escape. Though only Pugachov is left alive, this does not halt the search parties: 'trucks with soldiers continued to travel along the thousand mile highway for many days.'[100] The authorities also spend many months waiting for Soldatov to recover in order to shoot him, mainly to prove that nobody has the right to dictate his own future in Soviet Russia.

Shalamov has utilised this elastic principle, but in a number of ways. There are several methods in which characters are involved with the setting in both space and time. Firstly, there is reported physical setting. Secondly, there is movement within setting. Thirdly, there is character as setting. Finally, Shalamov frequently uses a spatial setting that does not involve a character's physical senses, but is mediated via their memories. This section will tackle these types of setting in order. The physical setting in *Major Pugachov's Last Battle* forms a background and demarcation to the plight of the escapees. The narrator informs the reader of a real, yet illusory boundary marker when he remarks, 'no one was permitted outside "the wire" without guards.'[101] The intention of the escape is indeed to penetrate this boundary and to do so it is necessary to affect a disguise. This disguise enables the convicts to become soldiers again and what is interesting here is that they are witnessed several times during their breakout. The guard and the duty officer both view the convicts through guard windows, whilst the tower sentry also 'notices' their progress. Shalamov inserts a barrier between the convicts and the camp guards. The convicts can move around and within these fixed locations because they are not detected. The buildings have become obstacles to the purpose for which they were designed. Equally, the safe guard barracks are invaded by outer chaos; To quote van Baak: 'if the house falls, history ends.'[102] The guard's history ends, as indeed does the history and future of sixty other men. The 'fall' of a guardhouse, although not in the literal sense of the word, is symbolic of a dramatic change in the lives of the current and future occupants. The continuity of its existence depends on the legitimate occupants reclaiming the building. In van Baak's words: 'The house is the chronotope of generations.'[103] Without occupancy, the house has ceased to function as a guardhouse. Another significant setting that affects the characters is the natural environment. As mentioned before, spring heralds a confidence in the convicts when '[l]ittle by little, the sun melted the snow…And the designated day arrived'[104] Metaphorically, the chains of winter are falling away for the convicts, but the chains never completely disappear. No escape can really be effected with these binds, and it is the snow-bound ravines and canyons that are the likely end point for many convicts.[105] Two other areas of background that appear are the forest and night sky. These constant features affect the convicts in several ways. With a clear night, although spring has arrived, there is no cloud cover and frost clings to the forest. The silence that descends after their hurried departure is a threat to the men. The 'twisted pines stood far from each other,'[106] thus offering no protection. Pugachov is depicted as isolated against the huge expanse of sky and taiga. The contrast between the individual and the cosmos could not be greater. Also, Pugachov exists in a period of silence and calm. Time has temporarily ceased to flow in this void and elements of the setting have receded. For example, the 'Big Dipper' or 'Great Bear' constellation has slipped down further to the horizon, perhaps as a metaphorical distancing from this time spent in the woods. It is not unreasonable to link the constellation with the Great Bear of Russia.

There is also a great deal of movement within each setting. Most of the characters named are in a state of change and the background reflects this. The environment is a reflection of actions or thoughts. The constant movement within and away from the camp and the charge for freedom involves both men and machinery. Although transport has already been discussed in Chapter 1, it has a special place here. In *The Train*, it will be recalled, the carriage was a static setting within a moving setting; however, the trucks mentioned *in*

Major Pugachov's Last Battle are used differently. The interior of the truck that Pugachov captures is not described and its journey has no textual substance. Its use is primarily as a delaying technique, one that forces the convicts to seek an alternative or more basic method of transport. They are effectively forced into the harsh landscape without aid. The truck remains as an instrument of the state by its inherent uselessness to the convicts. The convoy of trucks is mobilised in pursuit of Pugachov and they are compared with the river: 'The river was like any other river, but the highway was filled with trucks and people for tens of miles.'[107] Life has been added to the taiga and is in direct contrast to the isolating environment of the forest. This environment is hostile to Pugachov, as Kline notes: 'Kolyma landscape grows unnaturally large.'[108] The environment has not fulfilled the promise of freedom for Pugachov, and its vastness can be considered hostile. Shalamov accentuates the mountainside, which, like the sparse forest, is unwelcoming to Pugachov and his comrades. The narrator reports heavy traffic when Braude progresses to the battlefield. He also notes that 'trucks with soldiers continued to travel along the thousand mile highway for many days.'[109] The narrator has narrowed Pugachov's perspective to only focus on the chasing soldiers. The spacious environment is filled with the snake of travelling trucks and people and these now form the setting. Pugachov attempts to break away and split the convicts into two groups but this results in failure. He immediately runs back, thus drawing the setting back towards himself. The epicentre is the haystacks and is reinforced by the advancing soldiers in the meadow. They make up a circle that fills the convict's environment. When they attack, extreme changes occur in the characters. Firstly, many wounded are reported, until the narrative only reports deaths. The circle closes around the defeated men until all but Pugachov lie dead or dying. To locate the convicts in an area as large as Siberia should be like finding a 'needle in a haystack', but the vast environment has narrowed down to only a small concentric circle around the camp. This is perhaps suggestive of Stalin's influence over extremely large areas of the Soviet Union. Effectively, Shalamov is indicating that there is no escape from authority, even at these furthest reaches.

The narrator has further personified the haystack with the escapees. The stacks have become temporary, albeit unsafe abodes for the prisoners. The prisoners have metaphorically *become* the haystacks and as the deaths continue the narrator notes that '[a]nother haystack fell silent.'[110] The characters have become a part of the setting; they replace any natural flora or fauna. Earlier, the men followed a bear path and in doing so, adopted the bear's gait to avoid detection by hunters. It is fitting that Pugachov's final resting place is a bear's den. Like his men in the haystacks he occupies a much smaller place to escape the vastness of the taiga. This is a Freudian womb-state of security where Pugachov reminisces about his 'difficult male life'. He recalls two women who were crucial in his upbringing: one his mother, the other his schoolteacher. These women must have shaped his life and loved him without question. They occupy a particular setting in his mind and this leads on to the final stage of events. Shalamov draws forth many memorial settings that existed within the frame of the tale, but outside of current events. Each setting is directly relevant to the escape attempt, and reveals information about certain characters in the story. The narrator describes the environment as the 'white Kolyma desert,'[111] and the harsh conditions that destroyed the newcomers - 'hunger, cold, beatings and diseases' - lead to 'their self-esteem and bitterness [having] no point of support.'[112] He continues: 'The souls of those who remained alive were utterly corrupted.'[113] Here is a production line of ex-soldiers being delivered as an exchange for their fallen comrades. Indeed, the camps begin to resemble the war front, where heavy losses are replaced with new soldiers. Pugachov is a part of this process, but for him this camp is not the first. He reports how the events of the escape occurred in quick succession: 'He remembered the sentry shots, shouting, the mad, zigzag drive through the town, the abandoned truck....' and so on. His memory limits the setting and journey to brief specifics. The next catalogue of episodes after he has been sentenced is equally in the same style: 'cattle cars with bars on the windows and guards, the long trip to Eastern Siberia, the sea, the ship's hold, and the gold-mines of the far north.'[114] Each description holds meaning for his departure to Kolyma. Each phrase pinpoints an aspect of environmental imprisonment and is a restraint on his freedom. The last phrase 'And the hungry winter'[115] personifies Stalin's attempt to consume each and every threatening soldier. While these thoughts dwell on past settings, the narrator also speculates on the future. Several airports are mentioned, thus indicating numerous departure points, but after this no destination is mentioned. Braude also speculates about the future, on the basis of previous events. He describes events of several years ago when thousands died of cold. He uses this scenario to indicate the imminent future of the general. This memory portrays a vivid picture of indiscriminate blame and waste of life. The environment does not allow for mistakes, just as Stalin punishes scapegoats.

NOTES

[1] Scholes & Kellogg, p. 163

[2] Shukman, 'The Legacy of Propp', pp. 82-94

[3] O'Toole, *Structure, Style and Interpretation in the Russian Short Story*, p. 142

[4] That is, when structuralists do accommodate characters in their analysis. Rimmon-Kenan argues that this is because their 'commitment [is] to an ideology which "decentres" man and runs counter to the notions of individuality and psychological depth.' Rimmon-Kenan, p. 30

[5] M. Mudrick, 'Character and Event in Fiction', *Yale Review*, L, 1961, pp. 202-18. Cited in Rimmon-Kenan, p. 31

[6] D. Herman, 'Existential Roots of Narrative Actants', *Studies in Twentieth Century Literature*, XXIV, 2, 2000, pp. 257-69

[7] Greimas created the concept of 'actant', where characters can be defined in terms of their relationship to others, for example, sender-receiver. Reid clarifies this; 'They are distinguishable from actors, who occupy designated individual roles in a story.' I. Reid, *Narrative Exchanges*, (London: Routledge, 1992), p. 63

[8] O'Toole, *Structure, Style and Interpretation in the Russian Short Story*, p. 146

[9] Bolshakova, p. 8

[10] E. M. Forster introduced the idea of round or flat characters. In their simplest terms the former are dynamic and three dimensional, while the latter conform to a caricature or singular type. See Chapter 4, E. M. Forster, *Aspects of the Novel*, (Middlesex: Penguin, 1974), pp. 75-81

[11] Glad, 'Art out of Hell: Shalamov of Kolyma', p. 45

[12] C. Hollosi, Varlam Shalamov's 'New Prose', *Rusistika*, VI, December 1992, p. 21

[13] This follows the Greek concept of adventure time. The same motifs re-occur, as do the types of characters who remain static. Bakhtin, 'The Form of Time and the Chronotope in the Novel: From the Greek Novel to Modern Fiction', p. 504

[14] M. F. Oja, 'Shalamov, Solzhenitsyn, and the Mission of Memory', *Survey*, XXIX, 2, Summer 1985, pp. 62-9

[15] Kline, p. 389

[16] *Kolyma Tales*, p. 13

[17] Turgenev first formulated this binary pairing in the sketch 'Khor and Kalinych' from *Sketches From A Hunter's Album*. The binary was formulated systematically in his 1860 lecture entitled 'Hamlet and Don Quixote'.

[18] Hosking, 'The Chekhov of the Camps', p. 1163

[19] *Kolyma Tales*, p. 12

[20] Kline, p. 417

[21] Loc. cit.

[22] However, the narrator does not provide Glebov with information that would not already have been available to him. See Kline, p. 272

[23] The narrator, although reporting Glebov's thoughts, does not make generalisations about the characters. Shalamov does tend to refrain from assigning the narrator the role of preacher or authority figure. See Rimmon-Kenan, pp. 60-7

[24] Kline, p. 273

[25] Ibid., p. 272

[26] Loc. cit.

[27] *Kolyma Tales*, p. 12

[28] Although this study does not address Shalamov's use of Russian grammar, Kline's analysis of Shalamov's grammar is extremely relevant here: 'All the verbs describing completed actions are in the past perfective: the imperfective is reserved for repeated or continuous events and generalizations.' Indeed, throughout *Kolyma Tales*, there are numerous instances of repeated actions, events and characters. See Kline, pp. 272-6

[29] *Kolyma Tales*, p. 13

[30] Writing these tales had an obvious cathartic function for Shalamov, but he never came to terms with his imprisonment. If Shalamov had written in a more subjective way, one wonders whether his later life might have been different.

[31] *Kolyma Tales*, p. 11

[32] Oja, p. 67

[33] Tomashevsky in Lemon & Reis, pp. 78-87: i.e. where characters are portrayed as real and possess 'realistic' motivations for their actions.

[34] *Kolyma Tales*, p. 12

[35] Scholes & Kellogg (p. 177) argue that a unifying characteristic dehumanises a character. In this case, the character's lack of humaneness is the point of the characters' actions.

[36] *Kolyma Tales*, p. 12

[37] Ibid., p. 13

[38] I. Howe, 'Beyond Bitterness', *New York Times Review of Books*, XXVII, 14 August, 1980, p. 36

[39] *Kolyma Tales*, p. 13

[40] Ibid., p. 11

[41] Kline, p. 356

[42] *Kolyma Tales*, p. 11

[43] Kline, p. 440

[44] Ibid., p. 388

[45] This is perhaps an echo of Gogol's *The Overcoat*, where the tailor's toe is also subjected to particular scrutiny by the narrator. However, the dead man's toe is clipped and full of 'life', whereas the tailor's toe has a 'misshapen nail as thick and as strong as the shell of a tortoise.' *The Overcoat*, in N. Gogol, *The Complete Tales of Nikolai Gogol*, II, (ed.) L. J. Kent, (Chicago: University of Chicago, 1985), p. 311

[46] This beacon is reminiscent of the search for the Holy Grail, when Joseph of Arimathea preserved the blood of Christ in the Grail. Bagretsov has spilt his blood as an unconscious sacrifice for the quest.

[47] Kline, p. 394

[48] On this see van Baak, *Place of Space in Narration*, pp. 55-60

[49] Juri, Lotman, *Struktura xudozestvennogo teksta*, (Providence: Brown University Press, 1971) as cited in van Baak, *Place of Space in Narration*, p. 57

[50] Kline, pp. 389-90

[51] *Kolyma Tales*, p. 14

[52] Shalamov based this tale on second hand breakout accounts. Kline remarks that there were two such attempts from Kolyma, both resulting in failure. 'The first was by a group of 13-14 prisoners who disarmed the guards and disappeared for an entire summer. Their leader was a so-called "banderovite" or freedom-fighter from Western Ukraine. The escapees had a fight amongst themselves, split into two groups and were

soon caught. They tried to escape a second time later on, and there was a shoot-out. Many were killed. One of the wounded was a major, who eventually died. Shalamov was acquainted with him.' See Kline, p. 104

[53] Lévi-Strauss in Shukman, 'The Legacy of Propp', p. 88

[54] Meletinsky in Shukman, Loc. cit.

[55] From the end of the war until December 1946, some 1.6 million formerly armed personnel (including returning prisoners-of-war soldiers) passed through filtration and ultimately ended-up in the Gulag system. In July 1945, the NKVD issued orders to rename repatriates as 'enemies of the state'. See Kochan & Keep, *The Making of Modern Russia*, pp. 429-30. This tale reflects Stalin's paranoia and fear of these soldiers, whilst also fulfilling a 'what-if-maybe' function. The camps were not brought down by Gulag escapes, so maybe Shalamov is really asking 'if-only-this-had-happened-in-Russia-instead'.

[56] *Kolyma Tales*, p. 241

[57] A. S. Pushkin, *History of Pugachev*, Translated by E. Sampson, (Ardis: Ann Arbor, 1983)

[58] Shalamov did 'escape' from the camps once. He walked away from a lumber camp, as he disagreed with the camp's work-equals-food system. In view of his recent 10 year sentence, he did not receive an additional sentence. See Toker, *Return from the Archipelago*, p. 146

[59] A point to make here is the difference in oral and written culture. It would be reasonable to assume that Pushkin's written version is a synthesis of many oral versions. Shalamov's version is also another version, albeit in a different setting and time. The oral tradition always assumes the same indistinct world, whereas written works possess a social and historical location. Oral events are adaptable to the story-teller, whereas finished written works are located in the time frame in which they were written. Shalamov's story therefore retains a rigidity of space-time, whereas an oral re-counting of the tale will always differ from the written version. Scholes & Kellogg refer to this peculiarity of written and oral tales in *The Nature of Narrative*, p. 82

[60] Ibid., p. 218

[61] *Kolyma Tales*, p. 242. Howe asks the question 'Was Shalamov's survival enabled by the fact that, being 'guilty', he did have a unifying idea?' The vast majority of camp inmates did not have the slightest idea of why they were there and consequently has no sense of purpose or unity of direction. Pugachov's characters have strength in number and thus a unifying idea (of escape) was formulated. See Howe, p. 36

[62] *Kolyma Tales*, p. 243

[63] N. Frye, 'Historical Criticism: Theory of Modes' in Northrop, Frye, *Anatomy of Criticism: Four Essays*, (Princeton: Princeton University Press, 1957), p. 33

[64] Scholes & Kellogg, p. 268

[65] *Kolyma Tales*, p. 241

[66] Glad, 'Art out of Hell: Shalamov of Kolyma', p. 48

[67] A. Gereben, 'The Writer's "Ego" in the Composition of Cycles of Short Stories', *Essays in Poetics*, XIX, 1, April 1984, pp. 38-77. Gereben argues that there is an element of author in all texts, whether by author acknowledgement or implication. Shalamov's presence in *Major Pugachov's Last Battle* differs from the majority of other tales, simply because he has consciously distanced himself from first-person

narration. Because of this, the narrator is in charge of reporting events and not the author.

[68] R. Marsh, *Images of Dictatorship: Stalin in Literature*, (London: Routledge, 1989), pp. 196-7

[69] *Kolyma Tales*, p. 253

[70] Ibid., p. 254

[71] Ibid., p. 255

[72] Loc. cit.

[73] This hero, according to Greimas, is likely to be a social outcast with no ties and does not recognise 'legitimate' authority. Indeed, Pugachov does conform to this theory, if one places his comrades in the same position as Pugachov. They have had their ties permanently severed by the state. A. J. Greimas, *Du sens Essais Sémiotiques*, (Éditions du Seuil: Paris, 1970), pp. 232-3

[74] *Kolyma Tales*, p. 252

[75] Scholes & Kellogg, p. 166

[76] Lévi-Strauss found that there exists a universal structure to myths regardless of the content. Myths are a language with rules and grammar that the reader can instantly recognise. As Eagleton remarks 'myths think themselves through people rather than vice versa.' In T. Eagleton, *Literary Theory: An Introduction*, (2nd edition) (Oxford: Blackwells, 1997), p. 90

[77] *Kolyma Tales*, p. 241

[78] Ibid., p. 284

[79] Future orientation is 'what happens next?' and past orientation is 'what happened before?' The plot needs past events to convey understanding of the textual trajectory. Rimmon-Kenan, pp. 125-6

[80] *Kolyma Tales*, p. 241. By not answering his own questions, the author is utilising a monologic form of narration.

[81] This is a similar technique to that used in Shalamov's *Snake Charmer*, where the narrator presents someone else's story.

[82] *Kolyma Tales*, p. 242

[83] Ibid., p. 243

[84] G. Hosking, 'The Ultimate circle of the Stalinist Inferno', p. 166

[85] *Kolyma Tales*, p. 243

[86] Ibid., p. 244

[87] Chekhov often employs this feature in his plays. For example, Ivanov brandishes his gun at the beginning of *Ivanov* and uses it on himself at the end of the play.

[88] *Kolyma Tales*, p. 245

[89] The Greek adventure story frequently uses such words as 'suddenly' or 'just as' to denote cause and effect and to introduce time into the tale. Bakhtin, 'The Form of Time and the Chronotope in the Novel: From the Greek Novel to Modern Fiction', p. 506

[90] *Kolyma Tales*, p. 247

[91] Loc. cit.

[92] Ibid., p. 248

[93] Psychologically speaking, Pugachov has broken free form the chains of imprisonment, but with this comes a period of reflection. Once this period has been successfully dealt with, then Pugachov can move on to the future. These three steps are the necessary stages of a psychodynamic therapeutic approach. For example,

Frankl's 'will to meaning' or inner autonomy relies on a camp inmate's ability to focus on immediate survival aims to achieve a future goal. See Frankl, pp. 151-214 for a unique therapy borne out of his own camp experience.

[94] The controversial 'traitor' who was prominent in recruiting POW's for the Russian Army of Liberation.

[95] *Kolyma Tales*, p. 249

[96] Ibid., pp. 250-1

[97] Ibid., pp. 249-51

[98] J. Glad, 'Art out of Hell: Shalamov of Kolyma', p. 48

[99] Cobley, p. 19

[100] *Kolyma Tales*, p. 255 This is also reminiscent of the last four lines of a traditional verse on Pugachov, 'The Beginning of the Uprising on the Iaik':

> 'Fire soldiers, the foe do not dread,
> Save no powder, save no lead!
> When we capture this thief gory,
> Greatest will be our glory.'

From A. E. Alexander, *Russian Folklore: An Anthology in English Translation*, (Belmont: Nordland, 1975), pp. 318-9.

[101] *Kolyma Tales*, p. 243

[102] Van Baak, 'The House in Russian Avant-garde Prose: Chronotope and Archetype', p.5

[103] Loc. cit.

[104] *Kolyma Tales*, p. 244

[105] Seasonal cycles have always been incorporated into fiction, usually as a metaphor. One such basis for the metaphor is from the folklore: mortification, purgation, invigoration and jubilation. *Major Pugachov's Last Battle*, progresses through these stages albeit in a limited time scale. The death of all the escapees, guards and subsequent trials indicates a return to the mortification stage. On this see Scholes and Kellogg, p. 220

[106] *Kolyma Tales*, p. 248

[107] Ibid., p. 251

[108] Kline, p. 307

[109] *Kolyma Tales*, p. 255

[110] Ibid., p. 253

[111] Ibid., p. 242

[112] Loc. cit.

[113] Loc. cit.

[114] Ibid., p. 249

[115] Loc. cit.

Chapter 5

Setting

'As consciousness absorbs the forms of its material setting, it becomes increasingly desensitised and hence comfortable. Anguish occurs when awareness of reality is in operation; comfort is a quality of insensitivity and habit.' [1]

'Sublime symbolism, akin to Emerson's belief that every physical fact is a sign of a fact of the spirit, pervades his loving and sometimes bitterly awed descriptions of nature, as if Shalamov were repeating the question of the blind priest, his father, "Is it in this that God is?" and hearing no reply.' [2]

Analysis of setting has often been neglected in modern criticism owing to a precedent set in the nineteenth century. O'Toole explains that analytical approaches have tended to neglect descriptive writing for its 'cult of nature in poetry and prose, and the ease with which the "pathetic fallacy" was both exploited by writers and noticed by critics.'[3] There has been a drive to displace setting as a central feature of criticism: structure, point of view and plot have traditionally been the three main categories with which to draw information from poetry and prose. Character has been demoted to an aspect of plot and setting even more so. It has been argued that setting merely provides a background to character placement and an arena for structure: 'The setting "sets the character off" in the usual figurative sense of the expression.'[4] It is simply where the action occurs and although setting has a necessary place in prose, it acts as an environment for action. Setting has to function as a static environment, in order to foreground characters or action but when setting becomes dynamic, and is itself foregrounded, it is too easy to categorise its function as merely symbolic in relation to character or action. Setting, based on time, can function in three ways: as predictor, relief and reinforcement of events or character. The reader makes use of description to enrich his or her knowledge of a passage or even the whole text. Examples of these three functions are; the darkening clouds in Ostrovskii's *Thunder*, presaging a metaphorical storm; the cell in Solzhenitsyn's *First Circle* accentuates the prisoner's narrowed world; the characters' bewilderment amidst the chaos in Shalamov's *Bathhouse*. Setting, therefore, can be dynamic and is used for many other reasons than merely to emphasise temporal changes. Frye argued that the main purpose of a setting was to convey an 'image'.[5] This image, as O'Toole puts it, is both anagogical and analogical; that is 'in terms of the total order of words comprising a literary work' and 'in terms of its reference to social, biographical, psychological and cultural patterns in the world surrounding the work and in other literary works.'[6] The setting therefore, fulfils a crucial function in any work and has the ability to transcend the work itself. O'Toole has created a checklist which comprises four functions of setting that directly draw on inter-textual and extra-textual references. The full list (which covers over six pages) can be found in O'Toole's text[7], but I have précised the contents down to the following essentials:

Informative –   location; time; authenticity; social framework; social comment; character's personality; character's narrative function

Commentative – a background to fix a narratorial comment; moral comment

Structural –   change of scene; keeping characters still; changing characters; parallel settings; characters as setting; frame episodes; scale of setting; rhythm

Symbolic –   religious; philosophical; political; social; superstition; deformation of humans; nature

Setting can therefore be used to inform, comment, provide structure and finally provide symbolic meaning to a work. Its function is crucial to other levels of analysis, but it also exists independently as a level in its own right. If setting were not considered as such, then its function would be subsumed and lost beneath the other structural layers. This chapter aims to analyse Shalamov's use of setting and to test whether it fulfils the above criteria. A major impediment to this analysis is the lack of dominant descriptive passages in *Kolyma Tales*.[8] Hosking describes Shalamov's settings thus: '[His] nature descriptions are straight-forward, couched in the crude primary colours which are all that God had on his childhood palette.'[9] The descriptive passages' strength lies in the fact that one cannot 'get a razor-blade between the words.'[10] There are two reasons why Shalamov includes limited background description. Firstly, Siberia does not possess a changeable or dynamic landscape and natural scenes are often limited to snow, rocks, water, ice, ground, sky and trees. These topographical features of Siberia pervade the camp and consequently the convict's perspective. Man-made features are also usually limited: barracks, mess halls, hospitals, guard-towers and prison trucks. Secondly, when these features occur, they are intended to provide a definitive and understood background to the characters. For example, the light/dark in a barracks is frequently used to denote the binary of good and evil. The characters in *On Tick* play cards in semi-darkness, and emerge into the light as the narrative focuses on their actions. Indeed, binary pairings are often used by Shalamov and feature in most tales. Other instances that are commonly used are small/large, up/down and near/distant. An important point to consider is Shalamov's ability to manipulate the reader's expected function of these binaries. As mentioned in previous chapters, the concept of the house is that of safety and security. The 'house' in *Kolyma Tales* is not safe, and neither is the open landscape. Distant soldiers in *Major Pugachov's Last Battle* represent as much a threat as those in close proximity to the characters. In the words of Toker 'Shalamov creates the conditions for the reader's search for meaning instead of proclaiming or even encoding definite meanings in his text.'[11] He challenges the reader's preconceptions, by presenting expected and unexpected information. The reader, therefore, is challenged to find a specific and truthful meaning within the text and Shalamov does this by presenting many binary constructs. The terms of these constructs are not mutually exclusive and indicate Shalamov's idea that whenever a binary pairing is evident, there is no 'good' side, but always negativity. There is a third reason for Shalamov's use of limited imagery. For instance, as noted in previous chapters, the narrator assumes the position and knowledge of a zek, or at least a zek's perspective. The latter's focus is limited to food, warmth and sleep and nothing else would usually permeate a convict's consciousness. Snow, water, ice and rocks consistently engage a convict's senses. Equally, buildings suggest warmth, fellow convicts, food and death, and represent a major psychological determinant for survival. For example, an open door receives the chaos from outside, whilst a closed door provides a prisoner with time to 'live', before facing the uncertainty of the outside.

The tales chosen for this chapter are *Lend-Lease* and *Fire and Water* and in both tales the settings are not merely background elements, but are dynamic and accordingly figure both symbolically and as part of the plot. The tales emphasise the power of nature, albeit in different ways. *Lend-Lease* compares the longevity of stone and permafrost with Man's transient time on earth no matter how much he interferes with nature. Water in *Fire and Water*, although not taking on a specific persona (thus reducing the tale to symbolism), shows how unstoppable nature and unpredictable natural elements can be. The function of setting in both tales is to reveal the essential indifference that nature has towards Man, whilst highlighting Shalamov's fear and respect for nature's elements. In the camps, it was weather and the environment that killed a man, thus demanding respect. Any lack of respect was punished accordingly.

5.1 *Lend-Lease*

This tale demonstrates Shalamov's ability to change the focus of the setting, thereby drawing in large scale and minute detail. The narrator's focus encapsulates the immenseness of Kolyma, and at the same time reflects on how small a prisoner's viewpoint is. The convicts' world is ordered around this binary: 'I realised that I knew only a small bit of that world, a pitifully small part, that twenty kilometres away there might be a shack for geological explorers looking for uranium or a gold-mine with thirty thousand prisoners.'[12] Equally, the cavernous graves are filled with much smaller bodies, which are described in tiny detail. In this way setting for Shalamov can be seen as a vast jigsaw, where the broken pieces must assemble in order to form the whole, but can also be identified separately. Thus, the macro-universe has to be filled with a micro-universe where Shalamov and the rest of the convicts represent individual pieces of this puzzle. The vast taiga is not devoid of life, rather the opposite. It is metaphorically teeming with parasites, as a convict is full of lice. The focus on setting can either expand in order to encapsulate the vast environment or contract to capture ever-decreasing worlds. Thus, setting in *Lend-Lease* fulfils both these ideas, with a sliding scale of descriptive elements.

For example:

Taiga → grave → tractor → bodies → twisted fingers

This diagram is also indicative of the spectrum between life and death: 'At one end is full, human life, and at the other is death; but in between there is a descending scale of moral and even physical states which are neither.'[13] Man occupies many states of life, just as the environment is full of gradients. Near and distant objects are contrasted, as are descriptions of living fellow convicts. The bulldozer itself is dynamic and exists in several contexts within the tale. The background in *Lend-Lease* does not remain static, but is in a continual state of flux. Trees are felled, earth moves, graves appear and bulldozer marks indicate movement. But, ultimately, men and man-made objects are in relief against the background of nature where it is man who shifts and alters the scenery, and nature rebels against their work. Ironically it is man who, through excess logging, exposes the very bodies he once tried to hide.

5.1.1 Narrative Structure

At first glance, *Lend-Lease* does not possess a traditional narrative structure, as this 'tale' reads more like an essay than a story (which will be better explained in the next section). However, there is a progression of information concerning the gifts from the Lend-Lease programme, and they are reported in a definable temporal progression. What occurs through this essay-style tale is a build-up towards the final events. The bulldozer is mentioned on the very first line, but its physical presence is not reported until three pages later. From this point its abuse becomes the focus of the tale. In a way, the structure of this tale is based solely on Lend-Lease and the various items that are delivered to the camps. Apart from the tractor marks, there is not a single mention of scenic views or actual landscape until the peripeteia. The exposition briefly details the introduction of new items; yet with this comes a change to each item. Not all items are used in the way they were intended to be used. For instance, in the eyes of the convicts, the glycerine becomes 'American honey' and machine grease becomes butter. The text distances any physical placement of these items for two reasons. Clothes and foodstuffs do not reach the convicts in any recognisable form and therefore do not possess any tangible substance.[14] Important gifts like Spam, have become 'ephemeral'[15], and their tangibility is reduced to observations from a distance. Background reports change when the introduction of the bulldozer and its use is reported. Solid imagery is used and the tale develops along linear and temporal lines. The complication is prominent, and the need for food becomes secondary to more important events. Travel is important in marking this change with a journey away from the camp towards the awaiting abyss. The protagonist's sudden understanding of the bulldozer's function becomes apparent and the scale of the camp's hidden work is revealed. Nature's capacity for unloading its burden is not symbolic, but is a natural occurrence that destroys man's attempts to hide his own work. The tool of work is not even scratched by this re-burying, and although the grave is covered, the bodies 'did not disappear.'[16] The structure is shown below:

General Prologue –	Tractor prints
Exposition –	Gifts from beyond the sea
Complication –	Bulldozer's use in the camps
Peripeteia –	Narrator's realisation of events
Dénouement –	Power of nature
General Epilogue –	Job finished

5.1.2 Point of View

The narrator is fundamentally instrumental in the arrangement and symbolisation of setting in *Lend-Lease*. He is dynamic to the extent that he is the sole provider of information. This is not a narrator or a focaliser from within the camp's time frame, but a narrator from the future and there are fundamental differences between these two types of narrator. As previous chapters have shown, descriptions of setting are circumscribed and this is due to Shalamov's propensity to angle the focus purely from a near-death convict's perspective. This narrator takes a different viewpoint and for this reason setting plays a comparatively more important role in *Lend-Lease*. A near-death convict's perspective has been changed to the first-person singular and descriptions of setting are refracted with additional aphoristic information. He is an ex-convict, who is relaying these facts and maxims, not through a focaliser, but from a knowledgeable point in the future. There seems to be a single reason for this: the narrator has survived and since memory is an all-important factor in the tale, he is writing as he remembers events. The poet in the author emerges in this tale, because there is no need to rely on reporting from a near-death experience. He is free to make and manage symbols in this monumental event and indeed it is precisely because he has witnessed this event that his tale becomes an allegory of his survival and of the many others who died: 'Only now did I see and understand the reason for all of this, and I thank God that He gave me the time and strength to witness it.'[17] As Mandelshtam wrote, 'there were people who had made it their aim from the beginning not only to save themselves, but to survive as witnesses.'[18] Also as a survivor, he is the embodiment of life, when 'death is the natural thing.'[19] As the tale moves forward, the mood of the piece progresses from a light-hearted depiction of farce to a reverential portrayal of the dead.[20] The narrator is instrumental in this, and is careful to report particular events without implying his knowledge of further events. For example, although he has reported the bulldozer treads (thus indicating his knowledge of future events), he carefully side-steps any subsequent reference to them when describing the officer scenes.

O'Toole asks whether the narrator is 'authentic' in re-creating a setting, and in *Lend-Lease*, the narrator is instrumental in only reporting what 'he' sees.[21] The narrator in the first part of *Lend-Lease* only reports very specific facts, but goes into great detail surrounding the new items and their attributes. Spam undergoes a transformation from possessing nutritional value to no value at all. Here, the narrator points out 'once tossed in the pot, Spam from Lend-Lease had no taste at all'. He includes several comments and opinions in the text; the authorities are 'greedy'; there existed 'no better trucks in Kolyma'; and the dead were 'the fortunate ones.'[22] The narrator is primarily describing what he sees; however, he always adds a personal comment or enquiry. Thus, narratorial authenticity has to be questioned when the narrator confesses: 'I don't remember whether two or three laborers ran the circular saw at the wood-processing plant.'[23] Yet, the tale does not lose any validity because of this; in fact, this faltering statement heightens the narrator's authority. His very fallibility adds a semblance of reality and it is because of the narrator's fallibility and spatio-temporal distance from events, that the reader has a deeper understanding. The distance enables the narrator to roam from one aspect to another with ease. His style conforms to that of an outward looking narrator, inasmuch as it is the events and his reaction to events that dominate.[24] The environmental detail in the first part of the tale is purely focused on the causes and effects of the new goods, not on a solid background. For example, the reader's imagination can focus on a barrel of glycerine without its position being described. Likewise, it is possible to imagine the Russian adapted shovels, without their being put into use. Although the narrator is blinded as to the physical whereabouts of the sausages, the reader can see them, if only because of their 'magical jars'. The setting data are not fixed spatially, they are fixed in our imaginations. Thus, the narrator-reader relationship is fully interactive and images have depth beyond that which is described.[25]

The physical placement of objects begin with the introduction of the bulldozer. The narrator uses a specific technique to move the focus of the text spatially and temporally to the mountainside; 'interior monologue'.[26] The narrator does not report temporal markers as he moves from one item to the next. He does not report the food and clothing's spatial setting, thus highlighting their transitory nature; they will disappear, just as if they had never been there at all. The bulldozer arrives and occupies its own space, indeed, from the very first line, it possesses its own tread marks. It takes centre stage, reflecting 'the sky, the trees, the stars, and the dirty faces of the convicts.'[27] Thus, open spaces and vast expanses are metaphorically dwarfed by this arrival. When the bulldozer is not in focus, it still manages to possess a presence in the text: 'The sighs and groans…could be heard for a long time in the frosty air.'[28] Landscape is reported when the narrator focuses on the bulldozer's movement and the narratorial focus shifts once again back to the focaliser's workload. Comparisons are made between men, horses and 'horsepower'. The narrator adds an interesting question to the end of this sentence: 'the foreign bulldozer had come to help us (us?)'[29] In its frightening power the machine and its 'vertical blade' or guillotine represents merely another tool of death. The narrator reports that its use would increase human quotas to unworkable levels, thus decreasing a convict's lifespan. Shalamov demonstrates his fear of the mechanised rationality of a totally administered society and the bulldozer is the physical manifestation of this process.[30] The lifeblood (grease) of the machine becomes a food and its presence is centre stage. The bulldozer has the power of giving life, albeit fallaciously, to the convicts. The narrator ensures that the machine now represents not a gift, but an evil to the convicts and the environment. Trees become deformed in their fight for survival and assume grotesque features. For example: 'The trees on the mountain slopes don't look like trees, but like monsters fit for a sideshow.'[31]

In the second part of the tale the narrator is established closer to the scene. He is on the periphery of the camp, viewing the departure of the bulldozer.[32] He adopts the first person pronoun 'I' to place himself at the scene and further descriptions provide additional information to furnish the reader with an understanding of the setting. He reports the graves with additional symbolism and the bulldozer is finally revealed in its environment. Each movement, turn and scraping up of bodies by the bulldozer takes centre stage. The narrator and now his fellow comrades are the audience and the use of 'we' and 'us' draws attention to the spectators of this production. The narrator comments 'I and my companions knew that if we were to freeze and die, place would be found for us in this new grave.[33] The use of the plural only serves to emphasise the narrator's luck in being able to report this scene at a time when many companions were probably buried in a similar grave. The narrator does not show any compassion towards these nameless bodies as Bergsen observes 'Sympathy, like protest is a luxury.'[34] Thus, the singular 'I' is reporting this scene, but the plural 'we' experiences it. Therefore, the narratorial perspective changes from being outward-looking to inward-looking, whilst projecting the narrator's need to remember these events. The narrator is drawing attention to himself both as a witness and a human being, in order that the reader can empathise with his position. He also bridges the gap between 'factual and fictional autobiography, [where] the author has a real existence outside the story.'[35] By acknowledging the need to remember events, Shalamov draws attention to the creation of this tale, not as merely a piece of fiction, but as a work based on 'fact'. This is a part of Shalamov's narrative impulse to report the immorality of what he has witnessed. Cobley finds that in both historical and fictional accounts '[narrative impulse] might encapsulate a deeper human desire for a "moral" presentation, a sequence with an outcome.'[36] The narrator is shifting the role of witness to the reader, who then understands the immorality of the bulldozer's use and consequently the reader completes the work.[37]

5.1.3 Fabula and Sujet

A question to be asked, is whether this work can be called a tale in the full sense, or rather is it an essay that reports the result of the American Lend-Lease programme? Kline describes *Lend-Lease* as 'straddl[ing] the line between story and essay: [it] exhibits the framework of an essay, but is based on fictional material.'[38] Kline notes something else too: when a fictional work resembles an essay, its chronology ceases to be important. In other words 'the nature of the text reduces individual events to illustrations like those in an essay, thereby diminishing the importance of chronology or causality.'[39] Only two indications of date are reported in the tale: firstly, the narrator reports that work gangs dug the graves in 1938 and secondly '...six years of rain had not wrenched the dead men from the stone.'[40] Therefore, it is difficult to decide whether *Lend-Lease* is really mimesis or diegesis. This swift move from reporting general to specific information at the complication indicates a change in the tale's structure. Thus, the introduction of food and clothing merely indicate the misuse of these articles, and it is the abuse of the bulldozer that forms part of the main tale. It could be argued that the fabula is concerned solely with the bulldozer and the sujet fills in the historical background of the Lend-Lease programme. Temporality is limited to simple viewpoints, but there does not exist a temporal link between other Lend-Lease goods and the bulldozer: 'Linearity' Rimmon-Kenan notes, 'can also be exploited to arouse suspense or deliberately mislead the reader by delaying various bits of information.'[41] The author has created a temporary gap between what was initially reported (bulldozer tracks) and the bulldozer itself. Thus, a form of suspense has been created in delaying these two events.[42] Barthes calls this a 'hermeneutic' code; that is, marking an enigma and implicitly promising an answer. The introduction of the bulldozer tracks, although briefly mentioned is such an enigma and bears out Rimmon-Kenan's view of plot progression: 'on the one hand, [a plot device] seems to be pushing towards a solution, while on the other it endeavours to maintain an enigma as long as possible in order to secure its own existence.'[43] Thus, the bulldozer's actions will inevitably appear in the text, but only when all other information is imparted to the reader.

The camp and hillside form the two locations, with an intermediary period between the two. The transitional period is indicated by the climb, and consequently a feeling of temporality is noticed. Prior to this, events exist merely as the narrator's memories. The narrator comments 'Many logs had been abandoned because of the impossibility of the job, and the bulldozer was supposed to help us.'[44] This is an obvious cause for the introduction of the bulldozer, and indeed it arrives, but with a disclaimer: 'It had been assigned a totally different job.'[45] The early part of the tale therefore involves a form of temporality, but in no order or sequence. The tale also dispenses with any causality between the particular events. The barrel of grease therefore provides a focal point for several different events, though not arranged sequentially or in time. The narrator repeats himself over the security arrangements for guarding the barrel, thereby emphasising the power of this grease to be transformed into butter. This event is momentous for the convicts, but it is one of many events that convey a semblance of story. Between each episode additional information is included to invest a static object with symbolic significance. The grease has also been transformed into a stone, while being not only a stone but also a 'soft oily creature.'[46] The informing sequences of the tale heighten and further our understanding of simple objects.[47] Therefore, it could be argued that all objects included in the first part of the tale figure under both fabula and sujet. That is, when an object such as wheat is introduced, it is either transmogrified or other people are transformed by its presence. It takes temporality to transform objects and in this tale, the train of events ensures that the fabula is not far from the reported events. In effect, the narrator is adding real-time to the work.

The second part of the tale, although possessing a definitive temporal line, also fills in any causal gaps: 'I hadn't given any thought to why we were led to work for the last few weeks along a new road instead of the familiar path...but no one asked why we were being taken by a new path.'[48] This section on travel from the camp to the hillside answers the aforementioned question. The machine travels by the usual flattened path, a path created by man, whilst the convicts follow an alternative route. This results in a split between machine and man, although both arrive at the same destination. Symbolically, this can be understood to mean how man can choose to take either the straight or crooked road. This climb proves to be dangerous and causes the protagonist's blood to flow; but the painful quest reveals the truth. The logging area is devoid of trees, thus becoming a 'gigantic stage for a camp mystery play.'[49] The images are not merely reported, but the narrator mixes fact and mythological fiction. This place has been kept secret from the convicts, and the sujet has been deliberately manipulated to withhold the 'grave' information. In holding this information the permafrost has superseded the authorities. The convicts (and the reader) are last to be informed of this information. The fabulaic elements once again are reported with factual information and followed with more symbolism. However, the cause of the release of bodies, although hastened by tree felling and consequent earth movement, is greater than man's power: 'The north resisted with all its strength this work of man, not accepting the corpses into the bowels.'[50] This alternation between factual reporting and symbolism includes places beyond Kolyma's boundaries. The imposing guard towers and barbed wire of Kolyma surround the witnesses of this grave and this image is compared to Moscow. The narrator asks 'And what served as models for Moscow architecture – the watchful towers of the Moscow Kremlin or the guard towers of the camps?'[51] The enforcement of secrecy lies in the metaphorical towers, and it is probable that Shalamov is referring to the secrets kept behind the Kremlin's towers. The final sujet information summarises the nature of *Lend-Lease*: 'And if I forget, the grass will forget. But the permafrost and stone will not forget.'[52] The lack of temporal linearity during the first part of the tale now becomes apparent. The transient position of the convicts and their inevitable end in the same graves, does not allow them to report this re-interment. In fact, the system and indeed the Kremlin, is hoping that this information will never be released from between the guard towers of either the camps or Moscow itself. The tale then has not incorporated any such temporal changes, because like the stones, time has metaphorically slowed down, if not completely halted. This is the reason why this tale imparts its message through the sujet.

5.1.4 Characterisation

Traditionally, characters in a tale are a dominant part of the setting but they can also function as the setting themselves. *Lend-Lease* proves to be no exception, owing to its character-framing techniques. All characters are instrumental in revealing a particular character trait or framing a particular part of the tale. The setting draws out many character traits and functions, when a character is the subject of the narratorial focus. The wives of the Magadan generals are transformed by the new clothes, and in an almost Gogolian fashion, they are reduced to near-fistfights. The narrator reports on the 'emotional confusion [the goods] had introduced into the minds of the camp bigwigs.'[53] Thus, transformation of character is the operating idea of the new goods. The food in turn has been changed by the guards' own transformation. One guard becomes a small businessman and another guard has to guard grease, rather than convicts. The hillside lichen also transforms into life-saving 'honey' for escaped convicts and geological survey teams. Characters are also a function of setting, when they are used to frame particular events. For example, in the first part of the tale, the convict characters are key to the introduction of the new goods. These characters drive the narrative forward and occupy the scene of activity. Where an open space exists, it is completely filled by the convicts' presence. Examples are: the convicts in the camp; the negotiation of the mountain path and the audience for the bulldozer's activities. Equally, the narrator fulfils a quest-finding role and manoeuvres through the dangerous environment. He poses the question why the prisoners work here and specifies the arduous nature of their work detail. The characters are therefore seen in relief against the harsh background of the forest and are physically involved with the environment. The 'log-pulling' indicates a fight between men and nature, in which the convicts have the 'unbearable task of hauling and stacking the iron logs of Daurian larch by hand…to drag the logs…was an impossible task'[54] The wood is transformed into iron and the prisoners' strength in moving the logs is reported on a sliding scale of frailty. The logs take on a mystical God-like role and they are hoisted onto the shoulders of weak prisoners. However, this reverence is short-lived and the convicts are unable to accept this burden. The narrator comments that 'Many thick-ended logs disappeared into the snow, falling to the ground as soon as they had been hoisted on to the sharp, brittle shoulders of the prisoner.'[55]

Dead companions also feature as a part of the setting and function in several ways. Firstly, they are described as merely temporary tenants in the mountain, who are waiting to be ejected. They do not figure as 'characters' as such, because they should not possess living or dynamic features.[56] However, they have not 'died' nor decayed, but remain with recognisable human features. The narrator has reported the dead men's transformation into stone. Rimmon-Kenan observes that characters can reflect the characteristics of the surrounding landscape thus highlighting their own predicament or mood.[57] Shalamov has taken this analogy further and has metaphorically turned the men to stone. Secondly, the dead are also depicted as moving objects, objects that contrast with the immovable mountainside. Also, they are living and moving in contrast to the stationary convicts. It is only when the dead men have 'fallen', that the bulldozer can move in to transfer them to another pit. Only one convict is allowed to drive the bulldozer, and his role is a symbolic reference to the Oedipus complex: perversely, although he is a convicted parricide, it is his task to return the men back to the womb of the mountain.[58] He, like the dead prisoners, has also turned to stone, during the process of his work: 'On the stone face of Grinka Lebedev were hewn pride and a sense of having accomplished his duty.'[59] In this way both the driver and the dead convicts have become part of the setting and the environment. Thus, for Shalamov, 'the distinction between organic and inorganic, alive and dead, animal and vegetable, man and beast are no by no means clear or constant.'[60]

5.2 *Fire and Water*

This tale demonstrates the dual forces of fire and water, and the unpredictability of man's fate in nature's domain. However, unlike *Lend-Lease*, there exists here a natural dynamism that engulfs humankind in a variety of ways. Setting in *Lend-Lease* is dominated by man's interference with nature and nature's countervailing attempt to fight back. In this tale, nature is indifferent to man's needs or wants and arbitrarily destroys man's creations. For example, fire reduces houses to ashes, whilst water rips trees from the ground. It is these frightening qualities of an uncontrollable power, which bring life to man as well.[61] Fire brings heat and warmth to man, and water brings food for starving convicts. In *Fire and Water*, these binary forces of each element are revealed. Man may have harnessed both fire and water, but they can rage anywhere, even in a place as desolate as the taiga. The dry ground and the sun combine to create grass that is dry and brittle, which provides ideal material for burning. Three days of rain create a flood on the plains that spreads and engulfs everything in its path. The protagonist is shown as a fearless firewalker, but water 'could have saved the town, the geologists' storehouse, the burning taiga. Water is stronger than fire.'[62] Fire and water both form the backdrop for the protagonist, but in markedly different ways. The former is something to be admired, but the latter is a force to be afraid of. The protagonist walks amongst both these forces and survives, finally concluding that man is inconsequential to other men and social structures, but in Kolyma, nature also considers man irrelevant; whether he perishes or survives depends solely on good fortune alone.

5.2.1 Narrative Structure

The narrative structure in this tale follows a similar course to *Lend-Lease*. There are opening markers and varied settings that are either real and present or derived from remembrance. Like *Lend-Lease*, it splits into two separate parts, the first part providing the opening scenario, and the latter providing the development of the tale. It is clear from the first few pages that the extended prologue serves a dual purpose: primarily, it contextualises the tale and also describes fire's destructive power; secondly, it indicates a hierarchical order of power within the camps:

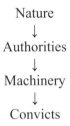

Nature
↓
Authorities
↓
Machinery
↓
Convicts

The convict will always come second when in competition with any of the above. The protagonist in *Fire and Water* finds that he does not have any fear of natural elements, as they are indifferent to his presence, in the same way that authority is indifferent to his life. The protagonist becomes immersed in the world of fire, and the narrator moves the focus of the tale around and within the flames, where he symbolises the destruction it leaves behind. As in *Lend-Lease*, the direction of the story is determined by a quest. Instead of finding the reason for their alternative route, this protagonist is hoping to gather mushrooms for food. The similarity in both tales is the fact that both protagonists were ordered to take this route and encounter the unexpected. Whereas the protagonist in *Lend-Lease* finds a mass grave and the gruesome use of the bulldozer, the protagonist in *Fire and Water* unexpectedly confronts deadly water. From this point on, his quest changes from mushroom collecting to finding a life-saving vantage point. Where the landscape was once fixed, it alters shape and becomes dynamic, just as the protagonist's perception has changed. Where he had his favourite spot to hunt for mushrooms, which represented safety in familiarity, he now has to search for safety in unfamiliar territory. The burning flames are a beacon and 'not an evening star,'[63] to guide him towards the peripeteia of safety. Distances are exaggerated by darkness, and even the morning light is sluggish to arrive, thus delaying the dénouement. The final part of the tale draws both symbols of fire and water together into a tiny vessel. Both are tamed within the hut and consequently by Man, but the 'tame water on a tame fire' quickly turns to natural anger as 'the water began to leap furiously in the pot.'[64] Fire can be contained, as can water, but together they form an even greater threat to humanity, especially during sleep. The structure is shown below:

Specific Prologue	– Descriptions of fires
Exposition	– Journey to seek out mushrooms
Complication	– Leaves path for better mushrooms and is caught by advancing water
Peripeteia	– Arrival at distant fire
Dénouement	– Returns safely to comrades and boat
Specific Epilogue	– Eats and sleeps in peace

5.2.2 Point of View

The use of narrator is similar to that discussed in *Lend-Lease*. Indeed, the tale splits into two distinct narratorial perspectives. In the first part, the narrator provides historical background information and in the second part, his views are refracted through a first-person focaliser. Also, common to both tales is the fact that the narratorial voice is from a future state, and not from the perspective of a near-death convict. However, the difference between the two narrators lies in the focaliser's location in the camp. In *Fire and Water* the focaliser is in a hospital for recovering convicts and this allows the narrator to make his focaliser informed and aware of his environment. His thought-processes are recovering, and he is therefore able to use memory freely; this is in contrast with the focaliser's need to remember events in *Lend-Lease*. This hospital is the source of his salvation and with his life returning, the focaliser has the freedom to take the luxurious opportunity of gaining better food. The trajectory of the tale is his physical journey, and this is achieved because of his subsequent psychological improvement. His unnecessary divergence from the path is a result of his forgetting that he is still in the camp, and therefore still under constant surveillance. Paradoxically, this idea is emphasised precisely because the narrator does not mention it. He just reports the chance to gain for himself and in doing so, distances himself from his incarceration.

The narrator is also selective in his framing and positioning of characters within the tale. In the first part of the tale, the narrator frames particular fires and describes both the effects and his position within the fire. He wanders through the fire in the town, and the narrator reports that 'inside the town it was clear, dry, warm, and bright.'[65] This is in contrast to the growling houses that 'shook their bodies, flinging burning boards on to the roofs of buildings on the other side of the street.'[66] The burning storehouse also possesses the previously mentioned centre/periphery dichotomy, and the narrator ironically comments that it was dark, but without the fire he could not have seen what was at risk. The centre of the fire also has become 'dry, warm, bright.'[67] This 'stage' marks the central area, where the narrator depicts safety, whilst around him is chaos. These forms of framing adopt Gestalt principles, and as the protagonist progresses through the fires, he becomes the 'figure' to the setting's 'ground'.[68]

Sequence inevitably implies foregrounding:[69] the narrator sustains focus on the protagonist throughout these fires, and consequently the fires are distanced from the protagonist. The narrator describes the fires with a certain detachment, and there exists no definite beginning or end to their occurrence. They only exist in the narrator's perspective, and there cannot be any other details to the events. The items retrieved from the storehouse are listed, and for all the convicts' courage in obtaining as much as they could from it, it is essential convict clothing that gets burnt. State mechanical items are worth more than state-issued clothing. The narrator's anguish at not receiving thanks is offset by his ability to experience childhood feeling once more. Fire is symbolised several times when the narrator is framed against various fires that he has either witnessed or followed. The infernal scenes he depicts are almost Dantean in nature.

Once the focaliser has been introduced, the narrator does not immediately use the new focus. He continues to commentate on the focaliser's work detail and importantly on the chef, Uncle Sasha. He summarises the chef's culinary expertise, and adds comment to an event that he did not attend: 'The creation (kasha) was a success.'[70] The narrator has respect for this chef and consequently, any cooking he does will be of an exceptional quality, regardless of the ingredients. From here, the focaliser takes over, and is marked by direct speech. The focaliser is 'used' by the narrator as a cinematic panning system, where the camera (focaliser) projects several viewpoints.[71] The focaliser provides all the delaying techniques to create scenes of foreboding: 'The river was roaring...the terrible muscular strength of the water...autumn night was black, starless, and cold,'[72] He also provides an abrupt lifeline amongst the dangers: 'Suddenly, a light gleamed from a narrow valley.'[73] The narrator with his use of the action adverb, 'suddenly', delays the description to report this new development. Ibsch cleverly observes that because of this adverb, 'description surrenders to the moment.'[74] The focaliser is an agent to space and he alone motivates description, and when he has to perform an action, then the narrative changes. The narrator progresses through various scenes where he either reports his environment or narrates the action. The focaliser continues the precarious nature of the quest by pointing out that 'distances are deceptive in the taiga.'[75] He controls the reader's perception of events and he reports the changes caused by the flood. New shores have been created, thus establishing a new and fresh environment. The night existed as a dark unseen period, before the light of the new day brought changes. The transitional period of night has also brought with it a different narratorial perspective. His fellow convicts are in the distance and are gradually brought closer into focus. He has acted out the dangerous events and participated in witnessing the changing scenery, from light to dark and back to light. What has transpired during this sequence of events is that the action is delayed by description and vice versa. Thus, the narrator/focaliser is instrumental in ensuring a fine balance between description and action.

5.2.3 Fabula and Sujet

The first sentence in *Fire and Water* provides information for the next two pages: 'I've been tested by fire on more than one occasion.'[76] This statement of remembrance leads on to many scenes and descriptions of fires that are in contrast to the protagonist's dilemma later in the tale. The first part of the tale tells of the destructive power of fire, and significantly is told in the past tense. Use of the past tense indicates that this passage will lead to a tale with a more current perspective. The method here echoes that used in *Lend-Lease*, and there is a similar use of fabula and sujet. There are no specific temporal markers to determine when these events occurred, other than general markers. That is, the protagonist at the first fire was 'as a boy' and the second fire 'as an adult.'[77] The rest of the fires are reported without any time markers. However, the descriptions of the fires are widespread and varied, as if the descriptions themselves represent the spreading fires. What these memories have in common is the sensation of the boy/man within the fire. They relay the boy's lack of fear of fire before quickly linking to the fire when he was a convict: 'childhood had long since slipped away.'[78] Again, the narrator moves the narrative smoothly onwards, but on to the general list of fires he had previously witnessed. These are non-specific fires and all occurred in the taiga; Shalamov has created parallel settings during this period in order to demonstrate where fires can occur. He also repeatedly depicts the effects: 'Fire was like a storm, creating its own wind, hurtling trees on their sides, and leaving a black path through the taiga for ever…I have often seen the Hippocratic death mask of a tree.'[79] He finally reports rain that would have 'saved the town, the geologists' storehouse, the burning taiga.'[80] This three-day rainfall begins the story proper, and water possesses friendly properties. Shalamov has created a complex interaction of elements that polarise their perceived functions. Where fire was once danger and water was a calming influence, Shalamov pacifies the destructive abilities of fire and enhances the strength of water. He does this by reducing fire to memorial experience and reporting water in the present tense.

Shalamov creates binary settings and introduces particular oppositions that work on the fabula and the sujet level. The characters in the hospital are given jobs to perform and have to undertake them, for '[a] patient in the convicts hospital couldn't feel secure if he wasn't doing something for the doctor, for the hospital.'[81] In effect, the patients are stuck between a rock and a hard place; they still have to work while sick or get sent back to the harsher camp work.[82] The narrator refers back and indeed forward to a time when the characters will be back inside the work camp, and this affects the reporting of the fabula. Their position in the hospital is therefore immediately changeable and this uncertainty explains the narrator's thoughts on fire and water. Where he praises one element, he denounces another, but ultimately, what the narrator reports does not affect the idea that both are dangerous to the convict. To work in the hospital temporarily extends your stay: nevertheless, a convict could be sent back immediately and the retrospective glances illustrate this fact. Thus, a hospital does not represent security, but a temporal anomaly in the convict's life.

The unreality of events continues when the narrator reports the mushrooms. They appear both in recollections and also during the unfolding of the tale. They initially take on un-mushroom like qualities, (that of snakes) but this symbolism extends to fire and water too. The water creates the mushrooms; the fire creates the snake effects in the grass, but the narrator assures us that 'there are no snakes in Kolyma.'[83] Mushrooms are associated with a magical or fantasy world and consequently nothing is as it seems. A mythical Eden is evoked, where mushrooms sprout overnight, but always accompanied by snake-like qualities. Again, the mushrooms are an indication of an irresistible temptation but will turn to dust at the end of the day. This links directly to the latter part of the tale, where the gigantic mushrooms have transformed into mere fragments.

The tale progresses when the narrator declares 'Today it was cold.'[84] The tale proceeds in a strictly linear pattern, bringing in relevant information to confirm forward movement, both physical and literal. The protagonist progresses along an established route, but when he digresses from the path he conforms to Eve's desire to gather fruit from the forbidden tree.[85] His greed in attempting to acquire better mushrooms is punished by the once safe water. It has already risen as a warning: 'The water was rising slightly, the current was swifter than usual, and the waves were darker.'[86] The mushrooms have taken on a grotesque size, but are 'so fresh, so firm, so healthy.'[87] The order of these two markers sets the changing priorities for the protagonist and his awareness of danger is quickly superseded by temptation. The river and the forest occupy van Baak's 'conflict space',[88] and challenge the protagonist's perception. The protagonist estimates the time to return to the path, but this return time is never reported nor is the time taken to pick mushrooms. These two temporal events fulfil Ricoeur's 'vacuous' text time.[89] The importance of this section is only in that they occurred, and descriptions of the water and the surrounding hills and forest play a major role.

The river takes on rhythmic qualities, as once did the fire in full roar. Thus, the scene has been transformed from a quiet place with little action, into a raging dynamic monster. The sanctuary of the campfire is in contrast to the river, but the water in the can possesses the river's anger: '[it] began to leap and squeak as it whitened with foam and heat.'[90] Thus, the water motif is not localised, neither just the river nor in the can, but is a force that transcends space. The water boiling indicates a suspension of time, in that wherever the protagonist travels, the water's anger is there to greet him. No reference to time is made until the protagonist descends the hill towards the boat and his fellow convicts. Thus, when he leaves the hillside, time is slowly reintroduced, and the duration of his time away from camp is indirectly implied in the two-day rations he consumed. The fabula of *Fire and Water*, therefore, can be seen as distinct from the reported sujet, inasmuch as the sujet has provided the cause of events and the fabula *is* the events. Even though the linearity of fabulaic events is reported, it concentrates solely on the sequence of events in the sujet. There is no formal link between the first and second part of the tale, but the former impacts on the latter in order to produce a combined ending. The alternation of fire and water is now presented together, where they form a reminder of their joint power: that of boiling water.

5.2.4 Characterisation

Both the main and secondary characters in *Fire and Water* have an input in the setting. Shalamov places great emphasis on a characters' positioning, not only within the frame of the tale but also within the frame of each setting. A major difference between the first and second part of the tale lies in the framing of the characters. The focaliser moves towards the fire, but steps away from the water, thus demonstrating his ability to move within a frame. Oja observes that the zek is in constant motion towards and away from death, but in both psychological and physiological ways.[91] In *Fire and Water*, the convict does not suffer from physical or psychological trauma and is able to physically move around thereby, metaphorically overcoming any impediment. It is this ability that places him in danger. He also moves between settings, temporally and physically. He is in the burning town and caught between the hill and the river. He also 'walked across luxurious blue moss a yard thick' and 'three of us set out across the river in a small boat.'[92] The protagonist therefore is freely able to move across settings, remaining in focus, while the settings move around him. He also remains in particular settings to emphasise safety. The camp on top of the hill is a refuge, as is the barracks. He sleeps in both scenes, thus highlighting the psychological prerequisite of safety in order to sleep. These resting periods within the tale are contrasted with activities outside his setting locale. Whilst he is resting in the cave the river level lowers and dawn breaks slowly around him. His drowsiness is time-consuming, without rendering him completely oblivious to external events and the boiling water also accompanies his sleep at the barracks. There are smaller events that are used to demonstrate the bridge between the natural and man's worlds. For example, when the protagonist enters the mushroom 'world' within the forest, the mushrooms encroach on civilisation: 'they surround every tent, fill every forest, pack the undergrowth.'[93] This two-way process between man and fungi occurs every day after the rain, and it is always temporary. Indeed, the characters in this story are also transient and their daily journey into the forest will stop once they have recovered their health. Other areas of framing are the protagonist's journey to locate the boat and his subsequent quest to reach the campfire. His way is barred at each turn, and he is forced to retreat and ascend higher and higher. The protagonist is located between the mountain and the rocky distant shore. He is in the weaker position, and therefore forced to ascend away from his destination with the water constantly forcing him further away. What is interesting here, is the protagonist's need to carry the mushrooms, no matter what. This burden, the cause of his distress, continues to weigh him down, and therefore his progress becomes slower and slower.[94] He is moving along and around immovable objects, such as the large rock. His progress is temporarily halted before salvation is detected in the shape of a tent, 'that was as low as a rock.'[95] In his descent, the destruction from the night before spreads out before him. Animate objects have been assaulted, with stones now appearing, both providing a hindrance as well as an aid in his long descent from the mountain. Thus, the character's progress is dependent upon his interaction with the setting, and to that extent he becomes an intrinsic part of the setting.

The protagonist's psychological make-up enables him to stand within burning towns and storehouses, and gain from the experience. Fear is a useful emotion in the camps, as it enables a convict to stand apart from dangerous environments, thus increasing his chance of survival. Shalamov's message in *Fire and Water* is quite simple in this respect: never become complacent or else superior forces will ensure your downfall. The protagonist has changed his perspective on life, although the events in this tale have not changed the other characters. The anonymous men around the campfire are similar to those found in the roadside cafeteria of *The Lawyers' Plot*. They act as nameless persons who occupy a donor role to the protagonist's receiver. Also, their position is framed by fire, a phenomenon that draws the protagonist towards them. They have become essentially redundant as hay-mowers during this flood, and therefore they occupy a transient role. Their position on the mountain offers a life-saving function for the protagonist, but one not without a metaphorical message. The protagonist receives a small amount of salt but no bread.[96] This could be interpreted as a lucky charm to ward off the Kolyma snakes or the snake-like mushrooms; mushrooms that could kill the protagonist.[97] The protagonist's two comrades also hinder his progress, but ultimately reward him with food. They sacrificed their mushrooms, but not their lives to save the major transport of this quest. Verigin and Safonov also act out several roles within the setting. As willing participants of the quest, they progress alongside the protagonist, but do not succumb to greed. Their subsequent disappearance enhances the protagonist's isolation, but they also provide verbal and directional information for both the protagonist and the reader. Kline remarks that 'frequent references to characters disappearing emphasise the lack of connectedness between the disparate elements which fill the literary space of *Kolymskie rasskazy.*'[98] They are the key to specific locational and temporal information that should have guided the protagonist. His presence is a constant reminder of his two missing companions. Gardner-Smith notes that absence itself can be used as a marking point: '…we may say that what is present in the text points always to what is absent, as figure implies ground.'[99] Their subsequent return is framed by distance: 'Far away, very far away.'[100] Their progress, although not reported in the text, foregrounds their positioning against the distant shore and emphasises the protagonist's perspective. All three men cease to be separated by nature's forces and they re-group in a human way. When the flood forces the protagonist to seek out substitute hospitality, it is also instrumental in keeping them apart. Their movement towards the near shore is not directly linear, but the boat misses the protagonist's spot by some distance. The protagonist describes the boat as on 'the other shore of life.'[101] The river therefore represents the distance between Heaven and the Underworld, with death's boat as the carriage between the two places.

NOTES

[1] Dipple, p. 48
[2] Toker, 'Stories from Kolyma: The Sense of History', *Hebrew University Studies in Literature and the Arts*, XVII, 17, 1989, pp. 188-221, p. 218
[3] O'Toole, *Structure, Style and Interpretation in the Russian Short Story*, p. 181
[4] S. Chatman, *Story and Discourse: Narrative Structure in Fiction and Film*, (Ithaca and London: Cornell University Press, 1993), p. 138
[5] Frye, pp. 95-115
[6] O'Toole, *Structure, Style and Interpretation in the Russian Short Story*, p. 183
[7] Ibid., pp. 187-192
[8] Hosking, 'The Chekhov of the Camps', p. 1163
[9] Loc. cit.
[10] During a private conversation, Solzhenitsyn is reported to have uttered this in appreciation of Shalamov's prose style. See M. Scammell, *Solzhenitsyn: A Biography*, (New York: Norton, 1984), p. 374
[11] Toker, 'A Tale Untold: Varlam Shalamov's "A Day Off"', p. 4
[12] *Kolyma Tales*, p. 282
[13] Oja, p. 66
[14] Rimmon-Kenan (pp. 55-6) state that descriptions are significant, but if an object is not described, this does not mean that it that it is not important. The location of the barrel of grease is crucial to the text, but the lack of physical description only accentuates the action surrounding it. In Gestalt theory, the barrel has become 'ground' to the 'figure' of the characters. This theory will be taken up later in the chapter.
[15] *Kolyma Tales*, p. 275
[16] Ibid., p. 283
[17] *Kolyma Tales*, p. 280. What is interesting about this statement is that Shalamov was proud of never having turned to God for sanctuary from his childhood to his period in the Far East. This, however, would seem to indicate that, although Shalamov turned away from God, he never denied his presence. In L. Toker, 'Stories from Kolyma', p. 218
[18] O. Mandelshtam in Oja, p. 67
[19] Hollosi, p. 21
[20] The mood of a piece can be defined by the characters' integration with setting. See Chatman, p. 41. In *Lend-Lease*, the polarity of 'light' and 'dark' scenes create an overall picture of terrible chaos, with the characters as principle architects in creating the differing moods. The narrator is, of course, the dominant force behind reporting characters' actions and situations and in *Lend-Lease* he chooses' to report the extremities of human action.
[21] O'Toole, *Structure, Style and Interpretation in the Russian Short Story*, p. 188
[22] *Kolyma Tales*, p. 275-8
[23] Ibid., p. 276
[24] On this see Scholes & Kellogg, p. 256
[25] All imagery in prose is imagined, but this device makes the reader work harder to contextualise it.

[26] This, like Stream of Consciousness is used to describe the inner movement of consciousness in a character's mind. Thus, the narrator is able to change perspective at will, drawing the reader along. See M. Drabble, *The Oxford Companion to English Literature*, (Oxford: Oxford University Press, 1996), p. 955

[27] *Kolyma Tales*, p. 277

[28] Loc. cit.

[29] Loc. cit.

[30] The bulldozer is symbolic of Stalin's drive for the mechanisation of Russia, which ideologically included mechanising people to function as automatons. Shalamov's ultimate fear was that the individual would cease to exist amidst the machinery of the state. P. Marvin, *An Intellectual History of Modern Europe*, (Boston: Houghton Mifflin, 1992), p. 476

[31] *Kolyma Tales*, p. 279

[32] Left and right have specific meanings here. To take the left hand path is to veer away from the good and on to the road of evil and misfortune. 'Left' in folklore (cf. Latin, *sinister*), has many negative connotations: 'left-handed compliment' and 'left-handed marriage'. In *The Wordsworth's Dictionary of Phrase & Fable*, p. 633

[33] *Kolyma Tales*, p. 282

[34] Quoted by Toker, 'Stories from Kolyma', p. 214

[35] Scholes & Kellogg, p. 257

[36] Cobley, p. 19

[37] Bolshakova, p. 4

[38] Kline, p. 251

[39] Ibid., p. 255

[40] *Kolyma Tales*, p. 281

[41] Rimmon-Kenan, p. 121

[42] A device also noted by Rimmon-Kenan is the use of permanent gaps where a point is raised in the text but not elaborated upon. Loc. cit. Shalamov does not tend to impart and forget information in this way, as he usually affects a form of closure after raising a point.

[43] Ibid., p. 126

[44] *Kolyma Tales*, p. 281

[45] Ibid., p. 282

[46] Ibid., p. 278

[47] This from of estrangement emphasises the key Formalist concept, whereby the familiar becomes transformed into the sum of its parts.

[48] *Kolyma Tales*, p. 280

[49] Loc. cit. Also, this wide expanse should represent freedom, and indeed the bodies are falling to freedom, but eventually they are all re-interred. For more information on wide spaces see I. Ibsch, 'Historical Changes of the Function of Spatial Description in Literary Texts', *Poetics Today*, III, 4, Autumn 1982, pp. 97-114

[50] *Kolyma Tales*, p. 281

[51] Ibid., p. 282

[52] Ibid., p. 283

[53] *Kolyma Tales*, p. 275

[54] Ibid., p. 277

[55] Ibid., p. 279

[56] Chatman, p. 140

57 Rimmon-Kenan, pp. 67-70. For example, a grey dreary sky may provide an indication or reinforcement of a character's mood.

58 Although in Glad's translation 'parricide' or 'parent-killer' is used, the original Russian specifies 'patricide', 'father-killer'. This reinforces the Oedipal association.

59 *Kolyma Tales*, p. 283

60 Oja, p. 66

61 Water also brought these prisoners to Kolyma in the first place.

62 *Kolyma Tales*, p. 497

63 Ibid., p. 500

64 Ibid., p. 502

65 Ibid., p. 495

66 Loc. cit.

67 Ibid., p. 496

68 Gestalt laws of organisation state that an object shown against a background will always occupy the figure position. Chvany (p. 12) illustrates this with a plum on a silver tray; the plum will always be the figure and the tray, the ground.

69 Chvany, p. 12. O'Toole in 'Dimensions in Semiotic Space' argues that Gestalt is too generalised a theory for detailed textual analysis. He advocates a more scientific investigation to locate all the relational levels in the semiotic space of a text. L. M. O'Toole, 'Dimensions in Semiotic Space', *Poetics Today - Narratology II: The Fictional Text and the Reader*, I, 4, Summer 1980, pp. 135-50

70 *Kolyma Tales*, p. 497

71 Chatman, p. 102. The focaliser reports many different scenes from different angles, thus mimicking a camera's roving technique.

72 *Kolyma Tales*, p. 500

73 Loc. cit.

74 Ibsch, p. 103

75 *Kolyma Tales*, p. 500

76 Ibid., p. 495

77 Loc. cit.

78 Loc. cit.

79 Ibid., pp. 496-7

80 Ibid., p. 497

81 Ibid., p. 498

82 Shalamov emphasises the idea that a convict is only worth his weight in gold, when he is working. An ill convict is still consuming food, and therefore is a burden on the state. Stalin still demanded his pound of flesh from the convicts in the hospital.

83 *Kolyma Tales*, p. 496

84 Ibid., p. 498

85 Overstepping the boundary to pursue forbidden fruit was mentioned in *Berries* in Chapter 2 – 'Point of View'. However, this time it is nature itself that takes revenge and not a vindictive guard.

86 *Kolyma Tales*, p. 498

87 Ibid., p. 499

88 Van Baak, 'The Place of Space in Narration', pp. 1-2. Conflict space is where the plot and a character's individual perception of the world combine. This is taken from Bakhtin's concept of 'chronotope'.

[89] Ricoeur, p. 39-40. 'Vacuous' times are excluded either for the reason mentioned above or in a general way. For instance, when a protagonist has fallen asleep and nothing can be reported. Sleep, like in other tales, is used to forward a tale and introduce a sense of unreality to proceedings.

[90] *Kolyma Tales*, p. 501

[91] Oja, p. 67

[92] *Kolyma Tales*, pp. 496-7

[93] Ibid., p. 497

[94] According to Slavic mythology, mushrooms can sap people of strength. See V. Ia. Petrukhin et al., *Slavianskaia Mifologiia*, (Moscow: Ellis Lak, 1995), p. 150-1. It could be argued that his burden is a penance for greed, and, like Sisyphus, he must always carry his burden with him.

[95] *Kolyma Tales*, pp. 500-1

[96] Salt and bread are traditional Russian gifts, especially associated with travellers. The protagonist's fellow convicts do not have any bread to give, but symbolically, the protagonist does not offer any mushrooms to his temporary comrades. Aesop's fable 'The Labourer and the Snake' and Krylov's variations on the same title, feature bread, salt and snakes. Indeed, in one variation the labourer (peasant) 'lies' with a snake as if she was his wife and is consequently shunned by his friends. He asks his friends if they tire of his bread and salt and they reply that the refusal of his hospitality will continue as long as he resides with the snake. It could be argued that the protagonist in *Fire and Water* is not offered any bread because he is residing with the 'snakes'. For all variations see L. A. Krylov, *Basni, proza, p'esy, stikhi*, (ed.) A. A. Devel', (Leningrad: Lenizdat, 1970), pp. 106-64

[97] There is a Russian and Ukrainian folk belief that salt frightens off evil spirits. Also 'The bread expresses a wish [on the part of the host] for [the guest's] wealth and good fortune; the salt is a defence from the hostile powers and influences.' In *Slavianskaia Mifologiia*, p. 364 or 387

[98] Kline, p. 420

[99] A. Gardner-Smith, 'The Occultism of the Text', *Poetics Today: Text and Discourse – Narrative*, III, 4, Autumn 1982, pp. 5-20

[100] *Kolyma Tales*, p. 501. Characters seen at long range, with limited detail, foreground when they move around a background. Thus, Verigin and Safonov's movements dominate the setting when they move towards the protagonist. On this in general see Scholes & Kellogg p. 168

[101] Loc. cit.

Conclusion

This study has sought to demonstrate the complexity and depth of each of the selected *Kolyma Tales*. Shalamov wrote each tale with such a precision and accuracy, that the reader finds himself immersed in the Gulag experience. One almost feels the imagery, detail and metaphor that arise from the tales, as if one were actually there. Shalamov has created great art out of the worst of human experience; indeed the higher the artistic value the greater the suffering that must be endured. The tales' contents enhance other Gulag testimonies, such as Solzhenitsyn's *Gulag Archipelago* or *First Circle*. There was strong opposition to their publication by literary and Government agencies, but as Glad notes: 'In the case of Shalamov it was evident that his stories were a major document of our time and any attempt to discredit them was doomed to failure.'[1]

Identifying the narrative structures in *The Lawyers' Plot* and *The Train* results in a better understanding of meaningless and dangerous journeys within and away from the Gulag camps. For instance, the reader is made aware only of what the protagonist knows in *The Lawyers' Plot*, and thus fully expects him to die. It is not only the convict who is reprieved, but also the reader in 'escaping' the final punishment of another convict death. There is no joyful triumph at this reprieve, because in the next story it could really happen. The complications in *The Train* delay progress, thus demonstrating the difficulty of a convict ever leaving the Gulag. Shalamov's use of the ignorant focaliser confounds and exemplifies the convict's position within the camp. Essentially, he wanted to 'get at the crux of what it is to be human, by examining the ways in which humans react in extreme conditions, at the depth of existence between life and death.'[2] This type of narration confines the focaliser's perspective, yet in doing so, broadens his (and our) understanding of the convict's environment. Where bread is important, it is only bread that appears in the text. Where the vast 'graveyard' is important, it is treated to a full inspection and commentary by the focaliser. Equally, when a convict dies, he receives just a sufficient amount of narrative. For instance, in *An Epitaph* (not discussed here) the narrator lists many deaths, and provides limited but essential background information on the lives of the dead. It is as if death is too inevitable and numerous an occurrence in the Gulag to warrant closer inspection. If Shalamov had written on the death of each and every convict he knew who had died, he would have still been writing into the next century. To write on each death would neutralise the power of estrangement, which the death of a single man always achieves. Although it was Shalamov's idea that at a state of near-death all men become alike, their deaths still possess a power of their own. He fought through his tales to repulse the familiarity of death and kept a sense of what it is to be human.

The plotting and presentation of each tale draws upon many techniques that enhance and structure a sequence of events. Memory plays an important part in a human's awareness of himself and his environment. Without a memory, a convict ceases to be human and exists at an animal's instinctual level. Words and thoughts are the first faculties to disappear and consequently the last to reappear. This mental state affects a convict's perception and in doing so, limits the scope of the sujet. The fabula of each tale exists within the frame of the tale, but is not reported in a strict linear order. Shalamov has created disorientation in each tale, and thus the sujet is important in recreating the facts. The sujet also introduces information from beyond the textual frame, whereby historical, social and political information is used to explain camp life. In *Major Pugachov's Last Battle*, the psychosis of physical and mental imprisonment was found to begin at the Kremlin and finish at the most extreme edges of the country. A single tale therefore does not possess any boundaries, as no form of closure can be said to apply. 'The Evil remains;' Toker warns, 'not all its stories have yet been told. Its picture is still to be pieced together.'[3] It was Shalamov's firm wish that history must not forget the Gulags. Indeed, Mikhailik refers to them as a Hell for those times.[4]

A Formalist approach is able to draw out these ideas of Shalamov's, whilst keeping the essential literariness of the tales intact. The short story is an ideal medium for this kind of analysis, and in Shalamov's case, the very brevity of his works enables a detailed analysis over a number of levels. Using one dominant level, and incorporating the other levels as subsidiary, this study attains a close reading of every tale. Shalamov incorporated many levels within the tales and when one finds meaning in one tale, it is not replicated in another. Each tale is one tiny part of the Kolyma mosaic and for the small selection chosen here, there are another 137 tales remaining.[5] Toker and Brewer have added much needed work on the ordering and thematics of the tales, but there exists a psychological perspective to themes which needs further investigation. Shalamov wrote these stories based on his need for the world to remember the Gulags and also to prove Man's ultimately base nature. Yet, Shalamov distances himself from events using a variety of narratorial and textual devices and consequently he is hardly ever active in the tales. As a result of this process, Shalamov's personality is not explicit and kept at a distance from the Shalamov as author of *Kolyma Tales*. This could be understood to mean that Shalamov is not writing these tales in the form of cathartic analysis. Shalamov never did 'mentally' leave the Gulag, a place that took up so many of his years, and as a result he suffered trauma for the rest of his life.

NOTES

[1]   Glad, 'Art out of Hell: Shalamov of Kolyma', p. 49
[2]   M. Brewer, 'Introduction to Masters Thesis', http://www.pitt.edu/~mmbst35/intro. html
[3]   Toker, 'Stories from Kolyma', p. 205
[4]   Mikhailik, 'Varlam Shalamov: v prisutstvii d'iavola. Problema konteksta', p. 214
[5]   'One may see the entire work as 147 signifiers, to which we may assign a particular meaning alone, but really only take on their true meaning within the system of syntagmatic and associative links with the others.' Brewer, 'Introduction to Masters Thesis', p. 1

Bibliography

Alexander, A. E., *Russian Folklore: An Anthology in English Translation*, (Belmont: Nordland, 1975)

Andrew, J., (ed.) *Poetics of the Text: Essays to Celebrate Twenty Years of the Neo-Formalist Circle*, (Amsterdam: Rodopi, 1992)

— Introduction to 'The Structural Analysis of Russian Narrative Fiction', *Essays in Poetics*, 1, 1984, pp. i-xxix

Baguley, D. A., 'Theory of Narrative Modes', *Essays in Poetics*, VI, 2, September 1981, pp. 1-17

Bakhtin, M., 'The Form of Time and the Chronotope in the Novel from the Greek Novel to Modern fiction', *PTL: A Journal for Descriptive Poetics and Theory of Literature*, III, 3, October 1978, pp.

Bakhtin, M. & Medvedev, P. N., *The Formalist Method in Literary Scholarship*, (Harvard: Harvard University Press, 1985)

Bann, S. & Bowlt, J. E., *Russian Formalism: A Collection of Articles and Texts in Translation*, (Edinburgh: Scottish Academic Press, 1973)

Bolshakova, A., 'The Theory of the Author: Bakhtin and Vinogradov', *in Essays in Poetics*, XXIV, Autumn 1999, pp. 1-12

Brewer, M., 'Varlam Shalamov's *Kolymskie rasskazy*: The Problem of Ordering', University of Arizona, Masters Thesis, 1995

Camus, A., *The Myth of Sisyphus*, (Harmondsworth: Penguin, 1980)

Chatman, S., *Story and Discourse: Narrative Structure in Fiction and Film*, (Ithaca and London: Cornell University Press, 1993)

Chvany, C. V., 'Foregrounding, Transitivity, Saliency (in sequential and non-sequential prose)', *Essays in Poetics*, X, 2, 1985, pp. 1-27

Cobley, P., *Narrative*, (London: Routledge, 2001)

Cohan, S. & Shires, L. M., *Telling Stories: A Theoretical Analysis of Narrative Fiction*, (London: Routledge, 1988)

Culler, J., *Structuralist Poetics*, (London: Routledge, 2002)

Dal', Vladimir., *Tolkovyi Slovar, zhivago velikorusskago iazyka*, IV, St. Petersburg, 1882, (Reprinted Moscow, 1978-80)

Diment, G. & Slezkine, Y., *Between Heaven and Hell: The Myth of Siberia in Russian Culture*, (New York: St. Martin's Press, 1993)

Dipple, E., *Plot*, (London: Methuen & Co., 1970)

Doležel, L., 'Narrative Semantics and Motif Theory', *Essays in Poetics*, III, 1, 1978, pp. 47-56

Drabble, M., (ed.) *The Oxford Companion to English Literature*, (Oxford: Oxford University Press, 1996)

Eagleton, T., *Literary Theory: An Introduction*, (2nd Edition) (Oxford: Blackwells, 1997)

Evans, I. H., (ed.) *The Wordsworth Dictionary of Phrase and Fable*, (Ware: Wordsworth Editions, 1994)

Falconer, R., 'Bakhtin's Chronotope and the Contemporary Short Story', *The South Atlantic Quarterly*, XCVII, 3-4, Summer/Fall, 1998, pp. 699-732

Feldman, R. S., *Understanding Psychology*, (New York: McGraw-hill, 1993)

Fizer, J., 'Has Socialist Realism been Identical with Itself?', *Russian Literature*, XXVIII, 1990, pp. 11-22

Forster, E. M., *Aspects of the Novel*, (Middlesex: Penguin, 1974)

Frankl, V. E., *Man's Search for Meaning*, (Washington: Washington Square Press, 1963)

Frye, Northrop, *Anatomy of Criticism: Four Essays*, (Princeton: Princeton University Press, 1957)

Gardner-Smith, A., 'The Occultism of the Text', *Poetics Today: Text and Discourse*, III, 4, Autumn 1982, pp. 5-20

Genette, G., *Narrative Discourse*, (Oxford: Blackwells, 1980)

Gereben, A. 'The Writer's 'Ego' in the Composition of Cycles of Short Stories', *Essays in Poetics*, IX, 1, April 1984, pp. 38-77

Glad, J., 'Foreword to Varlam Shalamov's *Kolyma Tales*', (Harmondsworth: Penguin, 1994), pp. ix-xix

— 'Art out of Hell: Shalamov of Kolyma', *A Journal of East and West Studies*, CVII, 1979, pp. 45-50

Gogol, Nikolai, *The Complete Tales of Nikolai Gogol*, II, L. J. Kent, (ed.) (Chicago: University of Chicago, 1985)

Greimas, A. J., *Du sens Essais Sémiotiques*, (Éditions du Seuil: Paris, 1970)

Hemingway, E., *The Old Man and the Sea*, (London: Cape, 1952

Herman, D., 'Existential Roots of Narrative Actants', *Studies in Twentieth Century Literature*, XXIV, 2, 2000, pp. 257-69

Hirschkopf, K., 'The Domestication of M. M. Bakhtin', *Essays in Poetics*, XI, 1, April 1986, pp. 76-87

Hollosi, C., Varlam Shalamov's "New Prose", *Rusistika*, VI, December 1992, pp. 3-71

Hosking, G., 'The Chekhov of the Camps', *TLS*, 17 October 1980, p. 1163

— 'The Ultimate Circle of the Stalinist Inferno', *NUQ*, Spring, 1980, pp. 161-8

Howe, I., 'Beyond Bitterness', *New York Times Review of Books*, 27, 14 August 1980, p. 36

Ibsch, I., 'Historical Changes of the Function of Spatial Description in Literary Texts', *Poetics Today*, III, 4, Autumn 1982, pp. 97-114

Jakobson, R., 'On Russian Fairy Tale', Selected Writings, IV, *Slavic Epic Studies*, (Hague: Mouton, 1966)

Jackson, R. L. & Rudy, E., (eds) *Russian Formalism: A Retrospective Glance*, (Yale: Yale Centre for International and Area Studies, 1985)

Jefferson, A., 'L Michael O'Toole: Structure, Style and Interpretation in the Russian Short Story: A Review Article', *Essays in Poetics*, VIII, 2, 1983, pp. 75-87

Kermode, F., *The Genesis of Secrecy on the Interpretation of Narrative*, (Cambridge: Harvard University Press, 1979)

Kline, L., Ph.D. Dissertation, 'Novaja Proza: Varlam Shalamov *Kolymskie rasskazy*', University of Michigan, 1998

Kochan, L. & Keep, J., *The Making of Modern Russia*, (London: Penguin, 1997)

Krylov, L. A., Devel', A. A., (ed.) *Basni, proza, p'esy, stikhi*, (Leningrad: Lenizdat, 1970)

Lane, M., (ed.) *Structuralism: A Reader*, (London: Jonathan Cape, 1970)

Lemon, L. T. & Reis, M. J., (eds) *Russian Formalist Criticism: Four Essays*, (Lincoln: University of Nebraska, 1965)

Marsh, R., *Images of Dictatorship: Stalin in Literature*, (London: Routledge, 1989)

Martin, W., *Recent Theories of Narrative*, (Ithaca, New York: Cornell University Press, 1986)

Marvin, P., *An Intellectual History of Modern Europe*, (Boston: Houghton Mifflin, 1992)

Mikhailik, Elena., 'Varlam Shalamov: v kontekste literatury I istorii', *Australian, Slavonic & East European Studies*, 9, 1, 1995, pp. 31-64
— 'Varlam Shalamov: v prisutstvii d'iavola. Problema konteksta', *Russian Literature*, XLVII, II, 2000, pp. 199-219
Morson, G. S. & Emerson, C., *Mikhail Bakhtin: Creation of a Prosaics*, (Stanford: Stanford University Press, 1990)
Mudrick, M., 'Character and Event in Fiction', *Yale Review*, L, 1961, pp. 202-18
Oja, M. F., 'Shalamov, Solzhenitsyn, and the Mission of Memory', *Survey*, XXIX, 2, Summer 1985, pp. 62-9
O'Toole, L. M., 'Dimensions in Semiotic Space', *Poetics Today*, I, 4, Summer 1980, pp. 135-50
— *Structure, Style and Interpretation in the Russian Short Story*, (New Haven & London: Yale University Press, 1982)
Petrochenkov, V., 'State-sponsored Persecution as Violence: Varlam Shalamov's *Kolyma Tales*', in W. Wright & S. Kaplan, (eds) *The Image of Violence in Literature, the Media and Society*, (Pueblo, Colorado: University of Southern Colorado, 1995), pp. 491-7
Petrukhin, V. Ia. et al., *Slavianskaia Mifologiia*, (Moscow: Ellis Lak, 1995)
Pomorska, K., *Russian Formalism*, (Edinburgh: Scottish Academic Press, 1973)
Pushkin, A. S., *History of Pugachev*, Translated by E. Sampson, (Ardis: Ann Arbor, 1983)
Ratushinskaya, I., *Grey is the Colour of Hope*, (London: Hodder & Stoughton, 1988)
Reid, I., *Narrative Exchanges*, (London: Routledge, 1992)
Reid, R., 'Discontinuous Discourses: Bakhtin in Modern Russian Literature and Bakhtin and Cultural Theory: A Review Article', *Essays in Poetics*, XVI, 1, 1991, pp 83-91
Ricoeur, P., *Time and Narrative*, I, (Chicago: University of Chicago Press, 1983)
Rimmon-Kenan, S., *Narrative Fiction: Contemporary Poetics*, (London: Methuen, 1988)
Romberg, B., *Studies in the Narrative Technique of the First-Person Novel*, (Stockholm: Almqvist & Wiksell, 1962)
Ronen, R., *Possible Worlds in Literary Theory*, (Cambridge: Cambridge University Press, 1994)
Salisbury, Harrison. E., *A New Russia?* (London: Secker & Warburg, 1963)
Scammell, M., *Solzhenitsyn: A Biography*, (New York: Norton, 1984)
Scholes, R. & Kellogg, R., *The Nature of Narrative*, (Oxford: Oxford University Press, 1971)
Shalamov, V., *Kolyma Tales*, (Harmondsworth: Penguin, 1994)
Shepherd, D., 'Canon Fodder? Problems in the Reading of a Soviet Production Novel', *Essays in Poetics*, XI, 1, 1986, pp. 22-43
Shukman, A., 'The Legacy of Propp', *Essays in Poetics*, I, 2, September 1976, pp. 82-94
— 'The Russian Short Story, Theory, Analysis, Interpretation', *Essays in Poetics*, II, 2, September 1977, pp. 27-95
Simpson, J. A., (ed.) *Oxford English Dictionary*, (Oxford: Clarendon Press, 1989)
Solzhenitsyn, A., *First Circle*, (London: William Collins, 1979)
Todorov, T., *Facing the Extreme: Moral Life in the Concentration Camps*, (London: Weidenfeld, 1999)

— *Introduction to Poetics*, (Brighton: Harvester Press, 1981)
Toker, L.,'A Tale Untold: Varlam Shalamov's "A Day Off"', *Studies in Short Fiction*, XXVIII, 1, 1991 (Winter), pp. 1-8
— 'Stories from Kolyma: The Sense of History', *Hebrew University Studies in Literature and the Arts*. XVII, 1989, pp. 188-221
— 'Towards a Poetics of Documentary Prose: From the Perspective of Gulag Testimonies', *Poetics Today*, XVIII, 2, 1997, pp. 187-222
— *Return from the Archipelago: Narrative of Gulag Survivors*, (Bloomington: Indiana University Press, 2000)
Tomashevsky, B., 'Literary Genres', in *Russian Poetics in Translation, V: Formalism; History, Comparison, Genre*, (Oxford: Holdan Books, 1978)
Van Baak, Joost., 'The Place of Space in Narration: A Semiotic Approach to the Problem of Literary Space. With an Analysis of the Role of Space in I. E. Babel's Konarmija', *Studies in Slavic Literature and Poetics*, III, (Amsterdam: Rodopi, 1983)
— 'The House in Russian Avant-garde Prose: Chronotope and Archetype', *Essays in Poetics*, XV, 1, 1990, pp. 1-16

Web Pages

Brewer, M., '"Authorial," Lyric and Narrative Voices in Varlam *Shalamov's Kolymskie rasskazy*: A Close Reading of Sententsiia'. On line at: http://www.pitt.edu/~mmbst35/shalamov.html (Consulted 06/06/2000).
Brewer, M., 'Introduction to Masters Thesis'. On line at: http://www.pitt.edu/~mmbst35/intro.html (Consulted 06/06/2000).
Marakenko, A. S., 'Lectures to Parents: Lecture 6 – Work Education'. On line at: http://www.marxists.org/reference/archive/makarenko/works/lectures/lec06.ht ml (Consulted 07/06/2002).
Paksoy, H. B., 'Crimean Tartars'.Online at: http://www.ku.edu/~ibetext/texts/paksoy-6/cae13.html (Consulted 13/07/2002).
Schwan, Mark, 'Raven: The Northern Bird of Paradox'. On line at: http://www.state.ak.us/local/akpages/FISH.GAME/wildlife/geninfo/ birds/raven.htm (Consulted 10/08/2002).
Starodvorskaya, Kate, 'Irkutsk'. On line at: http://www.mcn.org/ed/ross/ Kids/angara.htm (Consulted 17/11/2002).
van der Kolk, Bessel, 'The Body Keeps the Score: Memory and the Evolving Psychobiology of Post-traumatic Stress'. On line at: http://www.trauma-pages.com/vanderk4.htm (Consulted 20/04/2002).
Young, R., 'Shalamov, Tragedy and Poetry'. On line at: http://www.litkicks.com/BeatPages/page.jsp?what=VarlamShalamov&who=y oungrobert (Consulted 28/01/2002).

Index